COVER PHOTOGRAPH: Two ex-LNWR Coal Tanks 7710 and 27654, as yet not renumbered, arrive at Nantybwch with the 9.5am from Newport on 26th April 1948, the leading engine having been attached at Tredegar. W.A.Camwell/Stephenson Locomotive Society

BACK COVER PHOTOGRAPH: A view from Nine Mile Point No. 2 signal box showing Tredegar's Ivatt 2-6-2T 41204 with the 1.10pm Newport to Nantybwch in August 1952 as Stanier 2-6-2T 40171 waits in the sidings with the stock for the afternoon miners train to Nantybwch. A.C. Sterndale

SOUTH WALES VALLEYS

Railways and Industry in the
SIRHOWY VALLEY

NEWPORT TO TREDEGAR & NANTYBWCH,
INCLUDING HALL'S ROAD

JOHN HODGE

PEN & SWORD
TRANSPORT

AN IMPRINT OF PEN & SWORD BOOKS LTD.
YORKSHIRE – PHILADELPHIA

First published in Great Britain in 2020 by
Pen and Sword Transport
An imprint of
Pen & Sword Books Ltd
Yorkshire - Philadelphia

ISBN 9781526762566

Designed by Paul Wilkinson, Pen & Sword Books
Printed and bound in India by Replika Press Pvt. Ltd.

Pen & Sword Books Ltd incorporates the Imprints of Pen & Sword Books Archaeology, Atlas, Aviation, Battleground, Discovery, Family History, History, Maritime, Military, Naval, Politics, Railways, Select, Transport, True Crime, Fiction, Frontline Books, Leo Cooper, Praetorian Press, Seaforth Publishing, Wharncliffe and White Owl.

For a complete list of Pen & Sword titles please contact

PEN & SWORD BOOKS LIMITED
47 Church Street, Barnsley, South Yorkshire, S70 2AS, England
E-mail: enquiries@pen-and-sword.co.uk
Website: www.pen-and-sword.co.uk

or

PEN AND SWORD BOOKS
1950 Lawrence Rd, Havertown, PA 19083, USA
E-mail: Uspen-and-sword@casematepublishers.com
Website: www.penandswordbooks.com

CONTENTS

DEDICATION

I DEDICATE THIS book to the Manley family of Newport, of whom my mother was the only daughter. They lived at 52 Price's Street, Pill, and were a family of seven children, my grandparents having married in 1898. My grandfather Bert Manley (Albert George), born in 1877, was a huge man of 21 stone and was a boatman on the Newport Alexandra Dock. He always used to say that when he finished work, there was no need to secure his boat as only he was strong enough to use it! For all his size, he was a very gentle man who loved his family dearly. My grandmother (Elizabeth Jane) was two years older and was a lovely lady who always had a pot of stew heating on the fire, ready for any visitors. I remember visiting them with my mother one day and finding a huge conger eel in the kitchen sink, which my grandfather had caught that day and which would be his dinner.

Of their seven children, my mother (Lilian Doris) was the second eldest and only daughter, born in 1901, who later courted my father who would walk from Risca to Newport to see her, marrying in 1925. An elder brother, Albert, who died at an early age, was followed by my mother and five sons: George Francis, Wilfred James, Clarence John (Jack), William (Will) and Richard Charles (Dick). Four of these later worked on the railway, George and Jack in the Permanent Way Dept., Will as a Carriage & Wagon Examiner at Pontypool Road and Dick, first as a checker at Newport Goods, and then as a signalman at East Mendalgief box, outside Pill engine shed. Will had also achieved celebrity in the Pill Harriers Baseball team and was a notable sportsman. Wilfred died at an early age from rheumatic fever but the others lived until their seventies. George had married Olive and had two sons, my cousins Alan and Brian, and Jack married Edna and had three children, Elizabeth, Alan and Colin. Will married Agnes and had a son William, Dick married Grace and had no offspring. My lovely mother outlived them all and survived until her 94th year, just failing to celebrate that birthday. Both my grandparents died in the early to mid-1950s, in their seventies.

My father and mother settled at Grove Road, Risca, after marrying and later moved to New Park Road, Crosskeys, where I was born to join a brother and sister, in 1937. Our family moved from Crosskeys to Barry in 1942, due to my father's ill health, and remained there until I left to work for British Rail at Western Region HQ, Paddington, in 1970. My father died at 73 in 1974, my mother at 93 in 1995, my brother at 70 in 1996 and my sister at 77 in 2006, with the author now having clocked up 80+ years.

IN MEMORIAM – During the preparation of this book, I learnt of the tragic death of Gerald Davies in an accident at the Clydach Gorge in August 2019. Gerald was a good friend who helped considerably with material for this book and will be sorely missed from the South Wales railway fraternity. His knowledge of the Sirhowy and the LNWR in South Wales was unsurpassed after the death of W.W. Tasker whose collection he had inherited and made freely available. RIP Gerald.

ACKNOWLEDGEMENTS

SPECIAL THANKS GO to the late Gerald Davies of Tredegar and Alastair Warrington of Garndiffaith for their help with photographs and material, and also to Malcolm James of Rogerstone, Ray Lawrence of Oakdale for colliery data, and Tony Cooke of Oxford for his Track Layout information. Help with photographs is also acknowledged from Allan Pym of Ebbw Vale, and Tony Jukes of Oxford House, Risca.

Special thanks to the late Michael Mensing, who loaned me his colour negatives of workings over the line for me to print as part of his South Wales collection and to use as I saw fit.

References used include the following:
Barrie, D.S. & Lee, Charles: *The Sirhowy Valley and its Railways* – The Railway Publishing Co. Ltd. 1940
Cooke, R.A.: *Track Layout Diagrams Section 41*
Lawrence, Ray; *Collieries of the Sirhowy Valley*
Tasker, W.W.: *Railways in the Sirhowy Valley* – The Oakwood Press 1992
Tasker, W.W. *The Merthyr, Tredegar & Abergavenny Railway & Branches* – Oxford Publishing Company 1986
Tasker, W.W. *Memoirs of the Sirhowy Branch 1868-1960* – Treowen Press Ltd. 1994

I have made every effort to identify all the copyright holders of pictorial and archive material used in this book. If I have missed or wrongly attributed any material used, I apologise. Please email me at john_hodge@tiscali.co.uk so that we may rectify the position.

A **1946** shot of a then 3 coach service from Nantybwch to Newport with Coal Tank LMS 7834 in charge between Gaer and Hillfield Tunnels with the 11.8am from Nantybwch down service to form the 1.10pm return. The engine can be seen to have used little coal on the trip down the Valley and is well presented by Tredegar depot.
J.G. Hubback/John Hodge Collection

CHAPTER ONE

HISTORICAL INTRODUCTION

THE SIRHOWY VALLEY takes its name from the town of Sirhowy at the head of the valley where the Sirhowy Ironworks was established by Samuel Homfray and brothers in 1778 to take advantage of the raw materials of iron ore, coal and limestone as well as the soft water in the area. This became the first coke furnace to be established in the county of Gwent.

In March 1800, the Sirhowy Works owners Samuel Homfray, Richard Fothergill and Matthew Monkhouse were granted a lease by Lord Tredegar, Sir Charles Morgan, who owned much of the Tredegar area, to construct the Tredegar Ironworks, a mile or so below Sirhowy. This enabled them to work the lands involved to obtain iron ore and coal, with powers to build the furnaces necessary to produce iron and iron products. The cast iron from the Sirhowy furnace was soon conveyed to the new Tredegar Works where it was manufactured into finished products which would then need to be taken to the wharves at Newport for sea conveyance to the ultimate destination.

The Monmouthshire Canal Company (MCC)[1] had opened their canal from Crumlin to the wharves at Newport in 1796 with powers to build tramways within an eight mile radius of the canal to bring in traffic from works, quarries, etc. in the area, with the provision that if they did not construct such tramways themselves, the customers wishing to use the canal were empowered to make such tramways themselves. The Tredegar Ironworks Company (TIC) however did not opt for their traffic to be conveyed by

canal and proposed to build a tramroad over the 24 miles to Newport, the Sirhowy Tramroad. In a bid to force the traffic onto the canal, the MCC stated that if the Tredegar Company would abandon their scheme, they would construct a tramroad at their own expense by Christmas 1801 from Tredegar to Risca where it would join the canal for conveyance on to Newport. A draft agreement to this effect was offered dated December 1800, which the Tredegar Company did not accept.

The matter was referred to Parliament for the necessary approval, but what was actually sanctioned was considerably different. The Canal Act of 26 June 1802 gave the directors of the Sirhowy Tramroad Company, as had then been constituted, permission to make a tramroad from the Sirhowy Works over the sixteen miles to Nine Mile Point, at their own expense. The Monmouthshire Canal Company were to build the remainder to Pillgwenlly (for the River Usk wharves) at Newport, except for a mile within the Tredegar Park estate which would be up to Lord Tredegar (Sir Charles Morgan) to make himself, given that he would receive the tolls for passage over it. The tramroad would be double between Newport and Nine Mile Point to permit independent movement in both directions, but single between there and Tredegar, with priority for loaded over empty wagons. Also included in the provisions of the Act was authority for the partners to construct a five mile extension of the Sirhowy Tramroad to run from Rassa to Trevil Quarry where

1. For a full history of the Monmouthshire Railway and Canal Company, please see my *Railways & Industry in the Western Valley – Newport to Aberbeeg* (Pen & Sword 2016)

limestone and rock were quarried, which would be used in the works at Sirhowy and Tredegar.

The Act laid down that the authorised tramroads were to be completed by the end of September 1803 with the proviso that if the Canal Company's tramroad from Newport to Nine Mile Point was not complete by that time, the Sirhowy Company were empowered to complete it and for such work to be vested in that company. Benjamin Outram, who had been involved with the development of many tramroads, was consulted on the specification and recommended a gauge of 4ft 2ins and use of an edge-rail system with flat rimmed wheels on the wagons. The traders, who provided all the wagons, were happy with this as they preferred wagons with flat rimmed wheels which could then also be used away from the tramway.

A more detailed description appeared in a paper by T.G. Cumming in 1824 who described the Sirhowy Tramroad as being 'of 4ft 2ins width, composed of cast-iron plates, in 3ft lengths, having a flaunche [flange] on the plate and not on the wheel, forming nearly the angle of a square, the flaunche inclining a little inwards. The sleepers are stout blocks of stone, firmly bedded in the ground, with the extremities of each adjoining rail resting upon them, and made fast thereto by a pin passing through the rail and into a hole bored in the block 4 or 5ins deep, and there secured with lead.' The whole tramroad was laid out under the direction of John Hodgkinson to the specification of Benjamin Outram.

No firm date ever seems to have been agreed as to when the Sirhowy Company completed their part of the work down to Nine Mile Point, this still remaining the division between the two sections. However, the year 1805 seems to be the agreed date by which the tramroad was opened for traffic. Other reports pre-dating this may have referred to intermediate sections, especially those serving the Ironworks.

Many of the details of the development of the Sirhowy Tramroad are common to the development of the Monmouthshire Company's tramroad and railway as related in my book *Railways & Industry In The Western Valley (Newport to Aberbeeg)*, which readers are advised to consult.

The completed works between Nine Mile Point and Tredegar provided a carriage way alongside the seventeen miles of tramroad. At Risca, the Canal Company constructed a large stone viaduct to bridge the valley, probably the most notable engineering structure in the whole enterprise. The total cost of constructing the whole tramroad was about £74,000 or about £3,000 per mile, the split being: Canal Company £40,000; Tredegar Co. £30,000; and Sir Charles Morgan £4,000. The trams used averaged some 17cwt in weight when empty and could carry about 3 tons, but they had no springs or buffers and were connected by firm drawbars. Each train of trams was hauled by four or five horses with a wagon at the back of each train to convey a spare horse, these being fine strong animals which were well looked after. Stabling points for horses were at Tredegar, Rock (near Blackwood), Nine Mile Point and Risca. The speed of the trams in movement was controlled largely by sprags pushed into the wheels, as trams bearing down on the horses was highly dangerous. This problem was worse above Nine Mile Point from where there was an adverse gradient all the way to Tredegar.

A maximum speed of 4mph had to be observed and empty wagons had to give way to loaded wagons. Initially the only way this could be done was to crowbar the trams off the track but Richard Fothergill invented a turn-out system by which a train of empty trams could be held secure while a loaded train passed by. Rakes of fifteen loaded trams, some wood, some iron, normally formed a train. The plates which held the track

Boundary marker of the Sirhowy Tramroad Company.

Seal adopted by the Sirhowy Railway Company after conversion from the 1802 Tramroad to a Railway in 1860.

in position suffered much damage due to bad alignment and heavy loads passing over them and as a result, the maximum weight for any loaded tram was set at 56cwt.

Tolls were to be paid at various points en route and from 1810, private carriers were allowed to use the tramroad. A passenger service was introduced in 1822 by John Kingston of Newport, who provided a horse drawn vehicle known as the Caravan, while another was called the Waterloo coach, probably after the place of that name at Maesglas, Newport.

In addition to the main tramroad between Sirhowy, Tredegar and Nine

Mile Point, there were three branches constructed, one near Blackwood, another the Penllwyn Tramroad for 4½ miles from Nine Mile Point to collieries at Bryn, and a third, the Llanarth Tramroad from Ynysddu to the Rock Colliery at Blackwood.

However, all was not well in the relations between the Sirhowy and Tredegar Works management and in 1818 a legal dispute between them resulted in a split in which the Sirhowy Works were acquired by James Harford of Harford, Partridge & Co., owners of the Ebbw Vale Works from when the Sirhowy Works were operated as part of their works and supplied Ebbw Vale with pig iron where it was worked into wrought iron, the necessary connections between the two works being constructed via a tunnel. This left the Tredegar owners to continue the operation of the tramroad to Nine Mile Point on their own, working with the MCC and Lord Tredegar.

In his book *Origin and Progress of Rail and Tram Roads of 1824*, T.G. Cumming states that, 'Samuel Homfray & Co. of Tredegar Works have for the last 20 years been sending coal over the 24 miles to Newport over falling inclines of up to 1 in 79 with each horse capable of taking a 10ton load and returning with the empties, teams of five horses being employed.'

The increase in traffic to be conveyed to the Newport river wharves due to the amount of coal now being carried, as well as iron products, caused the directors to turn to the development of steam engine haulage in which much interest had been shown regarding the Richard Trevithick steam engine at Penydarren, Merthyr. Samuel Homfray Jnr, who had taken his father's place in the Company when his father became an MP, sent Thomas Ellis, the Tredegar Iron Company (TIC) Engineer between 1828-54, to see engines being produced by Robert Stephenson and as a result an engine, named *Britannia*, was ordered to be tried out on the Sirhowy Tramroad.

The engine was received in October

1829 and started working in the vicinity of the Tredegar Works. Just before Christmas it made its first journey to Newport along the Sirhowy Tramroad with Homfray and his friends on board. The journey caused many problems and though starting at daybreak it was dark by the time they arrived at Newport. The engine weighed some 9 tons but was a very rigid machine and was too heavy for the tracks in several places, causing breakages and dislodging the track on some tight curves, all of which had to be put right before the train could proceed. Then while passing through Tredegar Park, an overhanging tree dislodged and broke the engine's chimney which again had to be rectified before the train could proceed. With many lessons learnt, the train finally reached Newport where Homfray and his friends attended the Sir Charles Morgan cattle show. The engine returned to Tredegar, the defects were made good and it was then put to work regularly hauling trains of trams loaded with 50-60 tons of iron to the River Usk wharves, producing a 35 per cent reduction on the cost of the horse-drawn procedure.

Following this, two other engines appeared on the Sirhowy Tramroad, *Speedwell* and *Hercules*, built by the Neath Abbey Ironworks, but these suffered from the same problems of rigidity and continued to break up the tram plates, especially on the tighter curves, so that the Monmouthshire Canal Company was forced to issue an instruction that steam engines would be prohibited unless they were properly suspended on springs. Thomas Ellis continued to show his prowess in the development of the steam engine and built ten further engines for use on the Sirhowy Tramroad, weighing just under 20 tons each. By 1848, the newly built *St David* had hauled a train of 180 tons through to Newport. The *Bedwellty*, built in 1853, remained in traffic until 1882 and was not scrapped until some years later. Ellis whitewashed the

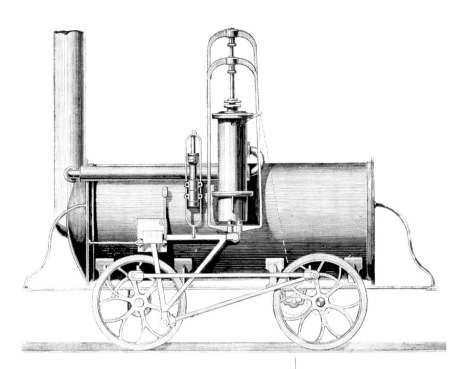

smokeboxes of his engines so that they could be easily seen approaching. He took on several apprentices at his Tredegar works, including Daniel Gooch. *Speedwell* was a smaller engine with only two coupled wheels, but between 1832 and 1848, the TIC under Thomas Ellis built eight six-coupled wheeled engines for use on the Sirhowy tramroad: *Tredegar, Jane, Lord Rodney, Lady Sale, Prince Albert, St David, Fanny* and *Charlotte*.

The Sirhowy Tramroad remained in the hands of these engines and wagons, though most of the tram plates needed to be replaced by wooden structures due to breakages, until about 1860, by when it had become much behind the times, with the Taff Vale Railway to Merthyr and the Rhondda Valley already opened as a full standard gauge railway from 1841 and the South Wales Railway as a broad gauge line from 1850. The MCC was also moving forward into the railway era and had now become the Monmouthshire Railway & Canal Co. (MRCC), and had declared its intention to construct a new Newport & Pontypool Railway by an Act of July 1845, a standard gauge line with full locomotive haulage with a full commitment to modify existing

The *Speedwell* built in 1830 by the Neath Abbey Iron Works for Thomas Prothero of Newport for service on the Sirhowy line.

The Tredegar
Iron Company's locomotive *St David* which was rebuilt in 1848. The original drawing by Thos. Ellis, Engineer states that the engine was built at Tredegar in 1830. He was the Tredegar Company's engineer from 1828-34, and other evidence shows he built no locomotives until 1832.

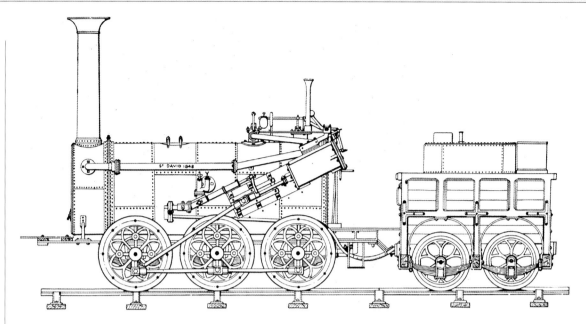

tramroads accordingly, eliminating horse traction after August 1849. Though this caused many transitional problems with track and wagons, some stretches of track having to accommodate wagons with both tramroad and railway gauges, the one running inside the other, the new arrangements came partly into force from 13 May 1850 throughout the MRCC, it being May 1855 before the MRCC Company Engineer R.B. Sayer was able to announce the completion of the changeover, though this excepted the section from Risca to Nine Mile Point, this being completed in November, though passenger operation was not involved.

The Sirhowy Company was thus many years behind the MRCC in their progress towards a transition to a standard gauge railway. There were claims that they were operating passenger services by 1849, though these were probably short-term services to and from the area around Tredegar Ironworks. They did not own any passenger stock or provide any signalling, which would have been a pre-requisite for authorisation. It would be May 1860 before the Sirhowy Tramroad Company secured the necessary Act to change the name of the company to the Sirhowy Railway Company, authorising the conversion of the line into a standard gauge railway. This Act also gave powers to extend the line

from Sirhowy to Nantybwch to make connection with the developing Merthyr, Tredegar and Abergavenny line, as well as converting the Trevil line to a standard gauge railway. A new routing of the line through Argoed and Blackwood was necessary to avoid running through the streets as previously, and a new routing was necessary through from Bedwellty Pits to Sirhowy. The routing authorised from Sirhowy to Nantybwch proved abortive and a further Act of June 1865 was necessary, following which the line was opened in November 1865. There were now to be four directors of the new company, initially Samuel and Watkin Homfray, Rowland Fothergill and William Henry Forman.

The Sirhowy Valley passenger service opened on 19 June 1865 between Sirhowy and Risca with running powers on to Newport Dock Street, and was extended back from Nantybwch in November. The 1860 Act had allowed three years for the Sirhowy Company to effect the necessary changes to become a standard gauge passenger and freight railway and it seems likely that the work was completed in this period but no passenger service was introduced until the stated date, possibly influenced by the following. By the start of 1864, it was commonly accepted that the Sirhowy Railway was up for sale, and that the MRCC had

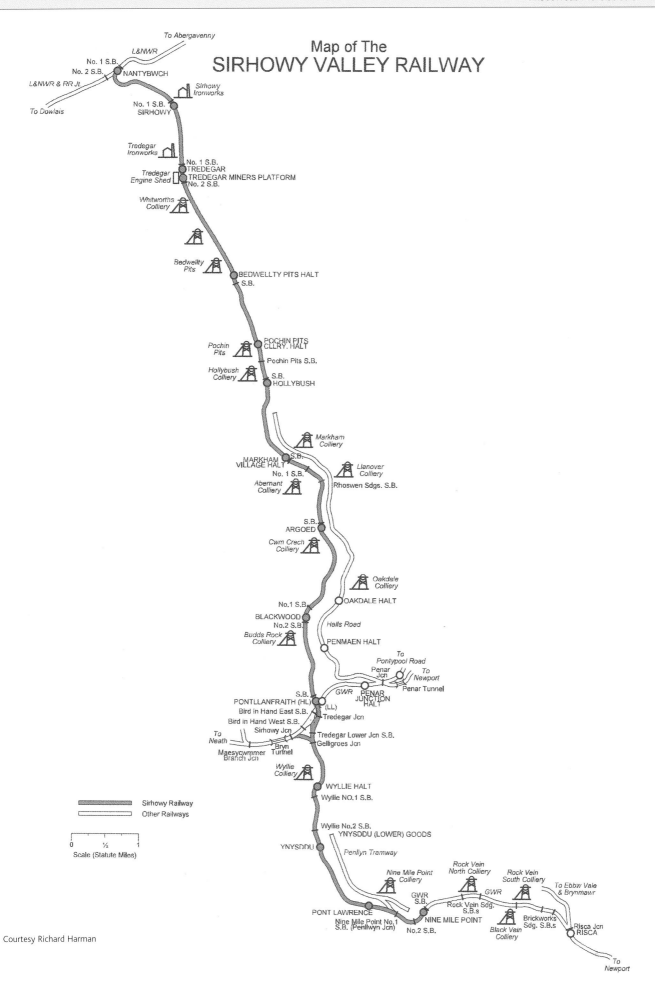

Map of The
SIRHOWY VALLEY RAILWAY

Courtesy Richard Harman

stated that they did not wish to acquire it, much to the disgruntlement of many of its shareholders. Starting dates for a passenger service were rumoured as April or May 1864 but still no action followed, probably explained by a reluctance on the part of the Sirhowy directors to move in the face of interest from both the GWR and London & North Western Railway (LNWR). The 1860 Act had authorised the Sirhowy Company to run services as far as Nine Mile Point and that the MRCC should provide the service on to Risca or Newport. This was clearly a most inconvenient arrangement and it was soon agreed that the Sirhowy Company would provide the service throughout, a further Sirhowy Railway Act of July 1865 stipulating that three services a day (except Sundays) were to run both ways between Tredegar and Newport 'without break or change of carriage'. Still with no firm interest from either of these two giant concerns, the Sirhowy directors decided to open their passenger service according to these criteria on 19 June 1865, and the company's independent existence was to continue for another decade.

The 1867 service showed three trains on Monday to Saturday and two on Sunday, all running between Sirhowy and Dock Street serving intermediate stations at Tredegar, Argoed, Blackwood, Tredegar Junction and Risca. Nine Mile Point was not served until 1869 when it had the suffix Quarry Mawr. Other stations were added as collieries developed in that area.

Neither the GWR nor the LNWR made any positive move towards acquiring the Sirhowy, this the more surprising as the LNWR were of course developing the Merthyr, Tredegar & Abergavenny (MT&A), which included Tredegar. In 1874 the Sirhowy directors opened negotiations with the MRCC and the GWR (who were about to merge anyway) for the sale of their undertaking. Those with the MRCC soon fell through but with the GWR went as far as a draft agreement with the GW also promoting a new line from Caerleon

on their new Pontypool to Newport line, across to Crosskeys and on to Nine Mile Point, which would take their Aberdare traffic away from the Golden Mile, and route it on to Aberdare via Tredegar Junction Lower and Sirhowy Junction also proposing to develop the Penllwyn Tramroad which was derelict at that time as party of a scheme to develop coal mines in that area. But all this came to nothing when it was revealed that the Sirhowy directors had been in secret talks with the LNWR and MRCC jointly, the latter also being in talks with the Midland Railway. The Midland however soon backed out leaving the LNWR/MRCC acquisition still possible. Collusion was rife and the LNWR then found that the MRCC had offered very favourable terms to the GWR to become part of the Paddington empire, the outcome being that both the big guns decided to take what they could when they could and the LNW agreed final terms to take over the Sirhowy while the GWR concluded a 99 year lease with the MRCC from 1 August 1875.

Three weeks later, the Sirhowy was vested in the LNWR, though the latter had started to work the Sirhowy services from 1 July. Shareholders in the Sirhowy Company received an equal number of shares in the LNW, in a very favourable exchange. The acquisition was ratified by the LNWR Sirhowy Railway Vesting Act of 13 July 1876.

The absorption of the Sirhowy within the LNWR left the GWR schemes for their new line from Nine Mile Point to Caerleon high and dry and with no route for their coal traffic from Aberdare to England. In order to provide for the latter, the GWR concluded an agreement with Lady Llanover to develop the Halls Tramroad for use as a railway which connected into their Taff Vale Extension Line at Penar Junction and would bring traffic down to connect into their newly acquired line at Crosskeys. However, this was still a tramroad and would require upgrading to a standard gauge railway.

Perhaps realising the value of being good neighbours within South Wales, the GWR and LNWR agreed a truce on the GW's Aberdare coal traffic routing and from 1 February 1877, they agreed that traffic could continue to run via Tredegar Junction, this being made permanent six years later. The GWR were very slow to develop Halls Road but the value of the acquisition was realised when in 1912 new collieries at Markham and Oakdale were opened which would be serviced off that line, despite the fact that a new connection into the Sirhowy line would have been easily achieved.

By company acquisition and securing running powers over the Rhymney Railway, the LNWR had acquired running powers to both Newport and Cardiff Docks, something they also emulated to Swansea via the Central Wales line, while the Midland Railway obtained footholds in the Swansea Valleys and the Neath and Brecon, a not inconsiderable hole in what otherwise should have been a GWR stronghold.

It would be the early years of the twentieth century before the next two events of importance affecting the Sirhowy took place. The first was down to the aspirations of the Barry Railway, who, following the opening of Barry Docks in 1889, had succeeded in accessing several routes in the Rhondda and Rhymney valleys with positive results though had largely failed to tap into the Tondu. In 1907, they made a bid to access the Sirhowy with an Act to support an ambitious plan to build a new line from east of Caerphilly to Nine Mile Point for access to the Sirhowy Valley and across to Crosskeys for the Western Valley. The works involved were very costly and difficult and in their own word 'unworkable' and though they continued their efforts, in 1911 they were withdrawn. These had been spearheaded by Archibald Hood who had taken over the reins at Barry after the death of David Davies, and whose success has never been

properly recognised.

The Grouping of 1922/3 saw the LNWR become part of the London Midland & Scottish Railway (LMS) while the GWR, which had absorbed the MRCC in 1875 (officially in 1880), remained running the lion's share of South Wales, with the Newport area being one of its most important and highest revenue earning areas. The Sirhowy Valley line continued to thrive during the first half of the twentieth century, with coal production buoyant, though with the passenger business badly affected by bus competition from the Red & White Bus Company who offered frequent services passing along main streets to and from Newport, a far better service than was provided by rail. During the war years, the railways throughout the country suffered from low levels of maintenance and renewal and with no money available to effect a recovery, were nationalised in 1948. Trains for the exclusive conveyance of miners were an important part of the service provided on the Sirhowy, especially after the opening of Nine Mile Point Colliery and the new collieries on the northern section of Halls Road which ran parallel with the Sirhowy line, Markham and Oakdale, which started production at the start of the century. These trains were timed to run at shift change and operated either twice or three times a day. Other than this, it was customary for a coach to be conveyed on the front/rear of service trains which ran at shift change times for the use of miners who could not use the miners' trains. Veteran coaches were always provided for the miners' trains and others, and these were (to coach enthusiasts) a feature of the Sirhowy services.

Excursion business at weekends which was a feature of rail travel on the Sirhowy, continued to thrive, especially local trains to Barry Island to where up to five trains ran in the 1920s and '30s on Sundays and Bank Holidays from stations along the MT&A and the Sirhowy Line, hauled by double-headed Coal Tanks, 0-8-0s and the Beames 0-8-4Ts. Long distance excursions also ran from starting points such as Blackwood and Pontllanffraith to destinations in the North of England and Scotland and rugby union internationals involving Wales produced regular excursions in the winter months to Edinburgh, Heysham for Dublin, as well as London for Twickenham, with local excursions for soccer matches at Newport and Cardiff, and other local events. (See separate section.)

As from 1948, a certain amount of rationalisation took place, including the placing of the former LMS areas in South Wales under WR control, this including the former MT&A line and the Sirhowy Valley. Things however moved slowly with former LMS engines still allocated to and working all services from Tredegar and Abergavenny Brecon Road depots. With the modernisation of motive power which began in 1951 with the production of Standard locomotives, the older types of engines were withdrawn, or existing withdrawal programmes speeded up, one of the casualties being the Webb Coal Tanks which had worked the Sirhowy services for over fifty years, though Ivatt Class 3 2-6-2Ts had been present on the line since 1948.

From 1954, the Sirhowy passenger service was cut back to operating between Risca and Tredegar/Nantybwch, instead of the through service to Newport. It ran as an auto train with a 64XX engine, 6439 being allocated to Tredegar for the purpose. This arrangement lasted until April 1959 when 6439 was transferred to Ebbw Junction, which did not then specifically provide a 64XX unless one was available, the resultant 57XX having to run round at both ends of the journey. With a change in both directions at Risca, and large gaps during the day, the service offered had little attraction against the frequent bus service along the main streets provided by the Red & White Co. From 1958, the demand could be covered with trains of only one coach, though the miners' trains operating from Nine Mile Point northwards continued

with trains of up to seven coaches involved. Long distance excursions were now a thing of the past, though a Sunday and Bank Holiday excursion still ran from Nantybwch (then Tredegar) to Barry Island powered by a former LNW 0-8-0 until the last had left, from when a 5600 Class officiated, the last running in September 1959.

The Western Region closed several country stations along the main lines in 1958 and it came as no surprise that the Sirhowy Valley service was on the list for withdrawal in 1960, in fact closing on 11 June, though the official date was the 13th. By then the Sirhowy service was provided with a pannier tank from Newport Ebbw Junction shed with one coach. The final day saw the usual one coach train make the normal service, with a special 3 coach train forming the normal 6.35pm from Risca which joined up with the engine that had worked the single coach at Tredegar and the two engines worked on to Nantybwch, returning to Risca (and on to Newport) with the 7.52pm booked service from Tredegar. (See Last Day for details.)

Coal services were still involved to those collieries remaining open along the Valley, though most had now closed mainly due to exhaustion, leaving only Wyllie and Nine Mile Point by the mid-1960s. The Aberdare to Severn Tunnel coal trains still ran via Sirhowy Junction on the Vale of Neath line, and Tredegar Junction Lower, but with the closure of the Vale of Neath as a through route in 1964, these trains were diverted to run over the Aberdare to Abercynon, Pontypridd and Cardiff route. However in November 1967, the Cardiff Division saw the chance to close the lower section of Halls Road from Penar Junction to Crosskeys by reversing coal services to and from Oakdale and Markham at Penar Junction, and running them along the Vale of Neath to Sirhowy Junction, Tredegar Junction Lower and down the Sirhowy to Risca and on to Newport, alongside coal traffic from Wyllie and Nine Mile Point. What they had missed was that the latter two collieries on the Sirhowy were both scheduled for closure by the end of the decade and when both closed in 1969, traffic to and from Oakdale and Markham had to be accommodated again along Halls Road to enable the Sirhowy line to be completely closed. Since November 1967, part of the closed Halls Road line had been recovered and had to be re-opened and re-laid to take the displaced traffic.

With the transfer away of most of the LMR engines during 1959, the WR had begun allocating 57XXs to Tredegar, the first officially recorded in February 1958. However, 4643 of Pill had been photographed working miners' trains in mid-1957, presumably either on trial or on loan to Tredegar depot, though never allocated. Seven further 57XXs were allocated and all but two remained there until after the closure of the passenger service on 11 June 1960, though two had been withdrawn meanwhile. From August 1960, power for the Sirhowy line was provided by Ebbw Junction, always in the form of a 57XX which returned to Ebbw each day, the amount of freight work on the Sirhowy now being negligible, Wyllie and Nine Mile Point being covered by Ebbw 42XXs for as long as they remained open, with workings from the Halls Road line described as above. The whole route was finally closed on 4 May 1970.

Signal Boxes
Distance from Previous Box
Nantybwch No. 1

Sirhowy	1m.12ch.
Tredegar No. 1	68ch.
Tredegar No. 2	20ch.
Ty Trist Siding	35ch.
Bedwellty Pits	1m. 12ch.
Pochin Pits	1m. 22ch.
Markham Village	1m. 34ch.
Argoed	
Blackwood No. 1	2m. 67ch.
Blackwood No. 2	
Pontllanffraith HL	1m. 64ch.
Tredegar Junction Lower	35ch.
Wyllie No. 1	66ch.
Wyllie No. 2	38ch.
Nine Mile Point No. 1	1m. 77ch.
Nine Mile Point No. 2	32ch.
Rock Vein Sidings	67ch.
Risca Junction	1m. 57ch.

Mileage from Newport High Street & Gradient Profile

Risca	6m.24ch. 186Reverse
Brick Works South	6m.71ch. 101R
Black Vein Coll.	7m.19ch. 101R
Rock Vein Coll.	7m.69ch. 148R
Nine Mile Point	8m.53ch. 181R
Pont Lawrence	9m.44ch. 100R
Ynysddu	10m.71ch. 102R
Bedwellty Pits	20m.26ch. 127R
Ty Trist Siding	21m.26ch. 80R
Tredegar	21.77ch. 80R
Sirhowy	22m.72ch 54R
Nantybwch	24m. 1ch. 42R
Wyllie No.1	11m.58 91R
Tredegar Junction Lower	12m.39ch. 99R
Pontllanffraith HL	13m.1ch. 99R
Rock Siding	88R
Argoed	16m.7ch. 88R
Markham Village	17m.48ch. 93R
Holly Bush	18.44ch. 107R
Pochin Pits	19m.31ch. 127R

As can be seen from the above, it was a solid climb for the entirety of the Sirhowy line, and though the incline was mostly reasonable, other than north of Tredegar, there were often problems for Coal Tanks which had poor adhesion on wet rails (not uncommon in the least) even on the five coach sets used until the mid-1930s and later on 3 coach sets, when the guard's assistance from his van was often very necessary. Banking was necessary for passenger and freight trains north of Tredegar, and at other points for coal services often at the discretion of the driver, given the load and conditions.

CHAPTER TWO

PASSENGER SERVICES

TIMETABLE TRAINS

When the line was opened for passenger operations in June 1865, the original intention was that the Sirhowy Co. would operate only as far as Nine Mile Point from where the Monmouthshire Railway & Canal Co. would be responsible for the continuation to Newport. The impracticality of this arrangement was soon realised and by the Sirhowy Act of 5 July 1865, a through service operated between Sirhowy and Newport Dock Street on the basis of one through service in the morning, afternoon and evening, this being

July 1865 timetable.

implemented in advance of the publication of the Act. Stations were provided at Sirhowy, Tredegar, Blackwood, Tredegar Junction and Risca, the trains then running non-stop to Newport. Perhaps surprisingly, a Sunday service was also provided with a train in the morning and one in the evening. All trains were composed of 1st, 2nd and 3rd Class coaches. Overall journey times between Sirhowy and Newport were 1hr 32mins in both directions, though the first up train from Newport only took 1hr 29mins. The timetable (or Time Bill as it was then called) can be seen opposite.

The Traffic Manager responsible for the preparation of the timetable and its operation was Robert Bond and the Locomotive Superintendent Benjamin Fisher, both located at Tredegar. The General Manager at the opening of the railway in June 1865 was S.H. Yockney.

The first variation in the service came in 1866 when a station was opened at Argoed, with Nine Mile Point and an extension to Nantybwch added in 1869.

An indication of the level of traffic to be handled is related by W.W. Tasker who recalled that on 11 June 1870, Blackwood Races were attended by over 7,000 people, many of whom would have travelled by train. The company's entire stock of coaches was required to be used to handle the crowds on the booked and special trains run and, in a few instances, goods trucks were noted attached to passenger trains loaded full of standing passengers.

Two major events occurred in the second half of the 1870s, first the acquisition of the Sirhowy Railway by

Sirhowy Ry. July 1865

Traff. Man. R. Bond.

	Week Days				Sundays		
Newport		9.45	2.20	6.40		8.50	6.0
Risca		10.10	2.45	7.5		9.15	6.25
Tredegar Jun.		10.35	3.10	7.30		9.40	6.50
Blackwood		10.43	3.18	7.38		9.48	6.58
Tredegar	7.45	11.10	3.43	8.8	6.30	10.18	7.28
Sirhowy	7.49	11.14	3.52	8.12	6.34	10.22	7.32
Sirhowy	7.53	12.18	4.46	8.16	6.38	3.58	7.36
Tredegar	8.0	12.25	4.53	8.20	6.45	4.5	7.40
Blackwood	8.27	12.52	5.19		7.12	4.32	
Tredegar Jun	8.35	1.0	5.26		7.20	4.40	
Risca	9.0	1.25	5.50		7.45	5.5	
Newport	9.25	1.50	6.15		8.10	5.30	

All 1, 2, 3 class. The Trains do not stop between Risca & Newport.

Weekdays					Sundays			
Sirhowy	7.53	12/18	4/46	8/16	6.38	3/58	7/36	/=pm
Tredegar	8.0	12/25	4/53	8/20	6.45	4/5	7/40	
Blackwood	8.27	12/52	5/19		7.12	4/32		
Tredegar Junction	8.35	1/0	5/26		7.20	4/40		
Risca	9.0	1/25	5/50		7.45	5/5		
Newport Dock St.	9.25	1/50	6/15		8.10	5/30		
Newport Dock St.		9.45	2/20	6/40	8.50	6.0		
Risca		10.10	2/45	7/5	9.15	6/25		
Tredegar Junction		10.35	3/10	7/30	9.40	6/50		
Blackwood		10.43	3/18	7/38	9.48	6/58		
Tredegar	7.45	11.10	3/48	8/8	10.18	7/28		
Sirhowy	7.49	11.14	3/52	8/12	10.22	7/32		

the LNWR and second the opening of an enlarged Newport High Street station to provide for the transfer from Dock Street of each of the Valleys services, the Western Valley services (now operated by the GWR) transferring on 11 March 1880 and the others later. This now provided the unique sight of GWR and LNWR trains using the same facilities at Newport High Street station.

The 1880 timetable showed little difference in the number of trains run, but the influence of the Church had removed the Sunday trains. The new century brought a marked improvement in the level of service provided, with seven trains each way to and from Newport, plus an additional Tredegar to Nine Mile Point on Saturday mornings. During the First World War, one service each way was withdrawn.

In 1900, new LNWR four wheeled coaches, formed into five coach close-coupled sets, were introduced on LNW operated lines in South Wales, these replacement coaches fitted with the Fay & Newall continuous brake and required the guard's assistance from his van when stopping, these remaining in service until 1935. The new sets were splendid attractive looking sets of coaches which stood out when seen against many of the coaches operated by the GW. The formation of the five coach

sets was a Brake Third at each end, then a five compartment Third at each end and a Composite coach in the centre with two Second and two First class compartments. With the introduction of improved bus services in the Valleys to and from Newport in the late 1920s, train services were badly hit by the improved frequency, easier accessibility as they ran along the main streets, increased calling points and cheaper fares. The first casualty for the Sirhowy train services was 1st Class travel for which there was little demand and the composite coach of 1st and 2nd class accommodation was removed from the five coach sets, reducing them to four.

At the end of September 1935, the four wheeled stock was withdrawn, some being transferred to use on the miners' trains where veteran stock was already widely employed. Sirhowy trains were henceforth made up of two or three 8 wheel coaches, cascaded from other railways taken over by the LMS at the Grouping, such as the LNW itself, Lancashire & Yorkshire, North of Scotland, Furness and LMS itself, either vestibule or corridor stock, which enabled the guards to go through the train to issue tickets, enabling booking offices to be closed at some stations which were then reduced to halts. W.W. Tasker states that an ex-Midland Railway six-a-side non-

TRAIN SERVICE
NANTYBWCH, SIRHOWY AND NEWPORT (Weekdays only)

	a.m.	a.m.	a.m.	a.m	a.m	a.m.		a.m.	p.m.	p.m.	SX p.m.	SO p.m.	p.m.	p.m.	SO p.m.	SO p.m.	SX p.m.	p.m.	p.m.	p.m.	p.m.	SO p.m.	SX p.m.	SX p.m.	SO p.m.	SO
Nantybwch ....dep.	...	7 12	8 24	8 48	9 21	9 48	...	11 8	12 55	2 0	2 55	3 18	...	...	4 15	...	...	5 12	5 55	7 35	8 25	9 10	9 30	10 5	10 10	10 5
Sirhowy ....arr.	...	7 17	8 29	8 52	9 28	9 52	...	11 12	1 0	2 4	2 57	3 23	...	...	4 19	4 42	...	5 16	5 59	7 41	8 30	9 14	9 35	10 9	10 14	10 5
Tredegar {arr.	...	7 20	8 33	8 56	9 32	9 56	...	11 16	1 4	2 8	3 1	3 29	...	...	4 23	4 45	...	5 23	6 3	7 48	8 33	9 18	9 43	10 13	10 18	11
{dep.	5 45	7 22	8 35	...	...	9 58	...	11 18	1 10	2 9	...	...	4 15	...	4 50	4 55	...	6 5	7 52	...	9 25	9 44	10 14	10 22		
Bedwellty Pits ....dep.	5 49	7 26	8 39	...	...	10 3	...	11 23	1 15	2 12	...	...	4 18	...	4 55	...	...	6 5	7 57	...	9 30	9 48	10 20	10 27		
Holly Bush ....,,	5 56	7 31	8 44	...	...	10 8	...	11 28	1 20	2 17	...	...	4 23		5 0	...	...	6 15	8 3	...	9 35	9 53	10 28	10 32		
Markham Village Halt ....,,	5 59	7 34	8 47	...	...	10 11	...	11 32	1 24	2 20	...	...	4 27		5 4	5 4	...	6 18	8 7	...	9 40	9 58	10 33	10 37		
Argoed ....,,	6 4	7 38	8 51	...	...	10 16	...	11 37	1 28	2 25	...	...	4 32		5 8	5 8	...	6 23	8 12	...	9 46	10 4	...	10 43		
Blackwood ....,,	6 9	7 44	8 56	...	...	10 21	...	11 43	1 34	2 30	...	...	4 36		5 14	5 14	...	6 29	8 18	...	9 52	10 9	...	10 49		
Pontllanfraith {arr.	6 14	7 49	9 1	...	...	10 25	...	11 47	1 39	2 35	...	...	4 41		5 18	5 18	...	6 33	8 22	...	9 56	10 14	...	10 53		
{dep.	6 15	7 50	9 3	...	...	10 26	...	11 48	1 40	2 37	...	...	4 42		5 19	5 19	...	6 34	8 23	...	9 58	10 17	...	10 55		
Wyllie Halt ....,,	6 18	7 53	9 6	...	...	10 29	...	11 51	1 43	2 41	...	...	4 45		5 22	5 22	...	6 38	8 26	...	10 1	10 21	...	10 58		
Ynysddu ....,,	6 20	7 55	9 8	...	...	10 31	...	11 53	1 46	2 43	...	...	4 46		5 24	5 24	...	6 40	8 28	...	10 4	10 26	...	11 0		
Pont Lawrence ....,,	6 23	7 59	9 11	...	...	10 35	...	11 57	1 49	2 46	...	...	4 49		5 27	5 27	...	6 44	8 32	...	10 9	10 29	...	11 3		
Nine-Mile-Point ....,,	6 27	8 4	9 15	...	...	10 40	...	12 3	1 53	2 51	...	...	4 53		5 32	5 32	...	6 50	8 37	...	10 14	10 33	...	11 6		
Risca ....,,	6 33	8 11	9 21	...	...	10 46	...	12 10	2 0	C	...	5 1	5 9		5 37	5 33	...	6 56	8 42	...	10 19	...	...	...		
Bassaleg Junction ....,,	AB	AB	AB	...	...	AB	...	AB	AB	AB	...	...	5 21		AB	AB	...	AB	AB	...	AB	...	...	...		
Newport ....arr.	6 49	8 27	9 37	...	...	10 58	...	12 23	2 16	3 20	...	...	5 29		5 55	5 50	...	7 10	9 0	...	10 37	...	...	...		
Cardiff ....,,	7 49	9 10	10 14	...	...	11 43	...	12 56	3 3	3 42	...	...	5 51		6 19	6 19	...	7 48	9 34	...	12 14	...	...	...		

	a.m.	a.m.	a.m.	a.m.	a.m	a.m.		a.m.	p.m.	a.m.	SO p.m.	p.m.	p.m.	p.m.	p.m.	p.m.	p.m.	p.m.	p.m.	SO p.m.	SX p.m.	SO p.m.	
Cardiff ....dep.	...	...	...	...	6 55	8 30	...	10 15	...	11 48	12 35	...	2 40	3 45	4 35	...	...	7 0	...	8 21	9 30	10 30	10 52	...
Newport ....,,	4 30	...	...	...	7 22	8 50	...	10 38	...	12 15	1 10	...	3 10	4 8	4 59	...	...	7 35	...	9 5	10 0	10 55	11 22	...
Bassaleg Junction ....,,	...	...	...	...	BB	BB	...	BB	...	BB	BB	...	BB	BB	5 6	...	...	BB	...	BB	BB	BB	BB	...
Risca ....,,	4 47	...	...	...	7 40	9 5	...	10 53	...	12 30	1 26	...	3 26	4 22	5 17	5 20	...	7 52	...	D	10 17	E	11 28	...
Nine-Mile-Point ....,,	4 54	...	...	...	7 47	9 11	...	10 59	...	12 36	1 32	...	3 32	4 28	...	5 25	...	7 58	...	9 29	10 23	11 14	11 34	...
Pont Lawrence ....,,	...	...	...	...	7 51	9 14	...	11 3	...	12 39	1 35	...	3 35	...	...	5 28	...	8 1	...	9 33	10 27	11 21	11 38	...
Ynysddu ....,,	5 1	...	...	...	7 56	9 18	...	11 8	...	12 44	1 39	...	3 39	4 34	...	5 32	...	8 5	...	9 37	10 31	11 21	11 44	...
Wyllie Halt {arr.	...	...	...	...	7 58	9 20	...	11 10	...	12 47	1 41	...	3 42	4 37	...	5 35	...	8 7	...	9 39	10 33	11 23	11 44	...
Pontllanfraith {dep.	5 6	...	...	...	8 1	9 23	...	11 14	...	12 52	1 44	...	3 45	4 41	...	5 38	...	8 10	...	9 43	10 37	11 27	11 47	...
{dep.	5 8	...	...	...	8 9	9 25	...	11 15	...	12 53	1 46	...	3 46	4 42	...	5 39	...	8 12	...	9 44	10 38	11 28	11 48	...
Blackwood ....,,	5 14	...	...	...	8 18	9 31	...	11 19	...	12 57	1 53	...	3 53	4 46	...	5 43	...	8 18	...	9 50	10 42	11 33	11 53	...
Argoed ....,,	...	...	...	...	8 23	9 36	...	11 25	...	1 4	1 58	...	3 58	4 52	...	5 51	...	8 23	...	9 55	10 49	11 42	11 58	...
Markham Village Halt ....,,	...	...	...	...	8 33	9 44	...	11 32	...	1 10	2 6	...	4 6	4 59	...	5 56	...	8 32	...	10 6	10 57	11 47	12 7	...
Holly Bush ....,,	...	...	...	...	8 37	9 48	...	11 37	...	1 14	2 10	...	4 10	5 3	...	6 0	...	8 37	...	10 10	11 1	11 51	12 11	...
Bedwellty Pits ....,,	...	...	...	...	8 42	9 55	...	11 42	...	1 21	2 15	...	4 15	5 8	...	6 5	...	8 42	...	10 18	11 8	11 56	12 18	...
Tredegar {arr.	5 34	...	...	...	8 47	10 3	...	11 47	...	1 27	2 20	...	4 20	5 14	...	6 11	...	8 47	...	10 24	11 15	12 2	12 24	...
Sirhowy {dep.	...	6 50	8 0	8 25	9 25	10 27	...	12 3	1 32	...	2SX32	2 55	...	5 15	...	6 12	7 15	8 5	8 50	9 35	10 30	11 21	12 4	...
Nantybwch ....,,	...	6 53	8 3	8 28	9 28	10 32	...	12 6	1 35	...	2SX28	2 58	...	4 33	5 18	...	6 15	7 18	8 8	8 58	9 38	10 33	11 21	12 7	12 31
.........arr.	...	7 1	8 10	8 40	9 35	10 37	...	12 13	1 42	...	2SX36	3 5	...	4 40	5 25	...	7 25	8 17	9 5	9 47	10 40	...	...	...	

AB—Calls at Bassaleg Junction to set down from Sirhowy line stations on notice being given by the passenger to the guard. BB—Calls at Bassaleg Junction when required to pick up passengers for Sirhowy line stations on notice being given at the station.

C—Calls at Risca to set down if required, on notice being given to the guard at Nine-Mile-Point.

D—Calls at Risca to pick up if required.

E—Calls at Risca to pick up passengers for the Sirhowy line on notice being given at the station.

SX—Saturdays excepted.   SO—Saturdays only.

corridor three coach set, composed of clerestory roof and gas-lit stock, was seen in operation in 1935-8.

During the first decades of the twentieth century, especially after the Grouping, the passenger service had been developed so that by September 1936, there were now five services to Newport during the morning, four in the afternoon and three in the evenings with variable SX and SO trains.

With the opening of new collieries, additional stations and halts had been opened and this resulted in there now being fourteen stations between Nantybwch and Risca, the additional being at Bedwellty Pits, Holly Bush, Markham Village Halt, Wyllie, Ynysddu and Pont Lawrence in addition to those already mentioned. Some of the older coaching stock was withdrawn following Nationalisation and replaced by

modern three-a-side LMS corridor stock which upgraded the comfort of travel considerably, but normally it was only one coach per train.

The continual downturn in passenger carryings on local services in South Wales during the 1950s (with the exception of the Cardiff Valleys where the introduction of Regular Interval services from September 1953 showed how potential could be realised) threw into relief lines such as the Sirhowy, Eastern & Western Valleys, Vale of Neath, etc., where no such modernisation in the way of regular interval working was possible and they continued to decline, other than on Saturdays, Bank Holidays and rugby international days. By 1953, the Sirhowy's twelve trains per day of 1936 had declined to eight (three in the morning, three in the afternoon and two in the evening) with long gaps such as

Passenger Service 1954.

24 — SIRHOWY BRANCH, BRYNMAWR, ABERGAVENNY, etc.

NEWPORT .... dep.	4 20	..	..	..	7 22	..	9 5	..	..	..	1 10	3 50	5e40	7 37	..	9 28
Bassaleg .... ,,	CR	..	..	..	7 29	..	9 12	..	..	..	1 17	3 57	5e47	7 44	..	9 37
Risca .... ,,	4 34	..	..	..	7 39	..	9 22	..	..	..	1 27	4 7	6 0	7 54	..	9 47
Nine Mile Point .... ,,	4 40	..	..	..	7 46	..	9 28	..	..	..	1 33	4 13	6 5	8 1	..	9 56
Point Lawrence .... ,,	..	..	..	..	7 49	..	9 31	..	..	..	1 36	4 16	6 8	8 4	..	9 59
Ynys ddu .... ,,	4 47	..	..	..	7 54	..	9 36	..	..	..	1 41	4 21	6 13	8 8	..	10 4
Wyllie Halt .... ,,	..	..	..	..	7 57	..	9 39	..	..	..	1 44	4 24	6 16	8 11	..	10 7
Pontllanfraith ...... arr.	4 55	..	..	..	8 2	..	9 44	..	..	..	1 49	4 29	6 21	8 15	..	10 12
Blackwood .... dep.	5 4	..	..	..	8 9	..	9 49	..	..	..	1 54	4 34	6 27	8 20	..	10 18
Argoed .... ,,	..	..	..	..	8 17	..	9 56	..	..	..	2 1	4 41	6 34	8 28	..	10 25
Markham Village .. ,,	..	..	..	..	8 22	..	10 1	..	..	..	2 6	4 46	6 39	8 33	..	10 31
Holly Bush .... ,,	..	..	..	..	8 27	..	10 6	..	..	..	2 11	4 51	6 44	8 38	..	10 36
Bedwellty Pits .... ,,	..	..	..	..	8 34	..	10 13	..	..	..	2 20	4 58	6 51	8 45	..	10 45
Tredegar .... arr.	5 40	..	..	..	8 41	..	10 20	..	..	..	2 27	5 4	6 58	8 51	..	10 52
Tredegar .... dep.	●	6 35	6 55	8 2	●	..	10 31	..	12 55	..	2 28	5 5	●	8 56	..	10 56
Sirhowy .... ,,	..	6 39	7 5	8 6	..	..	10 35	..	12 58	..	2 32	5 9	...	8 59	..	10 59
Nantybwch ...... arr.	..	6 45	7 11	8 12	..	..	10 41	..	1 5	..	2 38	5 15	..	9 5	..	11* 6
Nantybwch ...... dep.	5 41	..	..	8 44	..	..	10 56	..	..	..	3 20	5 55	..	9 24	..	●
Dowlais .... ,,	5 55	..	..	8 59	..	..	11 8	..	..	..	3 39	6 9	..	9 38	..	..
Merthyr .... arr.	●	..	..	9 28	..	..	11 36	..	..	..	4 7	6 36	..	10 3	..	..
Nantybwch ...... dep.	..	6 47	..	8 13	..	..	10 49	..	1 26	..	●	5 31	..	9 14	..	..
Trevil Halt .... ,,	..	6 50	..	8 17	..	..	10 52	..	1 30	..	..	5 35	..	9 17	..	..
Beaufort .... ,,	..	6 55	..	8 22	..	..	10 57	..	1 35	..	..	5 40	..	9 22	..	..
Brynmawr .... dep.	..	7 1	..	8 29	..	..	11 4	..	1 40	..	..	5 46	..	9 29	..	..
Gelli-Felen Halt .... ,,	..	7 6	..	8 33	..	..	11 8	..	1 45	..	..	5 50	..	9 33	..	..
Clydach Halt ...... ,,	..	7 12	..	8 39	..	..	11 14	..	1 50	..	..	5 56	..	9 39	..	..
Gilwern Halt ...... ,,	..	7 16	..	8 44	..	..	11 19	..	1 54	..	..	6 0	..	9 44	..	..
Govilon .... ,,	..	7 22	..	8 50	..	..	11 25	..	2 0	..	..	6 6	..	9 50	..	..
Abergavenny (B. Rd.) ,,	..	7 30	..	9 0	..	..	11 35	..	2 7	..	..	6 14	..	10 0	..	..
Abergavenny Jct. ... arr.	..	7 35	..	9 3	..	..	11 38	..	2 11	..	..	6 19	..	10 3	..	..

* Sats. only.

C.R.—Calls when required to pick up, for Sirhowy Line, notice to be given at the Station.

Change at Risca.

between 9.5am and 1.10pm from Newport northwards. The lack of attraction of such services paid the usual penalty in level of usage. In July 1954, the Western Region's Cardiff Divisional Office reduced the Sirhowy service to operating only between Risca and Nantybwch, with trains connecting in and out of Western Valley services, and being operated by an auto set and engine, the first and last services of the day running from/to Newport.

With only five services per day and over two hours gap between services, the timetable had no attraction and soon one coach sufficed to convey the dwindling numbers, some trains running with just one or two passengers. The down service was at 6.35, 8.50, 11am, then nothing until 4.50pm through from Nantybwch, with a following 7.52pm from Tredegar through to Newport. Northwards from Risca, there were trains at 4.35am (4.20am Newport Mail), 7.55am, 10.5am, 12.30pm and 6.32pm all to Tredegar. You wonder why they bothered!

With such a meaningless service, it came as no surprise when it was announced that the passenger service would be withdrawn on Monday, 13 June 1960. Even that meant that in practice it would be the previous Saturday.

The first fifty or so years of the twentieth century saw the passenger service dominated by the Webb Coal Tank 0-6-2Ts, which, though they had some problems with stopping when running downhill and had to be assisted by the guard from his van, were really masters of their task. Their punctuality was exemplary and my grandfather, who lived opposite the Risca Viaduct, used to say, you could set your watch by them on the passenger service. Following Nationalisation, four of the Ivatt 2-6-2Ts were allocated to Abergavenny and one or two of these worked from Tredegar each day, appearing on the Newport services most days during the early 1950s, some days in company with one of the

Stanier 2-6-2Ts, taking over the service entirely after the withdrawal of the Coal Tanks in about 1953, but themselves ceding place to a WR 64XX or 57XX from July 1954.

WORKMEN'S TRAINS
Winter 1953-54

From 1941 until the early 1950s, the Workmen's services on the Sirhowy included services to the Northern Aluminium Works at Rogerstone as well as services to each of the large collieries on the Sirhowy viz:- Nine Mile Point, Wyllie, Rock, Markham (on Halls Road), Pochin Pits, Bedwellty Pits and Ty Trist. Ordinary passengers could use the Rogerstone services (unlike the Miners' trains) and change at Rogerstone for Newport and the same in the other direction.

Rogerstone

4.26am Sirhowy to Rogerstone 5.23am
6.20am Rogerstone to Sirhowy 7.29am
12.26pm Sirhowy to Rogerstone 1.28pm
2.20pm Rogerstone to Sirhowy 3.33pm
8.26pm Sirhowy to Rogerstone 9.28pm
10.20pm Rogerstone to Sirhowy 11.29pm
These services were normally worked by Stanier 2-6-2T No. 40079

Miners' Trains

Trains called at all stations and halts and miners could join and alight wherever they needed. Trains were timed to connect with the start/end of shifts at the colliery at which the train terminated/started.

Nine Mile Point

4.10am Tredegar to Nine Mile Point 4.56am
5.39am Nine Mile Point to Tredegar 6.38am
2.55pm Tredegar to Nine Mile Point 3.52pm
3.14pm Nine Mile Point to Sirhowy 4.10pm

Wyllie

5.25am Sirhowy to Wyllie 6.9am
7.23am Wyllie to Tredegar 8.6am
11.8pm Wyllie to Tredegar 11.48pm
SO 2.25pm Wyllie to Sirhowy 3.12pm

Markham

5.52am Nantybwch to Markham Village
Halt 6.19am

3.0pm Markham Village Halt to
Nantybwch 3.34pm

Pochin Pits

6.1am Nantybwch to Pochin Pits 6.32am
(ECS to Argoed)

SX 2.30pm ECS Argoed to Pochin Pits

SX 2.50pm Pochin Pits to Nantybwch
3.19pm

SO 1.30pm Argoed to Pochin Pits ECS

SO 1.55pm Pochin Pits to Nantybwch
2.24pm

Summer 1958

Nine Mile Point, Wyllie, Pochin,
Markham (on Halls Road), and Ty Trist
collieries were still operating at this
time. The following trains were run to
convey miners to and from work at these
collieries:-

Nine Mile Point

M-S 4.10am Tredegar to Nine Mile Point
4.56am

& Wyllie

5.39am Nine Mile Point to Tredegar 6.38am

SX 2.55pm Tredegar South End to Nine
Mile Point 3.52pm

SX 9.43pm Tredegar to Nine Mile Point
10.33pm

10.57pm ECS Nine Mile Point to Wyllie
11.6pm

11.08pm Wyllie to Tredegar 11.48pm
(Workmen & Passenger)

SX 3.10pm ECS Nine Mile Point to Wyllie

SX 3.25pm Wyllie to Sirhowy 4.10pm

SO Q 1.55pm Tredegar South End to Nine
Mile Point ECS 2.2pm

ECS to Wyllie for 2.25 Wyllie to Sirhowy
3.10pm

3.15pm Sirhowy to Tredegar ECS 3.18pm

Markham

M-S 5.52am Nantybwch to Markham
Village Halt 6.24am

7.05am Markham Village Halt to
Nantybwch 7.40am

7.55am Nantybwch to Tredegar ECS 8.20am

SX 10.5pm Nantybwch to Markham
Village Halt 10.40pm.

10.56pm Markham Village Halt
to   Nantybwch 11.28pm.

SO Q 1.0pm Tredegar to Argoed LE 1.20pm

1.50pm Argoed ECS to Markham Village
Halt

1.55pm Markham Village Halt to
Nantybwch 2.44pm

2.50pm LE Nantybwch to Tredegar 3.0pm

SO 3.10pm Markham Village Halt to
Nantybwch 3.44pm.

Pochin Pits

M-S 6.01am Nantybwch to Pochin Pits
Halt 6.28am (ECS to MVH)

6.50am Markham Village Halt to Tredegar
ECS 7.8am

SX 2.0pm Nantybwch to Pochin Pits Halt
2.20pm ECS to MVH 2.30pm

SO Q 1.15pm ECS Tredegar-Markham
Village Halt 1.35pm

1.35pm Markham Village Halt ECS to
Pochin Pits

1.50pm Pochin Pits to Nantybwch 2.19pm

2.50pm LE Nantybwch to Tredegar 3.0pm.
or SO Q 1.30pm LE Tredegar to Argoed
1.55pm

2.30pm Argoed ECS to Pochin Pits

2.50pm Pochin Pits to Nantybwch 3.19pm.

3.20pm LE Nantybwch to Tredegar 3.30pm.

Tredegar Company
Collier's Pass for
travelling to and
from work on
Workmen's trains
valid between
Nantybwch and
Pochin Colliery
or between
Pontllanffraith and
Tredegar.

EXCURSION TRAINS
Main Line

Excursion traffic was very important to the LNWR and on most weekends until the start of the First World War, special charters or advertised excursions would run to the likes of Hereford, Shrewsbury (Flower Show), Blackpool, Manchester, Birmingham, Coventry, Glasgow and Edinburgh, especially at Bank Holidays. In season, rugby union specials would run to destinations featuring Wales Internationals, these being Cardiff or Swansea, London, Edinburgh and Heysham for boats to Ireland. Empty stock would be brought in from Crewe and other centres, and trains needed double heading unless a 4-6-0 worked through down the Sirhowy to the likes of Pontllanffraith or Blackwood to work the train throughout, this proving possible as such engines had to work down to Abergavenny to take over the train beyond. The usual practice however was for two Coal Tanks or an 0-8-0 (sometimes assisted by a Coal Tank) to work trains west of Abergavenny. Tasker recalls seeing LNWR 4-6-0 No. 88 *Czar of Russia* at Argoed on an excursion to Blackpool around 1922, but there are also photographs existing of Blackpool excursions being worked over the Sirhowy to Abergavenny route and back by two Coal Tanks. Excursion traffic ceased during the war but resumed again from about 1920 and by about 1930 the long distance trains had mostly ceased and been replaced by local services within South Wales, especially to Barry Island. However, rugby international excursions continued.

Some excursions from Aberdare ran via Sirhowy Junction and Tredegar Junction Lower onto the southern section of the Sirhowy to give a quicker access to Newport than via the Taff Vale line.

Barry Island

Though there were Saturday football excursions to Newport and Cardiff, the most frequent destination weekend and bank holiday excursions was Barry Island. There are records of excursions running under LNWR colours hauled by two Coal Tanks as far back as 1905. These originally started from Abergavenny Junction and ran along the MT&A, but the trains would soon be full and additional trains had to be started from Brynmawr, Nantybwch and Tredegar. It was also common for churches and schools to organise their own excursions on a charter basis, one notable origin being Holly Bush with a complete train starting from there and running non-stop. Up to five trains are reported to have run from the MT&A and Sirhowy line some weekends and bank holidays, when virtually all the stock available in the area would be worked to Barry, and additional stock had to be worked in.

Power was originally provided by double-headed Coal Tanks, with 0-8-0s and 0-8-4 tanks also employed, providing what must have been a feast of LNW power at Barry Island. The practice until the Grouping was for the Barry Railway to run empty coaches, utilising their running powers, to various locations in the Rhondda and Rhymney valleys to collect the day-tripper traffic and to convey them back in the evening, returning empty stock to Barry, but the Barry enjoyed no running powers over the LNW lines who therefore utilised and extended theirs by agreement to work excursions through to Barry Island. From the Grouping, the GWR was able to run out-and-back excursions from the Valleys under their own auspices and the employment of Barry engines on Sundays and Bank Holidays became confined to the booked service.

During the 1930s, there are reports of other types of power being employed with the G2 0-8-0s, such as a Hughes 2-6-0 and a 4F 0-6-0. Until 1935, trains were made up of 4 wheelers and

Tasker recalls a Sunday in 1933 when the train was made up of thirteen 4 wheelers and a 6 wheel brake third. By the early 1950s, these excursions had been eliminated from the MT&A with excursions from Abergavenny running via the main North and West line via Newport. The Sirhowy excursion traffic became confined to one train on summer Sundays and Bank Holidays starting first at Brynmawr, though this was then switched to the Western Valley, with the Sirhowy excursion starting from Nantybwch, a 6 coach train worked by a Super D, the four engines most employed being 49064, 49121, 49168 and 49409. The train was normally formed with a two coach LMS corridor set and four ex-GW non corridors.

There were two routes provided for these trains which ran either via Risca and Park Junction, or via Bird in Hand, Ystrad Mynach and Walnut Tree Viaduct, the latter becoming the regular route as the decade progressed. When the Risca route was used, the trains called additionally at Wyllie, Ynysddu, Nine Mile Point and Risca and then Cardiff General. Return trains via that route would probably have needed banking as more coaches are likely to have been conveyed.

Trains ran with common times as far as Pontllanffraith HL which were:-

49064 heads the Nantybwch to Barry Island Sunday excursion seen approaching Barry Dock station on 10 June 1957, carrying reporting number 52 which was the number carried before the later 56, by which the train became well known. John Hodge

A rare chance to see an LNW 0-8-0 carrying a Western Region Reporting Number on the smokebox as 49064 heads past Cadoxton Low Level box with the 7.35pm return excursion from Barry Island to Nantyhwch carrying 015 on 26 May 1958.
John Hodge

Nantybwch	Dep. 9.30am
Sirhowy	9.34 – 9.35am
Tredegar	9.38 – 9.45am
Bedwellty Pits	9.50am
Holly Bush	9.58am
Markham Village	10.03am
Argoed	10.08am
Blackwood	10.15am
Pontllanffraith	10.20am
Bird in Hand West	10/27am
Tredegar Junction Lower	10/22am
Hengoed HL	10/31am
Wyllie	10.26am
Ystrad Mynach North	10/35am
Ynysddu	10.29am
Ystrad Mynach South	10/37am
Nine Mile Point	10.36am

Thence via Llanbradach (Water Stop)
      Risca Junction 10.46am
Aber Junction, Penrhos Junction, Walnut
      Tree Viaduct, Park Junction 10/55am
Drope Junction, Wenvoe and Cadoxton to
      Barry Is.

In addition to the weekend excursions to Barry Island, regular Saturday excursions were run to Cardiff Queen Street during the 1930s via Ystrad Mynach, for shopping or events. These were also worked by a G2, 48899 often being favoured. On the Royal Gwent Hospital Carnival Day at Newport in the 1930s, all trains were strengthened to the load limit and all return trains ran late due to having to pull up twice at the platforms.

CHAPTER THREE

COAL & FREIGHT SERVICES

THE EARLIEST FREIGHT traffic over the Sirhowy Tramroad would have been coal from the local patches and levels, iron ore and limestone to Sirhowy and then Tredegar Ironworks, and iron and iron products from Tredegar Ironworks to Newport Wharves, the iron from Sirhowy Ironworks being conveyed to Ebbw Vale Works. However, many of the tramways from the local mines ran direct into the Sirhowy and Tredegar Ironworks and did not form part of the Sirhowy Tramroad as such. With the conversion of the Tramway to a Railway and commissioning in 1865, all traffic to Newport would have been conveyed over the new railway, plus other traffic such as bricks and metals from the likes of Waunfawr and Danygraig at Risca, together with colliery supplies such as pitwood.

Most if not all the coal mined at Whitworth, Ty Trist, Bedwellty and Pochin was consumed at Tredegar Ironworks but when this works closed in 1901, new markets were found for the steam coal produced, many of which were abroad, generating movement to Newport, Cardiff and Barry Docks, creating a requirement for a supply of empties to the collieries and a service for loaded wagons out. This traffic had previously passed over the Tredegar Iron & Coal Company (TICC) private line, but now it was chargeable for conveyance by the LMS. With perhaps two trains of empties per day required into each of these pits and two trains of loaded out, this would have meant an increased daily movement of up to 10-12 trains in each direction. Abernant Colliery, owned

by the Bargoed Coal Co., would have increased this number by probably another two trainloads per day. Train working was both to/from Abergavenny and Rogerstone, the latter more for collieries at the south end of the Valley, with trains for Cardiff and Barry Docks using the inter-Valley link via Bird in Hand.

Nine Mile Point opened between 1902-5 with trains required both north to Abergavenny, worked by Tredegar, and south to Rogerstone and Newport, worked by Ebbw Junction. This added to the requirement to serve Risca Colliery, which was served from Rogerstone with outward trains from the colliery to that yard and Newport Docks. Black Vein Colliery was the earliest large colliery on the Risca section and would have required one or two trains in and out per day. Many collieries advertised house and gas coal which was ordered in single wagon loads and required to be conveyed through marshalling yards to destination, initially Abergavenny or Rogerstone. Collieries receiving empties from Newport normally received these from Maesglas (or even Dock Street) as empties off shipment traffic.

Sirhowy Valley coal formed part of the supply to Scapa Flow via the Jellicoe Specials in 1914-18, with trains conveyed to Abergavenny Junction via the MT&A for onward movement to Scotland. Sirhowy steam coal was also supplied to LMS locomotive sheds, as Western Valley steam coal was to GWR and SR sheds, this traffic lasting until the 1960s.

Abernant Colliery at Argoed closed in

1932, and Bedwellty between 1939-41 but other than that, most other large collieries lasted until the late 1950s and '60s. Ty Trist, which would have required 2-3 trains per day, closed in 1959, reducing movements over the line by that amount in both directions. Budds Rock Colliery at Blackwood had closed in 1957, but this would have required one train per day at most. Pochin Pits closed in 1964, leaving only the two newer pits at Nine Mile Point and Wyllie in production until their demise by 1969. From this, it can be seen how coal services over the Sirhowy declined during the late 1950s and '60s.

Following the closure of so many station yards and collieries with land sale facilities, the NCB set up a large domestic coal yard at Sirhowy to act as a land sale and concessionary coal yard for use by coal merchants and this created a need to bring in coal by rail from collieries still producing domestic coal, such as in the Tondu and Cardiff valleys, for which two trains were run each day from Rogerstone. With the decline in use of domestic coal and pressure from British Rail to close the Sirhowy line, this depot was closed in 1963, leaving the only freight movement on the line south of Pontllanffraith.

It was the closure of Nine Mile Point and Wyllie that signalled the end of freight traffic on the Sirhowy. Coal from Aberdare to Severn Tunnel and England had been re-routed via Aberdare-Abercynon and Cardiff following the closure of the Vale of Neath as a through route in 1964. Coal from Oakdale which had been re-routed to travel over the Sirhowy Junction-Tredegar Junction Lower link and then down the Sirhowy to Risca was switched back to the southern section of Halls Road which had been closed in 1967 and partly recovered, as the savings to be made by closing Tredegar Junction Lower to Risca were greater than those for Penar Junction to Halls Road Junction at Crosskeys. The way was then open to close the Sirhowy line in its entirety which happened in 1970.

Analysis of Working Timetable for 1953

A copy of the 1953 WTT for the Sirhowy Valley has been created and is presented below. This shows both Passenger and Freight services, including Workmen's trains, EBV and LE movements. The line can be conveniently split at Pontllanffraith (Tredegar Junction Lower / Bird in Hand) as most of the trains using the southern section of the line came on/went off at that point, most en route to Aberdare. Those services above Pontllanffraith are serving the Sirhowy collieries above that station.

Services Over Southern Section (Below Pontllanffraith)
Aberdare Trains
Of the 10 SX services using the southern section of the line in 1953, eight were from Aberdare with coal for Severn Tunnel Junction Yard or through to England (loco coal), and of these all those to STJ returned with empties, as follows:-

Train		Pass Tredegar Junction Lower	Pass Risc
1.30am	Aberdare-STJ	4.7am	4.45am
3.45am	Aberdare-Moreton Cutting	5.42am	6.16am
5.45am	Aberdare-STJ	7.50am	8.31am
8.40am	Aberdare-STJ	10.46am	11.21am
10.40am	Aberdare-Salisbury SO	1.24pm	2.00pm
1.25pm	Aberdare-STJ	3.16pm	3.55pm
5.5pm	Aberdare-STJ	7.1pm	7.38pm
5.20pm	Aberdare-Maesglas	7.29pm	8.5pm
7.0pm	Aberdare-AD Junction	8.45pm	9.20pm
9.15pm	Aberdare-Salisbury SX	11.47pm	12.23am
10.30pm	Aberdare-STJ SX	1.02am	1.38am

Trains to STJ conveyed largely domestic coal and smokeless Phurnacite (from Abercwmboi) for onward marshalling to destinations across the south of England. Trains to Salisbury contained steam coal for Salisbury Engine Shed and probably also for Exmouth Junction as there was no direct train from Aberdare to Exeter. The train to Moreton Cutting carried loco coal for Didcot and Reading and possibly Oxford, though there were direct services of iron ore empties to Yarnton from Rogerstone. The Maesglas train had shipment coal for Newport Dock, and that to AD Junction coal for Newport and main line connections.

Return trains to Aberdare, mostly of Empties, were as follows:-

Train		Pass Risca	Pass Tredegar Junction Lower
4.20am	STJ-Aberdare	5.37am	6.15am
11.15pm	SX Salisbury-Aberdare	7.50am	8.18am
8.0am	STJ-Aberdare	9.45am	10.13am
11.40am	MX STJ-Aberdare	1.32pm	2.0pm
2.5pm	STJ-Aberdare	3.33pm	4.1pm
9.45pm	STJ-Aberdare	10.48pm	11.17pm
10.30pm	STJ-Aberdare	12.5am	12.39am
10.40pm	AD Junction-Aberdare	12.15am	12.52am

Nine Mile Point was served from Maesglas and Rogerstone by the 4.45am Maesglas-NMP arr. 5.52am. This service also worked small coal Risca Coll. to NMP as required.

8am Maesglas-NMP arr. 11.2am, returning at 12.15pm to Maesglas with shipment coal.

3.30pm Maesglas-NMP arr. 5.50pm returning 7.5pm NMP-Rogerstone.

Nine Mile Point was also served from the Tredegar end by a 7.20am service to Tredegar and the 3.30pm empties from Tredegar arr.5.50pm, returning at 4.30pm with traffic for the north via Abergavenny Junction

Empties were also provided by the 1.10pm SX (12.10pm SO) from Bird in Hand with wagons brought in from Ystrad Mynach.

A service at 4.25pm from Tredegar to NMP arr. 5.30pm departed again at 5.50pm from NMP to Ystrad Mynach conveyed coal for Cardiff or Barry Dock shipment. A second service ran at 6.30pm from NMP either EBV or loaded from NMP or from Bird in Hand with shipment traffic staged there, running to Ystrad Mynach.

Wyllie. The 7.30am from Rogerstone served all sidings and collieries en route to Wyllie (Danygraig Brickworks, Black Vein Colliery, Rock Vein, Nine Mile Point and Wyllie), loading back to Rogerstone at 4pm.

A direct service at 11.45am from Maesglas ran to Wyllie, returning at 3.50pm to Rogerstone.

There was also a 4.25pm EBV from Tredegar to Wyllie, loading back to Ystrad Mynach with Cardiff or Barry shipment coal.

Quakers Yard. A service ran from Rogerstone to Quakers Yard at 5.25pm calling at Nine Mile Point from 5.50 to 6.15pm and returned from Quakers Yard at 9.30pm to Rogerstone arr. 12.2am.

Services Over Northern Section (above Pontllanffraith)

Nine Mile Point. Services for traffic to the North via Abergavenny or for Merthyr ran from NMP to Tredegar at 7.20am and to Nantybwch at 4.30pm. Empties were also provided from Bird in Hand at 1.10pm (SX) and 12.10pm (SO).

There was also a 3.30pm Tredegar to Nine Mile Point which served Ty Trist (3.35-4pm), Pochin Pits (4.8-4.45pm), and Bird in Hand (5.10-5.30pm), arriving NMP at 5.50pm.

Rock Colliery at Blackwood was served by the 8.35am Bird in Hand to Tredegar which called at Rock from 9.0-9.20am, Bedwellty Pits from 10.42-10.58am and Ty Trist 11.3-11.20am.

Pochin Pits. Shipment traffic for Cardiff and Barry was cleared by a 10.45am

SX (9.45am SO) to Ystrad Mynach, and presumably if for Newport Docks, the train ran to Maesglas.

There was a 10.5am SO from Tredegar to Pochin and a 10.35am EBV SX from Tredegar to Pochin which both returned loaded at 11.25am.

Pochin was also served by the 3.30pm Tredegar to NMP from 4.8-4.45pm, which also called at Bird in Hand.

Bedwellty Pits. Empties were provided by the 8.20pm Ystrad Mynach to Tredegar which called at Bedwellty Pits at 9.41-10.5pm. Loaded were cleared by the 8.45am Tredegar-Bird in Hand between 9.5-11.20. On SO there was a 1.0pm empties from Abergavenny to Bedwellty, which presumably loaded back, though no time is shown.

Ty Trist was served for northern traffic by the 1.35pm empties from Abergavenny Junction which also called at Sirhowy (3.10-3.35pm) and Tredegar (3.40-4.20pm).

Loaded for northern destinations were cleared by the 5.5pm return to Abergavenny. This service is known to have been worked by an 0-8-0. Traffic for the south was cleared by the 3.30pm Tredegar to Nine Mile Point which called at Ty Trist from 3.35-4pm, Pochin 4.8-4.45pm and Bird in Hand 5.10-5.30pm (where shipment for Cardiff and Barry was put off) before arriving NMP at 5.50pm. A 2.30pm SO from Tredegar to Abergavenny Junction cleared traffic from Ty Trist as well as any northern traffic at Tredegar.

Bird in Hand. In addition to those services calling here, traffic for Ystrad Mynach was cleared by a 7.15pm service arriving at 7.41pm. In the reverse direction, a 7.5pm service ran from Ystrad Mynach to Tredegar with empties.

Local Services at the top end of the Valley ran at 7.55am Nantybwch to Tredegar, calling at Sirhowy from 8.0-8.32am and arriving Tredegar at 8.37am,

A returning train of empty minerals bound for Aberdare via Tredegar Junction Lower and Sirhowy Junction behind Aberdare's 7200 Class 2-8-2T 7216 working hard up the adverse gradient in August 1952. A.C. Sterndale

and also at 9.25am, calling at Sirhowy 9.30-9.50am and Tredegar 9.55am. There was also a 4.40pm Sirhowy to Tredegar arr. 4.45pm. The services starting at Nantybwch would have conveyed traffic off the MT&A for the Sirhowy, staged for onward connection from Tredegar.

Because of the weight of the trains involved, these coal services over the Northern section of the Sirhowy would have been worked by the 0-8-0s based at Tredegar and Abergavenny and also the 0-8-4Ts until their demise. From the southern end, most services were worked by the 4200 Class 2-8-0Ts and 7200 2-8-2Ts with the lighter trains powered by the 5700 Class 0-6-0T. As at 1953, Ebbw Junction based former B&M 0-6-2Ts would have worked some of the pick-up freights serving various sidings south of Pontllanffraith. In addition, Control services would be arranged to any colliery/yard when the booked service was unable to cope, especially where shipment coal needed swift clearance to the Docks.

Tender-first working was necessary southwards along the Sirhowy line as with Tredegar's 49316 as she heads a short train of coal through the station bound for either Ystrad Mynach or the Rogerstone direction on 3 October 1956. S.Rickard/J&J Collection

A Beames 0-8-4T heads a down train of coal in Tredegar branded wagons southwards through Pontllanffraith station in 1926, probably bound either for Rogerstone, Nine Mile Point to be handed over to the GWR for conveyance on to Rogerstone, or for Bird in Hand Yard or Ystrad Mynach from where perhaps the GWR will collect it for shipment at Cardiff or Barry Docks.

CHAPTER FOUR

TREDEGAR MOTIVE POWER DEPOT

THE ORIGINAL ENGINE shed at Tredegar was opened at the time of the conversion of the Sirhowy Tramroad to a Railway between 1860 and when the passenger service to Newport began in 1865. At that time, the railway was owned by the Sirhowy Railway Company but in 1876 it was taken over by the LNWR. In 1886, a new four road shed was built at the south-west end of the passenger station, and this survived, though not unscathed, until operations ceased on the line. The shed was designed to house sixteen engines, but these must have been tank engines, probably Coal Tanks which had been introduced to the LNWR (though not to the Sirhowy) in 1882, of which Abergavenny built up a large fleet.

A full record is available of the nine engines handed over from the Sirhowy Railway to the LNWR when they took over the line on 13 July 1875. These comprised two 2-4-0Ts which would have been used for the passenger service, six 0-6-0STs and one 0-6-0T, which would have been used mainly for freight but probably with some used also on passenger work. All were replaced with LNWR engines by the end of 1876.

The two 2-4-0Ts were the original Sirhowy Railway Nos. 1 and 2, and became LNW 2233/34. They had both been built in 1863 by Slaughter & Co., had 14x18ins. outside cylinders, 500 gallon capacity side tanks, with 4ft 6in driving wheels and 3ft leading wheels. No. 2233 weighed 22tons and No. 2234 23tons 10cwt. The first was sold to the Duke of Sutherland in November 1876 and the second to the Ebbw Vale Works in January 1880.

Of the 0-6-0STs, Sirhowy Nos. 3-7 were built by the Vulcan Foundry in 1859 (Nos. 6/7), 1860 (No. 3), 1863 (No. 5) and 1871 (No. 4), and became LNW Nos. 2235-39. No. 3 (2235) was rebuilt in 1875 and sold to the West Cumberland Iron & Steel Co. in December 1879. Nos. 6 and 7 were bought from the Tredegar Iron Co. All were scrapped during 1876. They were all larger engines than the 2-4-0Ts with 26x24in outside cylinders, 4ft driving wheels, 960 gallon tanks and weighed 34 tons.

No. 8, which became LNW 2240, was also an 0-6-0ST built by Vulcan in 1866 and was sold to the Ebbw Vale Works in January 1880. It was a larger engine than Nos. 3-7 with 17x24in outside cylinders, 4ft 6in driving wheels, had 1,000 gallons water capacity and weighed 36 tons 12cwt.

No. 9, which became LNW 2241, was an 0-6-0 side tank, built by the Worcester Engine Co. in 1867, was bought from the Metropolitan Railway in 1873 and was sold to the Newport Alexandra Docks & Railway in April 1879. It had 20x24in cylinders, 4ft driving wheels, had 1,100 gallons water capacity and weighed 45 tons.

Following the demise of the former Sirhowy Railway engines, they were replaced by LNWR 0-6-0 saddle tanks and 0-6-0 tender Coal engines, about which allocation not much is known. The first of the Coal Tanks at Tredegar may have been by transfer from Abergavenny in

SIRHOWY. RY.

List of Locomotives taken over by L. & N.W.R. 13.7.1875 as
per Crewe Official Records.

Note: The Crewe Capital List numbers of 1875 were book numbers only.

S.R. No.	Type	Makers	Works No.	Date Built	Remarks	L.N.W.R. No. Cap.List 1875	L.N.W.R. Dup. List No.	Date	W/D
1	2-4-0T	Slaughter & Co.		1863	Sold to Duke of Sutherland 11/76.	2233	1847	6/76	
2	"	"		"	Sold to Ebbw Vale S.C.& I.Co. 1/80.	2234	1865	9/76	

L.W. 3'0" C.W. 4'6" Cyls. 14" x 18" (outside). Tank 500 gals.
Weight: No. 1, 22 ^{T} 0 ^{C}. No. 2, 23 ^{T} 10 ^{C}.

S.R. No.	Type	Makers	Works No.	Date Built	Remarks	L.N.W.R. No. Cap.List 1875	L.N.W.R. Dup. List No.	Date	W/D
3	0-6-0ST	Vulcan	434	1860	Rebuilt 1875. Sold to West Cumberland I.& S.Co. 12/79.	2235	1870	9/76	
4	"	"	625	1871	New boiler 1863.	2236	1854	9/76	11/7
5	"	"	504	1863		2237	1991	9/76	9/7
6	"	"	424	1859	Bought from Tredegar Iron Co. ?	2238	1992	9/76	9/7
7	"	"	425	"	" " " "	2239	1990	6/76	6/7

C.W. 4'0" Cyls. 26" x 24" (outside). Weight 34 ^{T} 0 ^{C}. Tank 960 gals.

Nos. 4 - 7 were cut up on the dates shown.

S.R. No.	Type	Makers	Works No.	Date Built	Remarks	L.N.W.R. No. Cap.List 1875	L.N.W.R. Dup. List No.	Date	W/D
8	0-6-0ST	Vulcan	568	1866	Sold to Ebbw Vale S.C.& I.Co. 1/80.	2240	1859	9/76	

C.W. 4'6" Cyls. 17" x 24" (outside). Weight 36 ^{T} 12 ^{C}. Tank 1000 gals.

S.R. No.	Type	Makers	Works No.	Date Built	Remarks	L.N.W.R. No. Cap.List 1875	L.N.W.R. Dup. List No.	Date	W/D
9	0-6-0T	Worcester Eng. Co.	–	1867	Bought from Metropolitan Ry. 1873. Sold A (N.& S.W.Ry.& Docks. (No.5) 4/1879.	2241	1891	11/76	

No details given in Crewe Records as to which number it carried on Metro.Ry.

C.W. 4'0" Cyls. 20" x 24" Weight 45 ^{T} 0 ^{C}. Tank 1100 gals.

Additional dimensions not from Crewe Records:

Wheelbase   6'10" + 7'2"
        Total   14'0"
Heating Surface
        Tubes   1014.0
        Firebox   118.0
                Total   1132.0 sq. ft.
Grate Area   22.25
Pressure   130 lb.
Boiler   11'0" x 4'3"
Firebox   7'1" x 4'0"

1890, when Driver John Baker transferred between depots in the days when engines were allocated to specific drivers and 'he brought his own engine'. If this was so, this was eight years after the class was introduced in 1882, a design that would continue in production until 1897 and would become the mainstay of motive power on the Sirhowy and at Abergavenny for the next 60 years. Their normal load on the Sirhowy Valley passenger service was a set of five close-coupled four wheelers with first, second and third class. At weekends and on special occasions, two coaching sets were used on some services, producing trains of ten four wheelers which may have caused the Coal Tanks some problems in stopping when running downhill.

With the spread of bus traffic in the Valleys during the 1920s and early '30s, first class was withdrawn in 1933 and the centre coach of the five coach set was withdrawn, leaving a close-coupled four coach set of four wheelers until these were withdrawn from service in September 1935 and replaced by trains of three or two Vestibule and Corridor bogie eight wheelers drawn from a wide variety of origins in addition to the LNWR, such as Lancashire & Yorkshire, Furness Railway, North of Scotland Railway and Metropolitan Railway. Though tickets were issued at the larger stations, on train ticket issue was the practice to cover the smaller stations and halts. The Coal Tanks were good steamers and coped well with their load on the rising gradients climbing the valley, but the guard's assistance was critical in ensuring a safe stop at some stations in the reverse direction. On mineral traffic, the maximum load in both directions in the Valley was 49 wagons, though a banker was often necessary.

The LNWR introduced their Bowen Cooke designed G1 Class 6F 0-8-0s in 1912. They were superheated, developed from an earlier saturated design, many rebuilt from earlier Webb, Whale and Bowen Cooke compound and simple designs, introduced from 1892 onwards. Many of the G1s were later rebuilt with Belpaire boilers. Freight movement to and from Abergavenny was an important requirement at that time and they were soon allocated to both Abergavenny and Tredegar. During the First World War, two were allocated to Tredegar, Nos. 631 and 1329, both with cabbed tenders to facilitate tender-first freight working, which was involved down the Sirhowy Valley, which was beneficial as it ensured that water in the boiler covered the firebox crown. From 1921, these were developed into the G2 Class 7F with higher boiler pressure, many later being rebuilt with Belpaire boilers. Then from 1936, G1 engines were rebuilt with G2 Belpaire boilers and became the G2a Class 7F. They were also used on weekend and bank holiday excursion working, such as to Barry Island when they worked engine first in both directions, turning on the Docks at Barry. They were employed on all manner of freight working, and on passenger trains ranging from one coach to ten. Their single engine freight loading was 59 wagons and brake, both loaded and empty.

Allocations for Tredegar depot for 1917, 1 January 1922, 1925 and March 1928 are available as follows:-

1917:- 0-8-0 G1 Class 631 (with tender cab)
0-6-2T Coal Tank 6, 178, 216, 407, 442, 551, 682, 692, 699, 926, 957, 1005, 1250, 1252, 2010, 2358, 2460, 2490 (Total 18)
Total 19 engines

1 January 1922
0-6-0 Saddle Tank (Cabless)
0-8-0 Coal Engines with Tender Cabs:-
631, 1329 (both allocated since WW1)
0-6-2 Side Tank Coal Engines:- 693, 970, 1005, 1053, 1077, 1198, 1203, 1240, 1250, 1254, 1256, 2010, 2351, 2358, 2462, 3325, 3353, 3387, 3418, 3702, 3732, 3773, 3774. (Total 23)
Total 26 engines.

1925

Coal Tanks:- 693, 970, 1005/53/77, 1198, 1203/40/50/54/56, 2010, 2351/58, 2462, 3325/53/87, 3418, 3702/32/73/74 (Total 23)

Super D 7F 0-8-0:- 631, 1329 (both fitted with tender cabs)

Total 25 engines

March 1928

Coal Tanks:- 1005, 1198, 2351, 3767, 7573, 7608/64, 7738

Coal Tanks Classified as Passenger Engines:- 1207/54, 2462, 3670, 7611, 7812/18/22/40

Coal Tanks 5ft.6ins Driving Wheels:- 1423, 6640, 6745

Beames 0-8-4T:- 1976, 7933/43

Super D 0-8-0:- 8931/33/34, 9615

Total 27 engines

In 1925, there were twenty-three Coal Tanks allocated and 2 0-8-0s with tender cabs. By March 1928, this had become twenty Coal Tanks, 4 0-8-0s and three of the Beames 0-8-4 Tanks. Duties for the 0-8-4Ts included through running to Ystrad Mynach and Cardiff Docks via Rhymney Bridge, but they were restricted to a maximum of 20mph by the GWR on their lines and were subsequently banned. These engines were all withdrawn by January 1948, the Coal Tanks lasting until May 1955. With the progressive withdrawal of the Coal Tanks, three Stanier 3P and four Ivatt 2MT 2-6-2Ts had been allocated to Abergavenny and some were always sub-shedded to Tredegar working mainly the passenger service to Newport and the miners' trains, though with some freight duties. On Day 1 of Nationalisation, the Tredegar allocation was seven Coal Tanks, one Ivatt 2P 2-6-2T, two Beames 0-8-4Ts and six Super D 0-8-0s.

The depot was coded 31T by the LNWR and was a sub-shed of Abergavenny, though with its own allocation. All heavy maintenance and repairs of any significance were carried out at Abergavenny which led to replacement engines being provided from Abergavenny and the Tredegar allocation becoming somewhat fluid, a position that lasted until the 1950s.

The requirements of South Wales coal traffic over heavily inclined lines was one of the main reasons for the LNWR and then LMS building the Beames 0-8-4Ts introduced from 1923 and developed from the previous 0-8-2Ts. The first of the class (No. 380) arrived at Abergavenny on 28 May 1923 and was next day sent to Tredegar to start work. Though hugely powerful, they had a cramped cab due to having a dual screw and lever reversing gear, which took up a lot of room on the left of the cab, the screw for adjusting the cut-off and the lever for quick reversing and shunting. Due to their long wheelbase, they caused considerable damage to the track on curves and the GWR refused to allow them on the Rhymney Valley line, though they are known to have worked on Barry Island excursions, probably running via Risca and Park Junction They were also subject to derailment, especially on colliery layouts where the track was often not in the best condition. 0-8-0s had to be substituted where the 0-8-4Ts were restricted. On a gradient of 1 in 34 and in bad weather, they had started and run with loads of 31 vehicles or 209 tons, made up of 30 wagons and a 20ton brakevan. On a gradient of 1 in 40, they had started and taken 59 empties and a 20ton brake, a load of 392tons. On the 1 in 34 gradient, a passenger train of 14 vehicles (no tonnage details) was also taken with ease.

Though the passenger service was well within the capability of the Coal Tanks, the heavy weekday programme of miners' trains operated between Nantybwch, Tredegar, Pochin Bedwellty, Markham, Wyllie and Nine Mile Point required much longer trains, originally up to twenty 4wheelers on the Pochin trains, and later up to six or seven 8 wheelers.

These trains were in the hands of both Coal Tanks and 0-8-0s until 1936 when a new Stanier 2-6-2T, No. 79, was sent on trial from Llandudno Junction, especially for platform clearance trials and remained on the branch for a number of years, being joined by other members of the class, which were used on the passenger service to Newport, miners' trains and freight.

Following the introduction of the Ivatt 2MT 2-6-2T in 1946, four of the new design were sent to the area and one or two normally worked from Tredegar alongside the larger Staniers. With the progressive withdrawal of the Coal Tanks up to 1953, they took over the Newport service, until it was re-organised by the Western Region from July 1954 as an auto service to and from Risca. The Ivatts remained at Tredegar and were the last former LMS engines to leave in 1959.

Allocations are also available for the last day before Nationalisation and for 30 October 1948 for both Tredegar and Abergavenny, but these make no mention of the Stanier 2-6-2Ts or of 41201. Details for Tredegar are as follows:-

31 December 1947
Ivatt 2-6-2T 2P:- 1204
Coal Tanks 2F:- 7780/82, 7821, 27553/86, 27649/54
Beames 0-8-4T 7F:- 7937/39
Super D 0-8-0 6F & 7F:- 8921, 9064, 9161/68/74, 9409
Total 16 engines.

30 October 1948
2-6-2T Ivatt 2MT 41204 (no mention of 41201 at either depot, perhaps in works)
0-8-0 Class 7F 48921, 49064, 49161, 49409
0-6-2T Coal Tanks 2F 58880 (27553), 58885 (27586), 58895 (27654), 58915 (7757), 58921 (7782), 58925 (7794), 58930 (7816), 58933 (7829)
Total 13 engines.

As engines were regularly exchanged with others from Abergavenny, these lists can only be taken as a sample.

Engine Shed. The four-track shed roads were originally 165ft long but a fire pre-Grouping caused this to be reduced by about 50ft, the area concerned then becoming an open-air store at the back of the shed. Then around 1954, a fire at the front end of the shed destroyed the first three sections of the roof which remained open to the elements until closure, so that the shed had little covered space left. A coaling plant and water tower were provided on the east side of the yard.

At the Grouping, Abergavenny and Tredegar came within the Shrewsbury district, coded 4D and 4E respectively. Following Nationalisation, both depots were transferred to the Western Region and were placed in the Newport Division with Tredegar as a sub-shed to Abergavenny 86K, taking that code itself when Abergavenny closed in January 1958. Tredegar shed closed following the withdrawal of the passenger service on the Sirhowy Valley on 11 June 1960, when the miners' services were also withdrawn.

The Tredegar allocations given above are largely drawn from the book *Reflections on a Railway Career – LNWR to BR*, by John Maxwell Dunn, Acting Running Shed Foreman at Tredegar in the 1920s. He also lists the shed staff at the depot at that time as follows:

2 Shift Foremen
38 Drivers
38 Firemen
1 Chargehand Cleaner
21 Cleaners
3 Steamraisers
3 Fire Droppers
2 Boilerwashers
1 Tube Cleaner
2 Joint Makers
2 Coalmen
4 Fitters
1 Labourer
1 Clerk
Total Staff 119

He records that still in 1925 some drivers

Two views of the four road shed itself with the access tracks from the yard, on 28 March 1948 top and 16 August 1953 below. The 1948 view has a 2-6-2T and an 0-8-0 protruding from the shed both facing north with the yard well populated with ex-LMS passenger coaches, many veteran and parcel vans. Top SLS, Bottom HMRS

(presumably the senior men) had their own engines, and two drivers shared one regular engine. There were 35 turns on weekdays and 32 on Saturdays.

The work was divided into four links, the Top Link (involving eight sets of men) probably the senior men on the Passenger services, though the best earning freight turns could also have been involved. The Second Link involved six sets of men, the Third four and the Fourth link three, a total of twenty-one turns, the remainder preparation and disposal crews, Control Order crews, etc. The depot LDC represented the views of the senior men to the management at their regular meetings.

Following the closure of Abergavenny shed in January 1958, Tredegar took on a few more of the Abergavenny allocation but most were removed to the London Midland Region.

As the shed had been a sub-shed of Abergavenny (though with a shed code and allocation of its own), additional engines and men could be brought in from there. All heavy maintenance and repair of Tredegar engines was carried out at Abergavenny, and this resulted in replacements being provided by the parent depot, so it was standard practice for a few Abergavenny engines to be working from Tredegar at any time.

From June 1954, the WR took over operation of the passenger services from the original Coal Tanks and Ivatt 2-6-2Ts and truncated the service to operate only between Risca and Nantybwch for which an auto service was introduced with 6439 allocated. From April 1959, this engine was re-allocated to Ebbw Junction who took over the working with one coach, providing both auto and non-auto fitted panniers, the latter

Diagram of Tredegar Motive Power Depot as at May 1944, when coded 4E.

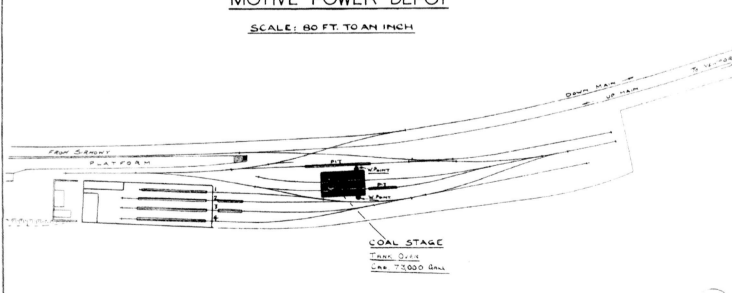

TREDEGAR

MOTIVE POWER DEPOT

SCALE: 80 FT. TO AN INCH

having to run round at the end of each journey. Through services from/to Newport started and ended the daily service.

The last of the former LNWR engines, 0-8-0 49064, left on 8 August 1959 with 41204 for Crewe (though 41201 remained). Several 5700 Class had by now been allocated to cover some miners' trains and residual freight services. 4643, though never officially allocated to Tredegar, was working from there from Autumn 1957, presumably on loan/on trial from Pill depot, three more in early 1958 (3700, 5790 and 7774) and another four in July/August 1959. 5790 and 7774 were condemned in February/March 1959, the remainder (3700/12, 7736, 8711 and 9662) all being transferred away (mostly to Ebbw Junction) in August 1960 when Tredegar depot was closed. All further provision of power for the Sirhowy line was made by Ebbw Junction until the eventual closure of the route in 1970.

The Webb Coal Tanks were the workhorse of the Sirhowy for over fifty years. Here 7822 forms the background to a posed group of shed staff in the 1920s. The Shed Foreman looks to be in the centre. Gerald Davies Colln

Coal Tank 27663 standing alongside the coaling plant in 1939. Built in July 1883 as LNWR 3709, she became LMS 7663 in 1923 and then 27663, being withdrawn in December 1947. Gerald Davies Colln

Standing alongside the shed, 58880 still carries the LMS branding over three years after Nationalisation on 24 March 1951, though it has been renumbered. J.J. Smith/Bluebell Railway Archive

A row of Coal Tanks stand together inside the shed on 20 August 1950, with 58925 and another forming the subject of the photograph, with an 0-8-0 on the next road. SLS

The huge Beames 0-8-4 tanks were introduced to Tredegar in 1923 and played a major part in both the freight and passenger working, being involved with many of the heavy excursion trains which they either worked singly or with a Coal Tank or 0-8-0 or even another 0-8-4T. They originally carried number plates as here with 1976, later renumbered to 7934, seen on shed in 1926.

They were not always kept in a clean condition and this one is so grimy that its number is invisible as is most of its LMS branding, on shed on 15 July 1933.

Under some shed masters, engines were kept in a more presentable condition as with 7933 preparing to go off shed in this 1930s view, the engine facing south which probably indicates that its first duty was to one of the Sirhowy collieries or on passenger working. W.A. Camwell/SLS

Another 0-8-4T which has been well cared for is 7931, again seen on shed in the 1930s facing south. W.A. Camwell/SLS

Another view of 7931 with the rear angle showing the size of the large bunker, reminiscent of the GWR 7200 Class.

Use of the ex-LNW 0-8-0s often involved tender-first working, though the many triangles and crossovers that existed often enabled engines to be turned, e.g. at Tredegar Junction Lower/Bird in Hand/Sirhowy Junction at Pontllanffraith. Here two of the long term Tredegar allocation, 49064, which often worked the Barry Island trains and 49121 which worked the final train over the MT&A on 5 January 1958, as well as the Barry Islands, stand together on shed in 1957. Pendon Museum Trust

Another view of 49121, this time standing outside the shed with another long term resident, 48921, on 22 September 1957.

Standing outside the shed on a southbound freight which it is working tender-first, 49064 shortly after its arrival back at the depot ex-works.

An historic picture of an 0-8-0 at Tredegar, dating from 1927 and showing No. 1891 with a fitted number plate. Alastair Warrington Collection

Two views of 49064 on shed on 2 May 1959, the first a rear view also showing an LMR 2-6-2T and a WR 57XX in the shed, while the second shows the engine preparing to go off shed, with the shed foreman standing alongside. Both R.O. Tuck/Rail Archive Stephenson

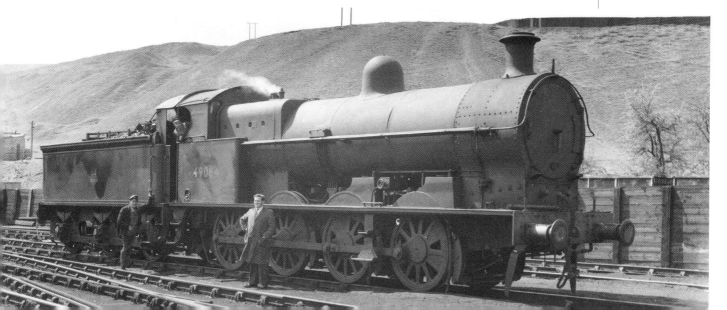

The four Ivatt 2-6-2Ts allocated to Abergavenny and Tredegar did valuable work on passenger and freight on both the MT&A and Sirhowy. In the first of three pictures of 41204 on 16 July 1959, she stands just inside the shed, the roof of which had been damaged by fire. H.C. Casserley

Standing just outside the shed, 41204 at the head of a southbound goods. Gerald Davies

On the final departure day, 41204 has just been coaled and made ready to depart, running bunker-first down the valley. S. Rickard/J&J Collection

Stanier 2-6-2T 40098 did valuable work on the Sirhowy, working passenger services to Newport, miners' trains and freight. Here she is seen under the coaling stage at Tredegar shed in a wide-angle view of the area with a train of empties in charge of a 57XX running south and another having its smokebox cleaned on shed. Ernie's Railway Archive

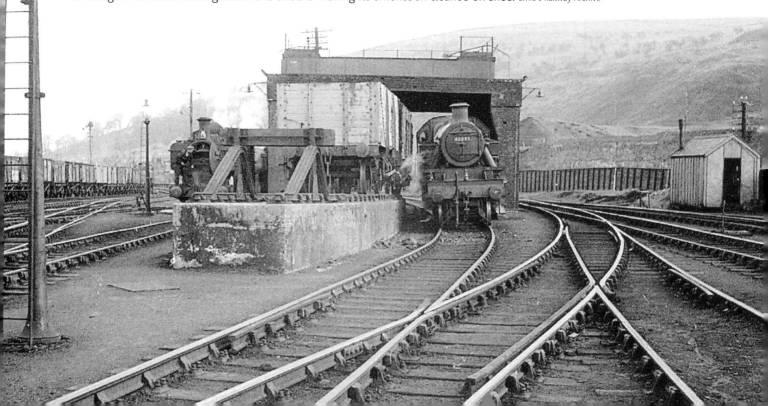

40171 was another Stanier 2-6-2T with a long association with the Sirhowy and is seen here in smart condition at the shed in April 1957. Alastair Warrington

A shed scene on 20 June 1959 with WR 5600 Class 6600, not a common class at Tredegar on shed, perhaps to work the weekend excursion to Barry Island, with 7721 and 41204. F.K. Davies

It was the original intention to work the Sirhowy service after transfer to the WR with railmotor services for which 64XXs were provided. Here 6412 stands on shed alongside 41201, which remained after 41204's departure, in this 8 August 1959 scene. The 64XX working was replaced by a 57XX and one coach in conventional working for much of the last months of the service. S.Rickard/J&J Collection

5727, which was never officially allocated but worked regularly at Tredegar, stands alongside the shed wall on 16 July 1959. The picture affords a good view of the South Platform used by miners' services, as well the crossovers into and out of the shed.
H.C. Casserley

Another Ebbw Pannier spending time working from Tredgar was 7736, which has been well cleaned and stands in the yard outside the covered shed in 1959.

Another WR 5600 Class on shed on 8 August 1959 was 6685 of Pontypool Road, perhaps to work the next Barry Island excursion.
S.Rickard/J&J Colln

The layout at the south end of the shed alongside the Miners' Plarform with 7771 negotiating the crossovers in 1958. The wagons contain coal for the coaling plant. D.K. Jones Collection

A group of shed staff taken during the 1920s with Coal Tank 970.

The staff on duty that day gather for a farewell picture alongside 49064 to which the depot snowplough had been attached for return to Crewe Works. S. Rickard/J&J Collection

THE LAST 0-8-0 LEAVES THE SIRHOWY

On 8 August 1959, the final ex-LNWR 0-8-0, 49064, left Tredegar shed and the Sirhowy Valley for Crewe. Bob Tuck and Sid Rickard had good relations with the shed and had been told of the final day arrangements. The 0-8-0 would first be sent to Ebbw Junction shed at Newport with Ivatt 2-6-2T 41204, still leaving 41201 at Tredegar. Bob and Sid were at Tredegar shed early on the morning of the 8th to record photographs of the engines being prepared for departure around 10am. The plan was to try to beat the engines by road to various photographic locations down the Sirhowy and beyond.

The pair are coupled and leave the depot, against the backdrop of the South End Miners' Platform.
S. Rickard/J&J Collection

Two views of the pair running south past Markham Village Halt, from where they had worked many a miners' train.
R.O. Tuck/RAS and S. Rickard/J&J Collection

The two are next seen running along the platform road at Pontllanffraith HL with the LNW signal off for their progress. R.O. Tuck/RAS

The pair pass Pontllanffraith HL box as unusual power is provided for the 10.5am Risca to Tredegar in the form of 6641 just transferred from Barry to Landore which found its way to Ebbw Junction and is being used for a day on the Tredegar line. S. Rickard/J&J Collection

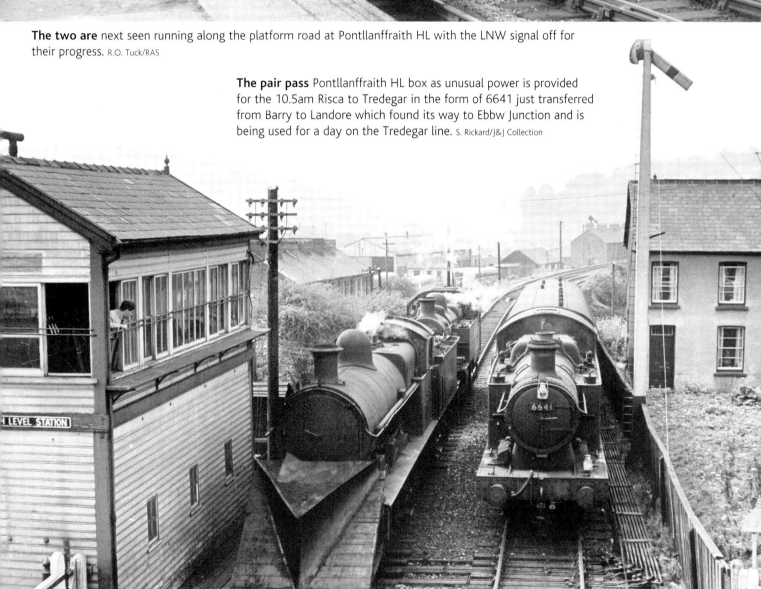

The two engines on their last journey from Tredegar are finally caught at Park Junction where they take the Western Loop which will enable them to run onto Ebbw Junction shed. S. Rickard/J&J Collection

CHAPTER FIVE

LOCATION ANALYSIS & ILLUSTRATION

Caveat – It must be accepted that there is always a problem in using layout drawings produced by the GWR/ LNWR as representing the total position in any area as sometimes the drawing appears to only represent the section of railway that was the subject of attention at that time. Other areas of railway could well be omitted leading to doubt as to whether they existed or not at that time. Also, there is a problem in terminology which affects collieries and sidings being referred to by different names at different times, perhaps under different owners. My attempt at describing collieries, works and sidings is conditioned by each of these features.

NEWPORT (High Street)

Though the Sirhowy Railway operated only as far south as Risca, the passenger service operated to Newport, initially to Dock Street, but from 1880 (when the new link was built) to High Street station. This is covered in a previous volume *Railways & Industry in the Western Valley – Newport to Aberbeeg*. The following photographs illustrate the operation between Newport and Risca.

Following the 1928 rebuilding of the station, some Valley services continued to leave from the main line down platform. Here Coal Tank 27563 waits to depart from Platform 1 with the 3.10pm service to Nantybwch, the first coach of which is a former LNWR 6 wheeler. Gerald Davies Collection

Two views of Tredegar's 58915 in charge of the 3.50pm service to Nantybwch on 4 May 1951 and seen standing with its two coach train at the west end of Platform 7, as an ROD 2-8-0 passes with a down freight in the first shot. The second shot shows the type of veteran stock used on these services at that time, often, as here, with a more modern coach accompanying. Both H.C. Casserley

A familiar sight to travellers running into Newport from Cardiff was the Sirhowy Valley train ready to depart from the west end of Platform 7. Here on 19 August 1950 we see Tredegar's Webb Coal Tank 7752, still carrying its LMS number, with two veteran LMS coaches. P.B.Whitehouse/M.Whitehouse

Seen standing at Platform 7 with the photographer standing in Godfrey Road Yard with the tracks leading to the turntable in the foreground, Coal Tank 7752, still carrying its LMS number, heads the departing Sirhowy Valley service. The crew have been approached by the photographer and pose together alongside the engine on the platform. P.B.Whitehouse/M.Whitehouse

The angle of the sun shows this shot to be of the 1.10pm service with a well presented Coal Tank in 1950. John Hodge

Another clean engine in the form of 58888 with an afternoon service to Nantybwch, headed by the usual veteran coach for miners use, in 1950. John Hodge

Standing further east on Platform 7, 58891 again has one veteran and one modern coach to make up the stock for either the 1.10 or 3.50pm train in 1950/1.

The Ivatt 2MT 2-6-2Ts were introduced to the Sirhowy Valley and Merthyr, Tredegar & Abergavenny line services immediately after being introduced in 1946, the first four of the class being allocated to Abergavenny/Tredegar. They went into service alongside the Coal Tanks though were ultimately to replace them. Here 41204 heads a Nantybwch service on 13 September 1951. H.C. Casserley

By the time of this shot on 7 April 1954, the Ivatt 2MT 2-6-2Ts had completely taken over in the area from the Coal Tanks and the 11.8am from Nantybwch now has 41203 in charge, as it is seen first approaching Newport Hillfield Tunnel and then departing with the 1.10pm return service. By now, former GW stock was also in use on these services as here with a brake second on the front and a van on the rear, the latter having been attached at Newport.
Both S.Rickard /J&J Collection

The 3.50pm Newport to Nantybwch approaches Park Junction on the section from Gaer Tunnel, composed of three vintage LMS coaches, some possibly of L&Y origin, behind Tredegar's 58911 on 16 April 1949.

RISCA STATION (5½ mp) to NEW RISCA COLLIERY (7mp)
Railway

The Sirhowy Valley line opened as a standard gauge railway about 1860, having been converted from the Sirhowy Tramroad which tended to serve each of the main works and collieries it passed, under the principles laid down in the original Canal Act which sanctioned the building of tramways to link works, collieries, quarries, etc. with the canal within an eight mile radius. As such, the tramroad served an industrial complex on the western approach to Risca located on high ground which then required a bridge or viaduct to be built to gain access to Risca. When the tramroad was replaced by a standard gauge railway in 1860, the new line of route into Risca was east of the tramroad viaduct (called the Long Bridge), with the double-track railway built on an embankment which gradually descended until it reached Risca on the correct level. The River Ebbw swings west at this point to continue its south-west course and a small viaduct was necessary to bridge the river, as in the case of the tramroad which had bridged the river further west. South of the new viaduct, the two track railway ran straight down to Risca station.

North of the viaduct, a plan for 1868 shows a trailing siding on the upside just past the 6mp used by a lime kiln company, though it does not show how the industrial complex of the original Copper Works and the later Morris Chemical Works was served following the railway construction, though this works was in existence at that time. A plan for 1878 (an important year for the area as the new Risca Colliery was opened further north this year) shows the full extent of a new trailing siding connection serving the complex. At the point where the siding leaves the main line, a loading bay for the Graig Lime and Stone Co. is shown (see photo) with a long siding leading to the Morris Chemical Works which occupied the site until 1895 (see below).

Some 6 chains further north, the Waunfawr estate was reached where a brickworks and a small coal mine – the Sun Vein Colliery – are shown on a plan for 1868, first with just one siding on either side of the running line, and then with an enlarged layout for the brickworks on the up side of the line in an 1878 plan, the area being controlled by two signal boxes, Brickworks Siding South on the down side at 6m.4ch. and Brickworks Siding North on the up side

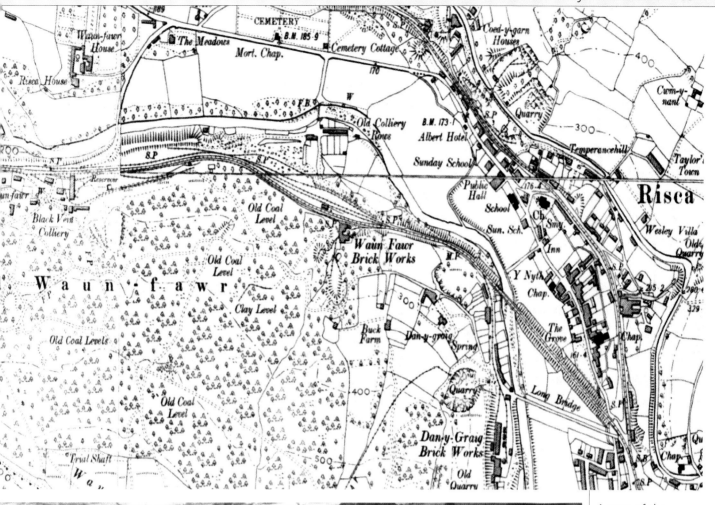

A map of the section from Risca station to Waunfawr at the turn of the twentieth century.
National Library of Scotland

Risca station before the line was quadrupled to give separate tracks to the Western Valley. An LNWR train stands on the down platform bound for Newport, probably formed with a five coach close-coupled set, including first class. The view is probably dated around 1905 when many photographs in the area seem to have been taken.

The junction between the Western Valley and Sirhowy Valley lines behind the signal box, from where a two track railway then continued south, until quadrupled in 1910.

The station after expansion due to the quadrupling of the line, so that separate platforms were now provided for the Western and Sirhowy valleys, the lines forming the Sirhowy route becoming the up and down reliefs south of Risca.

Looking up the Sirhowy Valley line from Risca Junction. What may be an Aberdare to Severn Tunnel Class H coal service waits at the home signal and will cross to the down main line for its onward journey.

Looking down the Sirhowy line from the bracket signal shown in the previous picture.

at 6m.20ch, both boxes closed in March 1954, when access was controlled by ground frame. Long loop sidings ran on both sides of the running lines from the South box right through to the 7¼mp on the down and to the 6¼mp on the up. The colliery sidings on the down side were part of the Old Black Vein Colliery (see below) and are shown on a later plan with four loop sidings on the down

side next to the running line, the colliery closing in 1921, replaced by the New Risca Colliery located on the down side beyond the 7mp.

A New Black Vein Colliery and Coke Ovens are shown on a plan for 1868 on the up side between the 6½ and 6¾mp. with access controlled by Black Vein Crossing signal box at 6m.53ch. This box was in existence in 1868 to control siding

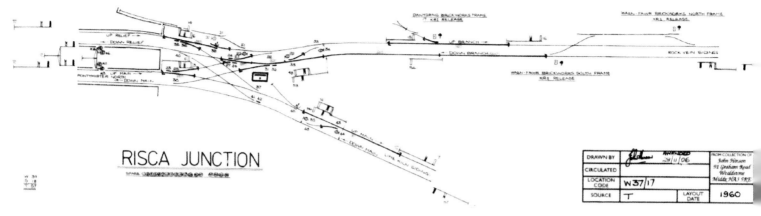

RISCA JUNCTION

DRAWN BY		ANNOTATED 28/11/06	FROM COLLECTION OF *John Hinson 91 Graham Road Wealdstone Middlesex HA3 5RE*
CIRCULATED			
LOCATION CODE	W37/17		
SOURCE	T	LAYOUT DATE	1960

A Signal Dept. drawing of the layout and signals at Risca Junction.

access but was reduced to a ground frame when a new box to control a level crossing at 6m.53ch. was opened in 1879, this remaining for controlling access to the sidings until 1954 but needed for the LC until the line closed in 1970. The coke ovens are shown much enlarged

A classic view at Risca for over fifty years was a Webb Coal Tank waiting at the Sirhowy platform to depart for Tredegar. Here LMS 7821, which was renumbered to BR 589XX but had not yet been changed, waits with the 6pm service in 1948. W.A. Camwell/SLS

on a plan for 1880 but would have been overtaken by the new facilities at the New Risca Colliery, sunk in 1878. Though three colliery loop sidings are still shown in situ on the up side on a plan for 1929, the Black Vein colliery itself closed in 1921, replaced by the New Risca Colliery, under the same ownership.

At the 7mp was Rock Vein Siding South signal box which originally

During the early 1950s the Coal Tanks were provided to Tredegar depot by Abergavenny who were responsible for maintenance. Here 58925 is seen waiting to depart with a service to Nantybwch formed of 3 coaches, the first for use of miners. These veteran coaches were often of Lancashire & Yorkshire origin.

The hillside vegetation features prominently in this shot of a 64XX crossing the junction to arrive at the down Western Valley platform. Courtesy Oxford House, Risca

controlled the site of the small Rock Vein Colliery (closed in 1898) but from the late 1870s controlled the entrance into the New Risca Colliery, opened in 1878. There were several sidings alongside the down line where colliery traffic was left and immediately west of these, the railway into the new colliery crossed a bridge over the Sirhowy River into the colliery complex with seven sidings fanning off to service waste tips. The colliery line then turned north to provide the siding facilities to service the colliery itself with four tracks under the screens and four alongside with several other tracks accessing other parts of the installation.

The inlet to the colliery sidings alongside the running lines was at Rock Vein Siding North at 7m.30ch. where a new box was provided by 1909, the facility lasting until the colliery closed in 1966, when it was closed in August 1967.

When Sirhowy services were first worked by the Western Region, 6400 Class Auto fitted engines were used, provided first by Tredegar with 6439 and then by Ebbw Junction. Here Ebbw's 6426 has arrived at the down Sirhowy platform with a service from the Valley in 1958 and has crossed over to the up platform for the return. Both W.A. Camwell/SLS

Following the withdrawal of Western Valley services in April 1962, Risca station lay desolate until the start of dismantling. This view on 1 June 1968 shows how much of the structure had been removed by then. Garth Tilt

Where once there was a railway ... The late 1970s scene following the lifting of the Sirhowy branch, after closure in 1970, as workmen use the former trackbed to walk home. Risca Junction SB has been demolished and the Western Valley route is now plain line, though still double track through the former Risca station, no longer a junction. Courtesy Oxford House Risca

The Long Bridge
or Viaduct built by
the MRCC to carry
the tramroad at
the bottom of the
Sirhowy Valley.
The tramroad was
routed via the hillside
Danygraig brickworks
which meant that
the viaduct was
necessary to bridge
the low level land
at Risca. Even years
after demolition, the
location was known
as the Long Bridge
with a bus stop of
that name on the
main road.
Oxford House

Industry

Union Copper Works, Morris Chemical Works, Danygraig Brick Works

On the approach to Risca, the original tramroad served an industrial site on the western side of the Valley near the River Ebbw, occupied by a Copperworks owned by Union Copper Co., between 1807-16. In 1816, this passed to the Morris Chemical Works which occupied the site between 1816-95. A plan for 1868 also shows a Lime Kiln plant with loading dock at the start of the siding serving the works with wagons branded Graig Lime & Stone Works Risca (see photo). In 1895, the Danygraig Brickworks was opened on the site by Southwood Jones to manufacture firebricks and the factory is still operating. When the tramroad was constructed, serving this site created a need for a long bridge or viaduct to be built by the MRCC between the works and the Canal. With the conversion of the tramroad into a double track railway in about 1860, the line of approach to the new Risca station (opened in 1850 for the MRCC service to/from Newport Dock Street, the Sirhowy service starting in 1865) was made east of the Long Bridge which was replaced by an embankment which carried the railway. From the day of opening, the Long Bridge (viaduct) then became redundant for railway purposes and was demolished at the beginning of the new century. The chemical works was served by means of a siding off the north end of a new five arch viaduct over the river, just south of the 6mp. This siding remained in use until finally taken out in February 1965, by when traffic to/from the Brickworks was passing by road.

A 1900 view of the Long Bridge, in very early stages of demolition, with the new trajectory of the railway approaching Risca. Access to the brickworks was maintained but only by a siding off the main Sirhowy line. Oxford House

The start of demolishing the Long Bridge c1905, and the end of the final arch over Cromwell Road, the main street in Risca. Courtesy Oxford House, Risca

The original tramroad deviated west to serve the Danygraig Brickworks en route to Risca. This building was where horses engaged on the tramroad were housed, the stables being the lower sections of the buildings.
Courtesy Oxford House, Risca

(Right) The Lime Quarry Loading Point at Danygraig Brickworks Siding, just north of the Viaduct, owned by the Graig Lime & Stone Works, Risca. Initially horses were used to move wagons.

The seal of the Union Copper Company, Risca opened in 1807 on the site of Roman lead mines. It became a Chemical Works owned by David Morris in 1816 and a Brickworks in 1892 owned by Edwin Southwood Jones.

(Right) One of the duties of the former Brecon & Merthyr 0-6-2Ts allocated to Ebbw Junction following the closure of Bassaleg depot in 1929 was the D04 8.15am Maesglas to Nine Mile Point which served the Danygraig Brickworks Siding en route. This view in August 1952 shows the engine, which has come bunker-first up the valley, putting off wagons in the siding and affords a view down over Grove Road, Risca, my grandfather's house being behind the engine's cab, and shows the road running out to join the main Cromwell Road with the church in the background and the Western Valley line running behind. A.C. Sterndale

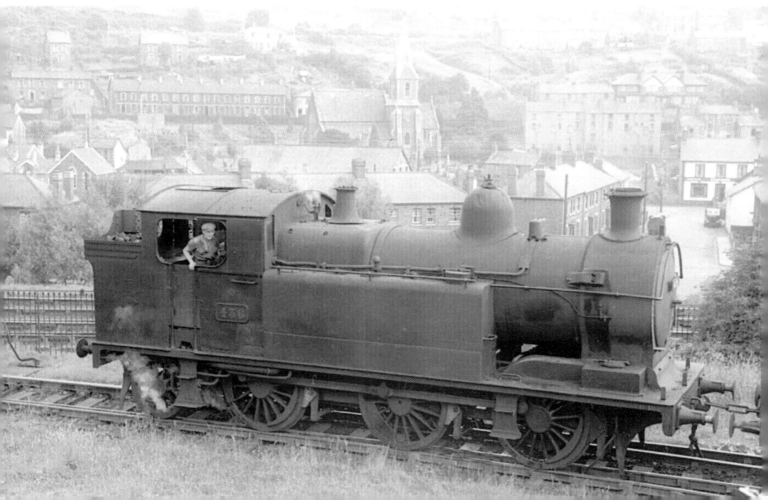

From my grandfather's house in Grove Road, I was able to climb up to the railway passing over the viaduct and, aged 12, recorded this view of a Coal Tank probably on the 1.10pm Newport to Nantybwch in 1950/1 while a southbound coal train runs down to Risca from either one of the Sirhowy Valley collieries or from Aberdare. The Risca Junction starting signal on the Sirhowy route was on the viaduct, the line being protected by short iron railings, which provided a good vantage point to lean over for photography. The crossover which can be seen in the foreground was to enable trains serving the brickworks to access the down line again. John Hodge

Another view from the same location, this time showing the five arch viaduct as an Ivatt 2-6-2T crosses with a northbound train formed of two ageing ex-GWR coaches, again in 1950/1. A down coal train is in the murky distance. John Hodge

The railway has gone and this view records the trackbed as it crossed the viaduct.
Courtesy Oxford House, Risca

A view from ground level off Grove Road of the five arch Risca Viaduct at the start of demolition.
Courtesy Oxford House, Risca

Waunfawr Brickworks and Colliery

Less than 200 yards to the north was the Waunfawr estate owned by Sir Charles Morgan. Records exist of small scale mining operations in that area going back to the 1670s. Commercial coal mining in this area appears to have started as early as the 1730s and in 1796, Edward Jones leased the mineral rights under the Waunfawr area from Sir Charles Morgan for an annual rent of £500. Jones opened a colliery at Waunfawr in 1796 near the site of the later brickworks and built a tramroad across the valley to connect into the Monmouthshire Canal. The colliery consisted of four shafts, one of which – the Old Ventilator shaft – used a horse to wind the coal. Jones was unable to recover his costs in the price he could sell the coal for and in 1800 went bankrupt. Partners were brought in and c£60k. injected into the venture, so that by 1810 they were selling coal to Swansea Copper Works.

A section of the Waunfawr Brickworks as seen in 1971 after the closure and recovery of the railway which ran in front of the works.

Part of the Waunfawr Brickworks with its tall chimney which was a landmark in the area.

The Waunfawr estate, a site of 1,000 acres, was acquired by John Russell in 1836 for £50,000 and in 1839 he sank a shaft which became the Black Vein Colliery. Other levels and small mines already existed or were opened in the area, such as the Sun Vein and Rock

Vein, the former being a very small mine working the Sun Vein seam that was normally inaccessible as it lay under other seams in the area but outcropped in a few places in the area, such as Nantyglo and Machen, on the other side of the mountain from Waunfawr.

A down coal train with a 1016 or 1076 0-6-0T at the head runs between brickworks North and South signal boxes, with the South box on the extreme right. The coal is best large and will either be bound for Rogerstone Yard or Newport Docks for export.

Black Vein Colliery

This was a sprawling complex on both sides of the railway, consisting of various pits and levels working different seams. John Russell and Partners formed the Risca Colliery Co. which opened the Black Vein Colliery in 1839 and in 1841 sank another shaft further to the north of the existing one called the New Black Vein Colliery, which became known as the Old Ventilator Shaft. The company prospectus of December 1845 reported that the Sun Vein and Big Vein Pits were being opened and would shortly be productive. These were just parts of the Black Vein Colliery, the Sun Vein being a level and the Big Vein a shallow pit. The Risca area is on the outcrop of the South Wales coalfield, where the seams come near to the surface and the Sun Vein seam was easily accessible here though not elsewhere, and formed part of the Black Vein catchment.

The Black Vein seam itself was highly productive, a much prized coal for steam raising but notoriously gassy to work, leading to many explosions and many fatalities. Until the New Risca Colliery was opened in 1878, the Black Vein Colliery was the largest working pit in the Risca area.

In 1847, the Black Vein Colliery was supplying steam coal to the Royal Mail Steam Packet Company, East India Co., Peninsular & Orient Co., Austrian Lloyds Co., with a 72,000 ton order for the Royal West Indian Mail Steam Packet Co., this with only 250 adult miners working underground, plus 50 youths under 18, and 15 boys under the age of 13 who towed drams of coal with chains strapped to their bodies. Russell's reasoning for this was that the narrow passages in which some mining was carried out were too restricted for men to be employed. Also in 1847, Russell formed the Risca Coal & Iron Co. with Thomas Brown to run the Black Vein Colliery and the Blaina Iron Works. He took over the Cwmtillery Colliery in 1852, sinking new shafts there in 1853/8, and in 1864 incorporated

Two views of Black Vein Crossing signal box, located south of Rock Vein Sidings SB, on 1 June 1968, where once stood the infamous Black Vein Colliery, known as the Death Pit from the number of fatal accidents that had taken place there, but now just a tranquil level crossing. Garth Tilt

Cwmtillery into his company.

With firedamp always a serious hazard, Russell allowed the highly dangerous practice of using naked candles for lighting, though Davy safety lamps were generally used. This contributed to the high number of explosions and fatalities at the Black Vein which impacted on the

availability of labour coming from the local area and Russell had to recruit from areas which were unaware of the dangers, such as Somerset, Dorset, Gloucestershire and Wiltshire. Explosions occurred in 1846 killing thirty-five, with others in 1849/53 but, on 1 December 1860, 146 men died with naked candle light igniting firedamp being blamed. The pit justifiably had the name of the Death Pit. The impact and repercussions of the high loss of life, coupled with legal arguments with Lord Tredegar over mining rights, bankrupted the company. In 1866, the Black Vein Colliery was bought by Thomas Rhodes who sold it on to the London & South Wales Colliery Co. in 1872. In 1878 the workings were listed as Risca Black Vein, Risca Red & Grey Vein, and Risca Clay Level.

With the poor safety record and reputation of the colliery, the age of the workings and the low reserves left in the present pit, the company announced in 1878 that they were to open a new pit north-east of the present one and across the River Sirhowy and the existing pit became known as the Old Black Vein Colliery. When the New Black Vein Colliery (or New Risca) opened in 1878, production continued at the Old Colliery on a limited but later revived scale until 1921 and it also served as a

Two views of the Risca Black Vein Colliery when in full production. The pit, which was very subject to firedamp, was opened in 1841 and closed in 1921.

In an abortive attempt to walk the track from Risca Viaduct to Nine Mile Point in the mid-1950s, I came to the remains of the Black Vein pit as Ivatt 2-6-2T No. 41203 heads the 3.10pm service from Newport. The signal which the train has just passed would be the outer home for Black Vein Crossing signal box. John Hodge

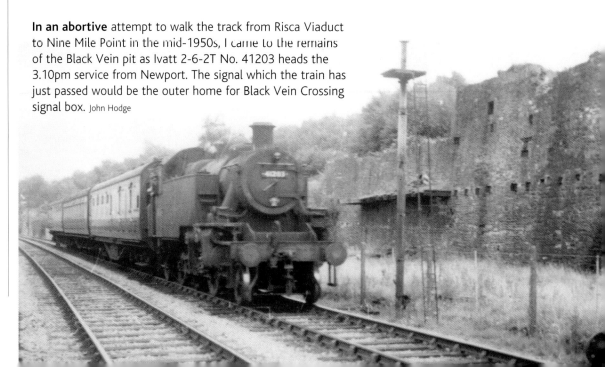

supplementary ventilation chamber for the new colliery. In 1892 United National Collieries Ltd. took control of both Black Vein collieries – the company later becoming part of the Ocean Coal Co. in 1928. Production continued at the Old Pit, which in 1905 employed 150, and this rose to 352 in 1908 and to 530 in 1915/6. Though the Old Pit closed in 1921, it was still listed in 1935, and remained standing for many years afterwards, the two shafts, 537ft deep, not being filled until 1968, and having to be filled again in March 1969 as the level of filling had dropped by nine feet in one and six feet in the other. The capped shafts now form part of the Black Vein Park alongside the new road that replaced the Sirhowy Branch Railway, and a memorial exists to all those who lost their lives working at the pit, located on the mountain opposite.

Level Crossing
Gates at Rock Vein Crossing.

Just north of the Black Vein Colliery was **Rock Vein Colliery**, a much smaller concern and owned by the same company. Little information is available on this colliery, other than that it closed in 1867 and may have been amalgamated

Map showing location of Rock Vein Colliery and New Pits which would become the New Risca Colliery, located across the River Sirhowy from the main Sirhowy railway. *Courtesy Oxford House, Risca*

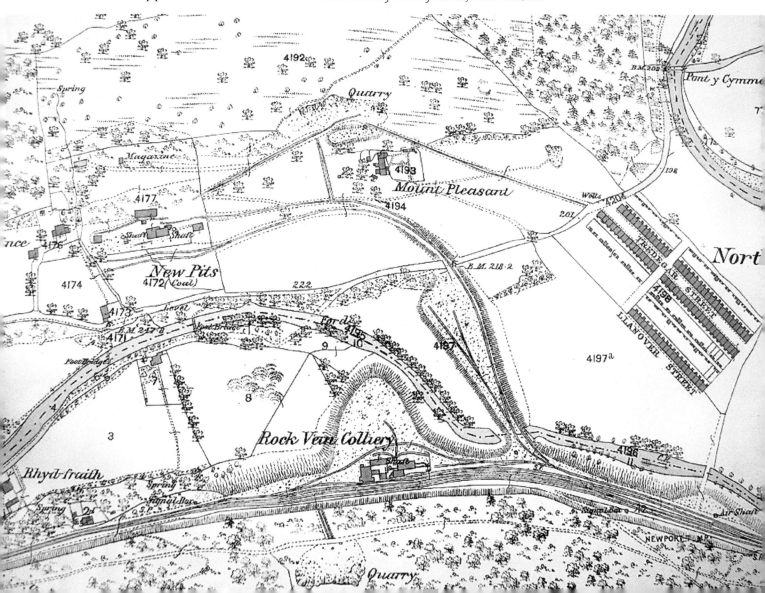

Remains of Rock Vein Colliery at site clearance in May 1969. A.J. Warrington

into Nine Mile Point when that pit opened as there was a section called Rock Vein, as well as the North and South Pits.

New Risca Colliery

In 1873 E.H. Watts (who gave his name to Wattsville) formed the London & South Wales Colliery Co. Ltd. and took over the Black Vein Colliery. Influenced by the problems of safety and probably high operating costs of the Black Vein Colliery, he decided to sink a new colliery to replace it, still with easy access to the highly productive Black Vein seam. The new pit would be only a short distance away to the north east, on the other side of the railway, on land across the Sirhowy River. Two shafts were sunk in 1875 to access the Black Vein (Nine Feet) seam and this was reached at a depth of 288 yards in the case of the downcast, with the Five-Feet seam reached at 320 yards for the upcast ventilation shaft. The new colliery was to be known as the New Black Vein (Risca) Colliery. In course of time, it was also known as the Rock Vein North Colliery (as it was close to the small old Rock Vein Colliery), North Risca, North Black Vein and New Risca. It was eight miles north of Newport on the east side of the Valley with seven rail sidings accessing the waste tips, fanning out from the bridge across the river. It was based on a target production of 1,000 tons of coal per day, employing 1,050 men and 102 horses, being the first colliery in South Wales to use electric lighting at the pit bottom.

The Black Vein seam was the reason that the collieries at the south end of

A view of the New Risca Colliery, located on the downside of the line, via a trailing at Rock Vein Siding North signal box, near the 7¼mp., ¾ mile north of Risca Black Vein Colliery, located on the upside. The New Colliery was opened in 1875, and closed in July 1966, employing more than 2,000 miners during the 1910s and '20s when annual production reached 450k.tons, but declining by half both in miners and production after Nationalisation and finally closed through exhaustion and being uneconomic.

the Ebbw and Sirhowy Valleys were sunk. The seam averaged some 10ft. in thickness and had a low ash content of about 6 per cent, with a low sulphur content of 0.6 to 1.5 per cent, with a reputation for being the finest coking coal in the world. Risca coal was in great demand for express locomotives on the railways both at home and abroad.

In May 1892, the London & South Wales Colliery Co. Ltd. was re-formed into United National Collieries Ltd. to manage the Risca and Abercarn, National (Rhondda Fach), and Blaenrhondda Collieries with Watts, Watts & Co. as their sole Shipping Agents, one of the largest shipping companies in the country with six offices in the UK and a further six on the Continent. They were also shipbrokers, coal exporters and colliery owners. E.H. & F.S. Watts, as well as having a controlling interest in United National, were also shareholders in the Abercarn Coal Co. which re-opened the Prince of Wales Colliery in 1883 following the major explosion there which killed 268.

In 1880, manpower was 800 with output in 1889 346,000 tons and in 1894 405,000. In 1896, the new Risca Pit employed 840 men underground and 168 on the surface, working the Black and Lower Black Vein seams. Data for 1900 showed 1,201 at the new pit and 106 still at the Old Black Vein colliery.

The Company prospectus for 1913 stated that:

'The Company are at present constructing an up-to-date coal washing and coking plant, comprising a Coppee coal washery capable of washing 2,000tons of colliery slack every day, and a battery of 45 Coppee by-product coke ovens. The greater part of the coal leaving the washery will be as Washed Nuts, Beans and Peas, while some 300tons per day of washed small coal will be delivered to the coking plant. The gas produced during the carbonisation of the coal amounting to 1bn. cu.ft. per annum will be treated in the bi-product plant for the production of Tar, Sulphate of Ammonia and Crude Benzol. The waste heat from the Coke Ovens will be used for raising steam in a special range of boilers adjacent to the Coke Oven, where about one ton of steam will be produced for each ton of coal charged into the ovens.'

In 1915, the company's properties were quoted as Risca Old and New Black Vein Collieries, National Colliery, Wattstown

and the Standard Colliery, Ynyshir (purchased in 1914), with a combined value of almost £0.5m and a share value of just over £1m, the company having made a profit between 1903-14 of £1.049m.

Following the disaster at the Universal Colliery, Senghenydd, in October 1913 when 439 miners were killed due to a gas explosion, Risca colliers embarked on a one-week strike in November 1913 over the danger of explosion from gas at the pit, the occurrence of firedamp being a continuous known working hazard. With the return of men from the war, employment figures for 1918-23 show just over 2,000 men employed with an output in 1923 of 450,000 tons.

In 1928, United National Collieries came under the control of the Ocean Coal Co. and though the 1930 level of production was still 450,000 tons, it was with around 500 less staff. The Depression years of the 1930s saw the level of employment at the Risca Pit fall to under 1,000 between 1932-37, and to as low as 626 in 1934. This was also the period of union unrest over non-union employment which caused stay-down strikes and walk-outs at both Risca and Nine Mile Point. In November 1937, safety concerns

Four views of the New Risca Colliery in operation at the peak of production.

came to a head when Risca miners refused to allow shot-firing during the working shift for fear of explosion, and went on a four-week strike, this escalating in a ballot of all 13,000 miners employed by the Ocean Company which resulted in them all striking and a victory for the safety cause.

Production continued to fall and in 1940 was down to 300,000 tons with 1,020

A former 850 Class 0-6-0T No. 1966 was also employed at Risca Colliery and is seen there on 27 October 1947.

A former Barry Railway Class F No. 780, which had been fitted with pannier tanks to replace the previous saddle tanks, was bought on withdrawal by the New Risca Colliery and is seen working at that colliery in April 1952. SLS

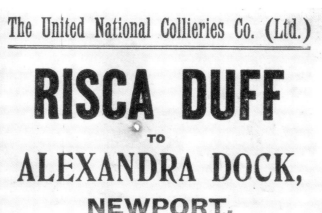

Gold coloured identity disc No. 277 issued to staff by United Collieries Limited, for use at Risca Collieries.

Two wagon labels as used by Risca Colliery. The first is an original Monmouthshire Railway wagon label for truck No. 7248 issued on 16 July 1878 for traffic to Messrs. J. Rees & Co., Tranch Colliery, Pontnewynydd via Newport. Note there is no weight on the label. The second is issued by United Collieries and is for Risca Duff to Alexandra Dock, Newport. Note this is not specific to a vessel but is for a pool of wagons all loaded with Risca Duff which can be drawn on as required to satisfy an order. Again, no weight is shown. The label is coloured gold. A.J. Warrington

miners. By Nationalisation it was down to only 175,000 in 1948 with 661 men. The 1950s saw production only reach 200,000 in two years with employment in the mid-700s. By 1960/1 output had fallen to just over 100,000 tons p.a. and the number employed to less than 500. In June 1962, 21 miners staged a 33 hour stay-down strike over the NCB's decision to remove power loading from the colliery, which they viewed as a precursor to closure.

For the financial year ending April 1965, the NCB reported a loss of £106,000 for Risca Colliery, an average of 90d per ton. They repeated that the economically workable reserves of coal at the pit were coming to an end and suggested that the men's best interests would be served by moving to other more prolific pits in the area. A date of closure was announced

for 20 May 1966 but this was actually deferred until 9 July 1966. The shafts were finally filled in June 1968.

NINE MILE POINT
Railway

The Nine Mile Point from Newport and boundary between the GWR and LNWR was just south of the original two platform station, and was actually at the eight mile marker, the extra mile represented by the Park (or Golden) Mile over the land of Lord Tredegar on the outskirts of Newport. The GWR signal box which controlled the line across the river to Wattsville Goods as well as the start southwards from the station was at 7m.78ch. The exact boundary was at the 8mp and was at 15m.38ch. coming south over the LNWR, measured from the junction with the MT&A line at Nantybwch which was 0.00. Under agreement with the LMS, the GWR closed their box in September 1932. The original GWR station had two platforms of equal length as the line curved south but by the new century, the up platform had been staggered, moved north and shortened, possibly as part of the alterations made following the opening of Nine Mile Point Colliery in 1902/3. There was a goods shed on the down side near the north end of the down platform in 1868 but this had gone on a plan for 1878. This plan showed sidings on the up side serving Evans Quarry which by 1920 were in the name of Pennant Stone Quarries Ltd. A plan for 1920 showed three long sidings on the up side alongside the running lines as they curved east with No. 2 signal box at 15m.19ch. sited to see both ways around the curve.

On the down side, the Penllwyn Tramroad track fed into the running lines. The Penllwyn Tramroad ran from Nine Mile Point to Ynysddu Lower. It was opened in 1824 and was the same gauge of 4ft 2in as the Sirhowy Tramroad. It served small mining installations and yards until the end of the century and in 1908, the LNWR, following the opening of Nine Mile Point Colliery, took over the former tramroad to Ynysddu Goods Yard and to Wattsville Goods.

With the opening of Nine Mile Point Colliery, a new junction and signal box, No. 1, opened at 14m.68ch. in June 1908, coal from the new colliery having previously joined the main line at the station. The new connection into the colliery crossed the Sirhowy River just before the main line junction, and the former Penllwyn Tramroad line connected out of the new colliery line almost at the junction to run alongside the down line before connecting into that line just past No. 2 signal box. No. 1 signal box was closed in November 1967 when the connection onto the colliery branch was covered by a ground frame.

Industry

Nine Mile Point Colliery opened between 1902-5 located on a branch off the main Sirhowy line at No. 1 signal box, under the ownership of Burnyeat, Brown & Co. It was also known as the Sirhowy Valley Colliery until 1912, also as the Sirhowy Black Vein Colliery and as the Coronation Colliery, but the evocative Nine Mile Point won through! The East and West Pits were sunk to the steam coal seams of the Lower and Middle Coal Measures to a depth of 395 yards, while the Rock Vein Pit was sunk to 300 yards to access the Rock Vein seam (No. 2 Rhondda) of the Upper Coal Measures for house coal. The washery and screens could handle 3-4,000 tons per day, equivalent of up to eight 500ton trains, with ten tracks running under the screens for the different types of coal produced. The sinking of the shafts was not without dangers, as seven men were killed when the sinking process to the Black Vein seam was being carried out in the region of the Merthyr Vale or Pengam Fault and the Risca Fault which run down the Valley.

In the record year of 1913, Nine Mile Point was in full production with 2,105 men employed. In that year the company advertised as follows:-

'Burnyeat, Brown & Co.Ltd.
Proprietors of:-
    Insole's Smokeless Steam Coal
    Sirhowy Black Vein Steam Coal
    Rockvein Bunker Coal
    Insole's Abergorki Loco Coal
    Insole's Merthyr Smokeless Washed
        Nuts and Peas
On the Lists of the English, French,
    Italian, Roumanian, Russian, German,
    Brazilian, Dutch, and Spanish
    Governments, and the Principal
    Foreign Railways and Steamship
    Companies
Shipping Ports, Cardiff, Newport,
    Swansea, Port Talbot
Sole Agents:- Watts, Watts & Co. Ltd.
Offices at:-London, Cardiff, Newcastle-
    on-Tyne, Blythe, Liverpool, Glasgow,
    Newport, Algiers.'

Between 1904-15, the company made profits of £761k. Their prospectus of 1913 stated:-

'Nine Mile Point Colliery, which first started work six years ago, is steadily increasing its output, which is expected in the near future to cap the figure of a million tons per annum. It is responsible for the celebrated "Sirhowy" Black Vein Steam Coal and the "Rock Vein" Steam Coal which is in great demand for bunker purposes.'

Industrial relations were however poor with much disagreement between the workers and the managers causing 24 strikes in 1917-19. Unrest, with resultant loss of production, was so bad that the company closed the colliery in October 1923 and in November 1928 due to constant disagreements about payments. In 1928, the company became a subsidiary of the Ocean Coal Company and industrial relations deteriorated even further, involving police baton charging in February 1929.

Manpower had risen to over 2,000 in 1910-13, 1920/5 and 1932 but after 1935 fell away to 1,100-1,200 in most years until Nationalisation. Output figures held up at 550,000 tons in 1923, and 650,000 in 1941/2. Figures for the number employed at the three pits varied as shown by:-

	1923	1930
East Pit	789	589
West Pit	441	350
Rock Pit	506	420
Surface	288	264
Output tons 550,000, pa		

In 1935, further unrest centred on Nine Mile Point which escalated to world interest, when 78 miners decided to stay down in the West pit over the importation of non-union labour by the Ocean Coal Co. from all parts of the coalfield. The strike quickly spread to other collieries in the area, especially Risca with crowds marching to other local collieries to encourage action there. By 19 October

Map of Cwmfelinfach, as at the turn of the twentieth century, the future location of Nine Mile Point colliery.
National Library of Scotland

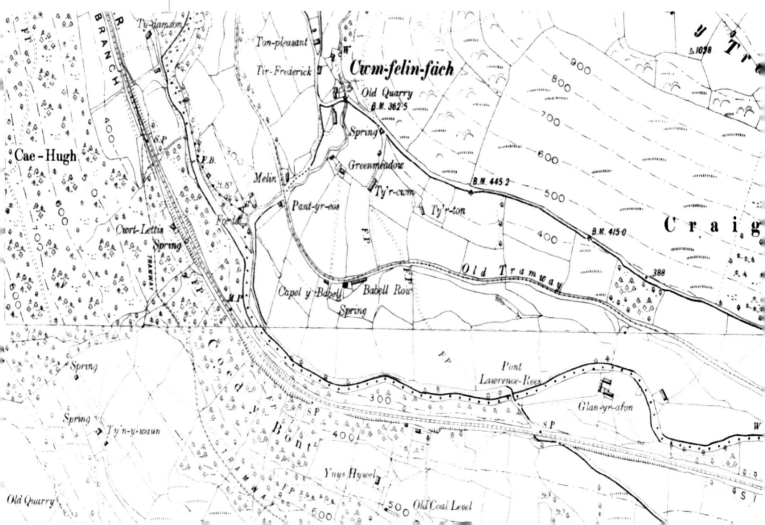

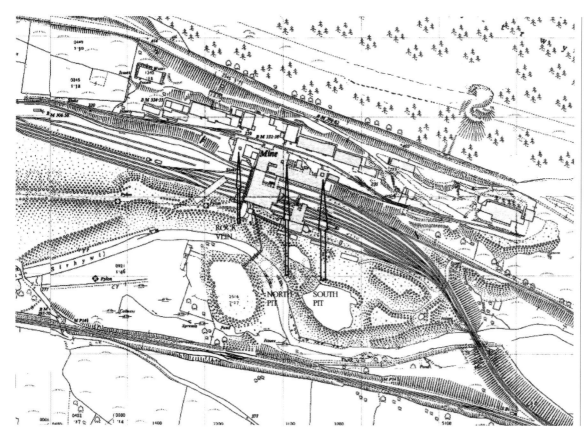

Map of Colliery workings at Nine Mile Point showing the three shafts to North Pit, South Pit and Rock Vein.
Courtesy Oxford House

1935, there were 30,000 miners on strike throughout the coalfield and hurried negotiations between the Ocean Co. and the South Wales Miners Federation were necessary to resolve the problem by banning the use of non-union 'scab' labour.

At Nationalisation, Nine Mile Point employed 1,027 men underground and 234 on the surface and was working the Five-Feet, Lower Black Vein, Black Vein, Big Vein and Rock Vein seams. Coals from the steam coal seams were still classified as Type 301B Prime Coking Coal for use as foundry or blast furnace coke, and both with low ash and sulphur content. In 1954, the Rock Vein Pit was closed and the colliery transferred from the South Western Division's Monmouthshire Area (No.6) to the Rhymney (No.5) No. 3 Group. During the 1950s, output fell to mostly around 300,000 tons, though in 1958 it was only 235k., this with a constant manpower of just over 1,100. In 1961, the colliery was again transferred, this time into No. 2

Nine Mile Point No. 1 Signal Box. There were three boxes, No. 1 controlling a head-on up line junction, Box 2 only 31ch. south controlling access to the Pennant Stone Quarries sidings and a head-on down connection into colliery lines, and GWR box, closed in September 1932 giving access to Wattsville Goods and the colliery, affording a triangle with the previously mentioned down line connection. No. 1 Signal Box controlled the junction into the colliery, off which came a new connection to the Penllwyn Tramway right opened in 1908.

Two views of the junction into the colliery, the second showing more of the colliery.

Group of the Rhymney Area No. 5, where it joined Wyllie and Risca.

Examples of the working levels of the seams being worked in the 1950s are available and show:-

No. 2 Rhondda (Rock Vein) 48ins.
Two-Feet-Nine 15ins.
Four-Feet (Big Vein) 26ins.
Six-Feet 41ins.
Nine-Feet (Black Vein) 115ins.
Yard/Seven-Feet 69ins.
Five-Feet/Gellideg (Lower Black) 72ins.

Empty wagons lined up awaiting acceptance into Nine Mile Point in the 1920s. Note the rake of new wagons for coal factor Philip Thomas, trading from Cardiff, Tredegar Co., E.D. Williams and C. Pond who owned collieries on Halls Road.

Problems with flooding were experienced in November 1963 in the area of the

An excellent view of the colliery and sidings with a variety of wagons on view, United National, Burnyeat Brown and Ocean, with inwards timber for the colliery and a shunting engine above the second Ocean wagon.

Nine Mile Point Colliery, Cwmfelinfach.

Lower Black Vein seam, the water coming from old workings ten yards above the existing ones. This obviously had an adverse effect on output and by March 1964 output per man shift had fallen from the previous 23cwt to 7cwt. Thirty-five men were transferred to the nearby Risca colliery and output rose to 16cwt pms. By then however losses were running at £1 5s for every ton mined, with a total loss to the colliery of £14,000, output in 1963 being 130,600 tons. The NCB announced they wanted 150 men from the West Pit to transfer to Penallta Colliery at Ystrad Mynach, and that the East Pit would close by the end of 1964. Despite initial resistance from the colliery Lodge, Nine Mile Point was closed on 25 July 1964. The NCB's official reasons for closure were adverse geology and the colliery now being uneconomic. However, the NCB's own figures showed that

the colliery had 18m tons of workable reserves and that losses in 1963 had fallen from £305,000 to only £8,000 in June 1964, or £2 6/6d per ton to eleven shillings.

No. 2 SB in August 1952 with empty wagons in the sidings opposite awaiting clearance back to Rogerstone or Maesglas. A.C. Sterndale

NINE MILE POINT No. 2

LAYOUT & SIGNALS

Nine Mile Point No. 2 Signal Box Diagram – Layout and Signals.

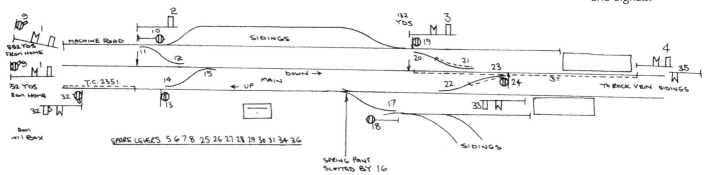

This superb view from No. 2 Box shows Tredegar's Ivatt 2-6-2T 41204 getting away from the station with what is probably the 1.10pm service from Newport to Nantybwch in August 1952 as Stanier 2-6-2T No. 40171 waits in the sidings with what will be the next northbound miners' service at the end of the morning shift. Loaded wagons await removal from the up sidings while others are standing in the down sidings. The train has just passed the up home signal for No. 2 box whose down starter can be seen on the left. The houses of Cwmfelinfach, mostly occupied by miners from the pit, form the backdrop to this picture. A.C. Sterndale

It was generally felt that the level of militancy shown by the workforce had not helped to guarantee the colliery's future at a time when there was probably a surplus of individual production units in the area. Following closure, the majority of miners were transferred to Penallta (249), Bargoed (71), Risca (44) and Wyllie (23).

Nine Mile Point station consisted of two staggered platforms, the up platform the more northerly. This is the view taken from the north end of the down platform and shows the down siding which was stop-blocked at the platform end, and the three up sidings which were beyond the up platform, on 12 July 1958 containing a passenger coach and a freight brake van. H.C. Casserley

With the amount of demolition and clearing up required following the closure, the last train of empties provided to the colliery and loaded out was in 1969 to cater for amounts of coal from reclamation. I arranged for the last train of empties to be provided following a request from the NCB Supplies Co-Ordinator Bernard Gurner at Ystrad Mynach, with whom I worked closely while replanning coal movements in South Wales at that time.

A conference between the train crew of the 12.30pm Risca to Nantybwch at the up platform on 7 June 1960 as the engine has failed. Malcolm James

On 12 July 1958, the SLS ran a special tour which included the Sirhowy Valley which is seen leaving the down platform behind Radyr's 6434 running with a Y Special target. H.C. Casserley

Another SLS Special ran on 7 May 1960 with Ebbw's 6426 seen making a call at Nine Mile Point where members were able to have a last walk-about. John Beardsmore

A **view** of the up platform taken from the final down train on the last day of the passenger service, 11 June 1960. E. Wilmshurst

A posed picture from the early years of the century, probably linked to the special train standing in the siding behind the up platform. It seems likely that the people on the platform were the guests, but the five gangers have found their way into the photograph.

A 1939 picture showing the staggered platforms, probably on the visit of the District Auditor with briefcase who is standing at the south end of the up platform with the station master and another.
Alastair Warrington Collection

A view of a Brecon & Merthyr 0-6-2T at Nine Mile Point is rare enough but here we have three views of 436 working Turn R12, a Rogerstone to Nine Mile Point pick-up service which has served Danygraig Brickworks at Risca en route. Whether by arrangement or otherwise, the engine is running head-on back to Rogerstone which enables the photographer, who was travelling on the engine, to get the best of views. In the first, the return train is easing round the curve from the colliery and then runs along the sidings near No. 2 box, where it will pick up more wagons. A.C. Sterndale

An Ebbw Junction 2-8-0T brings a train of coal across a bridge over the Sirhowy Rover, possibly en route to Uskmouth Power Station against the background of the Colliery Baths and Canteen left and the row of houses on the right is Morrisville, just north of Wattsville, on the main valley road A4048 to Cwmfelinfach. At the top centre, a small shed on the path up the mountain was the explosives store.

The Penllwyn Tramroad after conversion to a railway as it passed derelict houses near Nine Mile Point.

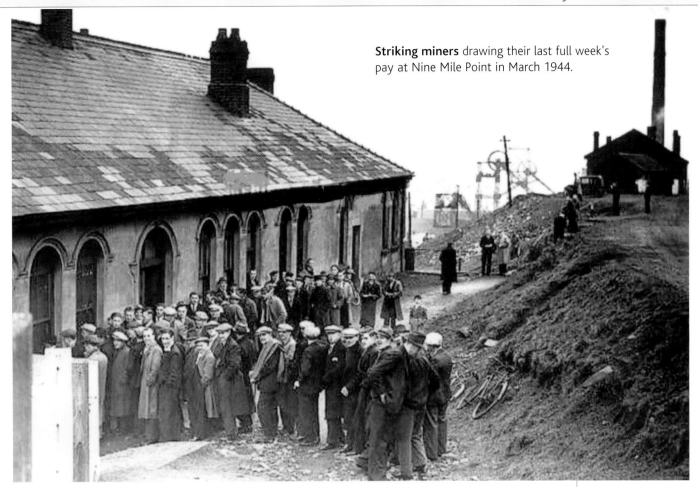

Striking miners drawing their last full week's pay at Nine Mile Point in March 1944.

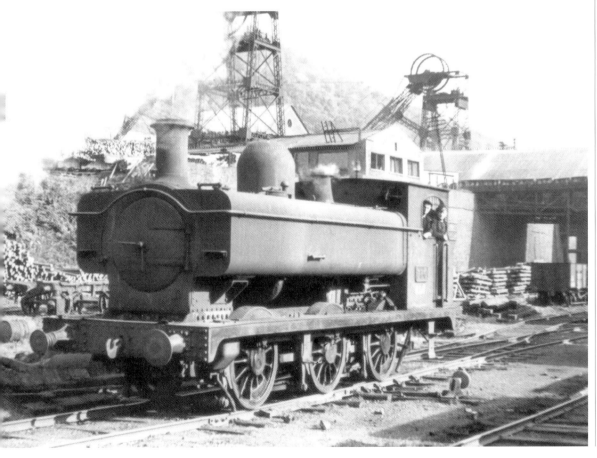

In addition to working later at Risca Colliery, ex-Barry Railway Class F No.780 was first employed at Nine Mile Point where it is seen on 27 October 1947. It underwent an overhaul there before moving on to Risca Pit.

A.J. Warrington Collection

Another view of the same engine at Nine Mile point, here working wagons of pitprops. This former Barry Railway engine was withdrawn by the GWR in May 1936, having been Barry No. 138. It was converted by the GWR from saddle to pannier tank in 1927 at Swindon. A.J. Warrington Collection

This former Hunslet Engine Co. 0-6-0T dates back to 1908 and was used at Risca Colliery until 1937 as No. 978 before becoming Ocean Coal Co. No. 1. It is seen in derelict form at Nine Mile Point in May 1946. It was withdrawn from service in 1951. B. Roberts, IRC

Burnyeat Brown Wagon Label in gold with the Class 1 traffic in red. The label was for Large Coal and did not carry a weight, though this was checked first at the colliery and then on the hoist at Newport Dock, where the weight would often be lighter due to water content at the colliery running off before it was unloaded. The wagon would go into a pool of wagons held at Maesglas/Mon Bank, which would be set against the amount shipped and details passed back to the colliery for future levels sent. A.J. Warrington Collection

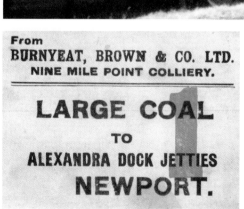

From **BURNYEAT, BROWN & CO. LTD.** NINE MILE POINT COLLIERY.

LARGE COAL TO ALEXANDRA DOCK JETTIES **NEWPORT.**

Ten ton wooden coal wagon owned by Burnyeat Brown, branded Insoles Merthyr Smokeless Steam Coal. A.J. Warrington Collection

PONT LAWRENCE HALT

Pont Lawrence at 14m.44ch. from Nantybwch was alongside Nine Mile Point Colliery, the installation being across the Sirhowy River and was opened largely for use by the miners there on 1 October 1911. It was 24ch. north of Nine Mile Point No. 1 signal box which controlled the branch leading into the colliery. Pont Lawrence Halt remained open until the closure of the passenger service on the Sirhowy Valley on 11 June 1960, after which miners were conveyed by contract bus services.

Pont Lawrence platforms looking south towards Nine Mile Point.

Coal Tank 7752 heads a down train to Newport, possibly the 9.10am from Nantybwch, formed of two well-presented vintage coaches on 19 August 1950.
P.B. Whitehouse/M. Whitehouse Collection

The same formation returning north possibly as the 11.10am Newport to Nantybwch on 19 August 1950.
P.B. Whitehouse/M. Whitehouse Collection

A postcard of Ynysddu station with the staff posed on the up platform. There was a signal box at the end of the down platform between 1902-31. Malcolm James Collection

YNYSDDU

Until 1874, the Sirhowy Valley line was single. At the 13¾mp between Pont Lawrence and Ynysddu, Lord Tredegar had a private siding on the up side consisting of two tracks which accessed his tramroad to his Wentlodge Colliery. The private siding was opened in 1879

A map of Ynysddu at the turn of the twentieth century. National Library of Scotland

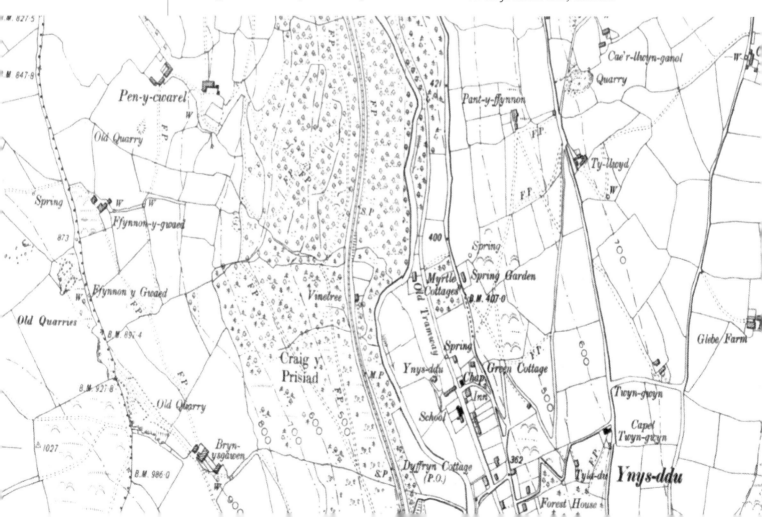

and closed in 1935, with removal in 1936, the tramroad having been taken up by 1920.

Just north of the 13½mp was a private loop siding on the down side owned by Duffryn Chemical Works as at 1878, egress at the south end controlled by the Chemical Works Siding Ground Frame at 13m.35ch, finally taken out of use in 1926.

The Duffryn Chemical Works became the Ynysddu Chemical Works in 1904 and from July 1913 the siding was used by the Mynyddislwyn UDC until 1926 when use of the siding appears to have ceased.

Ynysddu Station was a short distance further north at 13m.17ch., consisting of two facing platforms of equal length, both platforms being extended southwards

A view of the station on 12 July 1958. The platforms were extended at the south end between 1878-1909. H.C. Casserley

A view of the station in its woodland surroundings from a semi-elevated position. John Beardsmore

The station buildings on the up platform as seen on 12 July 1958.
R.K. Blencowe

between 1878-1909. A signal box was located at the south end of the down platform at 13m.18ch. shown opening February 1902 when it replaced an earlier box and closing by 1931.

The Penllwyn Tramroad served quarries above Wattsville and also ran to Ynysddu Lower Goods Depot which opened in July 1911, also serving Cwmfelinfach Goods which opened July 1911 and Wattsville Goods from January 1913. The Penllwyn Tramroad

6412 works an auto service from Risca up the Valley with the engine on the front of the auto formation. SLS

was opened in 1824 but carried no traffic between 1887-1903. It closed beyond the approach to Cwmfelinfach Goods on 1 December 1937, while the colliery company took over the line to Wattsville Goods as part of the access to Nine Mile Point in January 1913. The remnants of the Penllwyn Tramroad were closed in August 1939.

The Llanarth Tramroad connected out of the Penllwyn at Ynysddu and ran on to Penllwyn Colliery at Pontllanffraith and on to Rock Colliery at Blackwood. Until 1908 an occasional horse-drawn tram was worked along the tramroad to preserve the right of way but was closed in 1920 following the closure of the small mines it served.

WYLLIE HALT and COLLIERY
Railway

The line was doubled between Pontllanffraith and Nine Mile Point in 1874. The Sirhowy Valley line ran north beyond Ynysddu towards Tredegar Junction (later Pontllanffraith HL) and from 1924 passed the new Wyllie Colliery on the up side with Wyllie No. 2 signal box, also on the up side, which controlled

the egress southwards from the colliery at 12m.71ch. opened in that year. Wyllie No.1 was also located on the up side controlling the north inlet to the colliery at 12m.32ch. Both boxes were reduced to ground frames on 20 November 1967, all being removed on 9 September 1968 after colliery closure.

Industry
Wyllie Colliery

This was the last colliery to be opened in the Sirhowy Valley and in Monmouthshire, on 23 August 1924. As such, it was a modern colliery in many aspects with long inwards (three) and outwards (four) sidings, with five tracks passing under the screens to take each of the coals produced. In the early years of the new century, the Tredegar Iron & Coal Co.'s (TICC) collieries at the top end of the Sirhowy Valley were becoming exhausted and they decided to probe the untapped steam coal seams of the Middle and Lower Coal measures of the central Sirhowy Valley. In 1906, they negotiated with Lord Tredegar for the mineral rights to his lands between Holly Bush and Ynysddu, and as a result opened

A Risca to Tredegar service timed to leave Ynysddu at 2.30pm has no passengers for there on 7 May 1960 with engine 9644 of Ebbw running bunker-first up the valley. Note the facilities provided at this small station, Ladies and Gentlemen's Waiting Rooms and Booking Office. R.E. Toop

Two views of Wyllie Halt on 12 July 1958, looking south with the colliery buildings in the background. Wyllie No. 1 SB was at the south end of the up platform and controlled the entrance into the colliery. The station was opened with the colliery in 1926 for the mining community but closed in June 1960 while the colliery survived until 1968, with transport undertaken by road. H.C. Casserley, R.M. Casserley

three new pits at Markham, Oakdale and Wyllie, the first two located on the line which the GWR had purchased from Lady Llanover in 1877, and was known then as Halls Tramroad, which they converted to a standard railway by the new century.

Wyllie Colliery was named after Lt Col Alexander Keith Wyllie, a director of TICC, and in 1922 a subsidiary company, Tredegar Southern Collieries Ltd., was formed to run it. The colliery was originally to have been at Gelligroes, a mile further up the Valley, but this was

Wyllie Halt looking north towards Ynysddu on a wet 12 July 1958. H.C. Casserley

abandoned due to excessive water found during preliminary sinking operations, and the project was further delayed by the war, making Wyllie the last colliery to be sunk in the county. Access was a problem as there was no proper road to the site and a new road over a mile long had to be constructed during the months

A train from Risca runs into Wyllie Halt past the No. 1 SB with Ebbw Junction's 3747 working the one coach service on 12 July 1958. The colliery sidings can be seen in the left distance with the pit shaft. H.C. Casserley

An Ivatt 2-6-2T heads north on the up line, probably to work a miners' service to Nantybwch as a 57XX heads south on a service to Risca. SLS

previous to the opening of the mine in August 1924. The new pit was electrically equipped throughout and all modern facilities were provided. A colliery village for miners and their families was constructed, as was the case at Markham also, for which the railway provided a railway station. Most of the steelwork used to construct the colliery was made at the TICC plant at Tredegar.

There were two shafts, 50 yards apart, the South Pit (629 yards deep) sunk between November 1924 and August 1926 and the North Pit (598 yards deep) between January 1925 and September 1926. The Big Vein seam which was 73in thick was reached at 323 yards but work was first started on the Upper Rhas seam. They continued sinking to the Old Coal seam so as to prove the accessibility of all the seams. Electricity supply was from the Oakdale Colliery powerhouse and covered the two winding engines, compressors, ventilating fans and switchgear as well as all staff facilities. The capacity of the electric winders was two trams per wind, equivalent to a total wind of 171tons per hour. No horses were used at the colliery.

By July 1928, output was 7,000 tons per week, the coal being of excellent quality. A washery was installed in 1930 with a washing capacity of 125 tons per hour.

The Chairman's report for July 1938 however made mention of underground problems which had been known to

exist when the pit was sunk but which had to be accepted, revolving around a large number of faults and disturbances in the two seams which had been most intensively worked. On the east side of the pit was an upthrow fault of considerable displacement which had occurred nearer to the shaft than was anticipated, but he was pleased to announce that they had now worked around the displacement to reach a good section of coal beyond.

By 1928, manpower at Wyllie had reached 971 and gradually rose to 1,406 in 1934, the highest level ever involved. Output in 1930 with 1,248 men was 350,000 tons , reaching the highest level for the colliery in 1940 of 400,000 tons with only 855 men, average earnings being between £8-12 per week. With Nationalisation in January 1947, Wyllie was placed in the No.6 (Monmouthshire) Area, Group No.3, at that time employing 639 men underground with 126 on the surface, working the Five-Thirty-Yards and Five-Twenty-Yards seams. In 1961, the colliery was moved into the No.5 (Rhymney) Area with Nine Mile Point and Risca.

When the colliery was in full production, its coals were classed as types 203 and 204 Coking Steam Coals, the 203 weak to medium caking and the 204 medium to strong, both low volatile, low sulphur and ash content and mainly used for steam raising in boilers for foundry and blast furnace cokes and for coking blends.

Manpower after Nationalisation and until the end of the 1950s was 8-900, but after 1960 fell to the mid to high 600s. Output between 1948 and 1958 was normally between 190-250,000 tons pa. but during the 1960s fell to less than 200,000.

As with other pits in the area, profitability suffered during the 1960s and in 1967 the NCB announced that Wyllie was losing £15,000 per month and that its coals had a high sulphur content

A one coach auto working, as Ebbw's 6426 propels a Nantybwch to Risca train, both pictures showing the full station and signal box. SLS

The one coach train conveys a parcels van on its service to Risca on 28 May 1960 with power by an Ebbw Junction Pannier.
E.T. Gill/R.K. Blencowe

making it difficult to sell. Because of these problems, they announced closure of the colliery on 23 March 1968. The shafts were filled but were not capped until November 1979. At the time of closure, there were 645 men employed there and

they were dispersed to several collieries in the Rhymney area, most going to Windsor Colliery. Later attempts by Oakdale to work the remaining reserves of Wyllie into the 1990s, resulted in failure, that colliery closing in 1989.

The view northwards along the down platform from a society special three coach auto.

Wyllie No. 1 signal box at the south end of the station controlling the inlet into the colliery.
John Beardsmore

Wyllie No. 2 signal box south of the colliery, controlling the exit from the colliery sidings.

WYLLIE No. 2

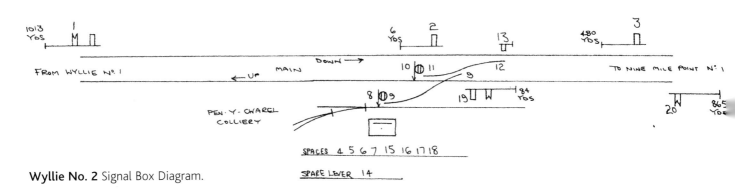

Wyllie No. 2 Signal Box Diagram.

Wyllie Colliery from the south end.

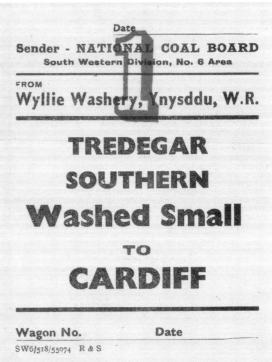

A wagon label from Wyllie Washery for Tredegar Southern Washed Small to Cardiff Dock.

PONTLLANFFRAITH (HL)

Pontllanffraith was an important railway junction location, as this was where the Sirhowy line met with the Vale of Neath. Until 1 July 1911, its railway location on the Sirhowy was known as Tredegar Junction. The Sirhowy and GWR (former Taff Vale Extension) lines formed a large triangle south of the two passenger stations, the Sirhowy line passing over the GWR line south of both stations. The Sirhowy line ran down to Gelligroes Junction en route to Ynysddu while the GWR swept around the base of the triangle to Sirhowy Junction where it joined with a chord line from Gelligroes, making a triangle. In the middle of the triangle were Bird in Hand sidings, until 1948 an important interchange point for traffic between the two railways, though losing its importance after Nationalisation. Approaching Gelligroes Junction on the Sirhowy line was Tredegar Junction Lower signal box at

11m.45ch. and it was as this name that the area was best known.

The Bryn Tramroad also ran in this area from north of the LNWR station at Bryn Siding ground frame to a point south of Bird in Hand East box and then took a southerly direction alongside the Taff Vale Extension line.

By 1900, Bird in Hand yard had fully developed with signal boxes controlling the north and south connections, East Box controlling the eastern end of the through running lines to Sirhowy Junction off both the GWR and LNWR lines and the connections off the Vale of Neath line into the three exchange sidings, and also from the LNWR line into the two sidings on that side of the yard. Bird-in-Hand West signal box controlled the west end section of the running lines to Sirhowy

Map of the area at the turn of the twentieth century, showing Sirhowy Junction centre left, the triangle to Gelligroes Junction Tredegar Junction Lower, Bird in Hand and Tredegar Junction LNWR and Pontllanffraith GWR. National Library of Scotland

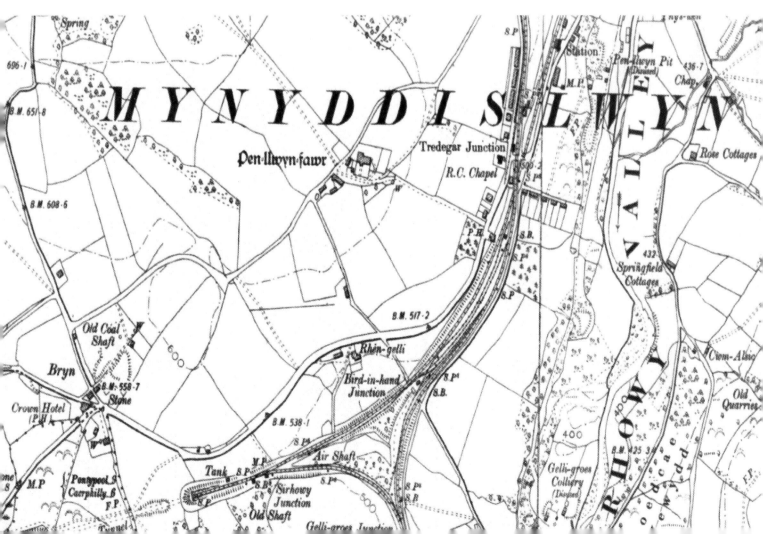

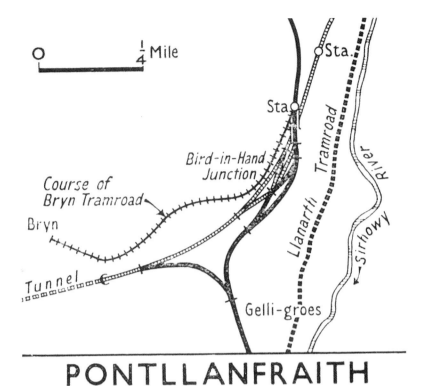

PONTLLANFRAITH

Plan of line from Gelligroes Junction Tredegar Junction Lower to Sirhowy Junction, Bird in Hand and Tredegar Junction Pontllanffraith HL, also showing the course of the Bryn and Llanarth Tramroads. From Sirhowy Junction a connection was made at Hengoed HL with the Rhymney line for Ystrad Mynach Sidings where freight traffic to Cardiff and Barry Docks was exchanged with the Rhymney and Barry Railways.

Junction and the egress from the Bird-in-Hand sidings, plus two more sidings between the box and Sirhowy Junction East box closed in June 1939, leaving just the West box to control the yard until that also closed in May 1961. By that year, all the sidings between East and West box had been taken out of use, leaving just the two sidings between the former West box and Sirhowy Junction which were closed when the Vale of Neath line closed as a through route in June 1964.

The third side of the triangle was the

A close-up of the tracks in the area as at 1900 and after singling in June 1961. Courtesy R.A. Cooke

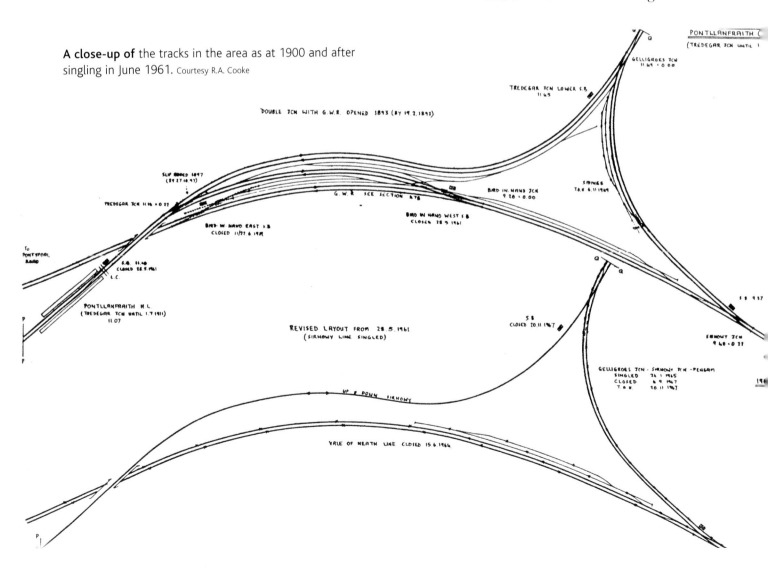

chord line between Gelligroes Junction and Sirhowy Junction, originally single and doubled on 19 February 1888. Gelligroes Junction, the southern tip of the triangle, was covered by Tredegar

Junction Lower signal box located just north on the Sirhowy line at 11m.45ch. The original box was renewed in 1882 and lasted until 20 November 1967 when it was closed, the line having been singled on the Sirhowy Valley on 28 May 1961.

Another view of Tredegar Junction Lower SB alongside the Sirhowy line running south to Gelligroes Junction with the line coming in from Sirhowy Junction on the left in the shade. Gerald Davies

Looking towards Bird in Hand West SB from Tredegar Junction Lower showing Bird in Hand Junction and the Vale of Neath line coming round from Sirhowy Junction, on 6 June 1963. Jeff Stone

A close-up of Bird in Hand Junction on 6 June 1963 with the Sirhowy line from Pontllanffraith on the left and the Vale of Neath line from Sirhowy Junction on the right. Jeff Stone

> This was double line and a drawing for 1881 showed a tramroad linking into a loading point from Gelligroes Colliery, with two sidings on the inside of the

Approaching Bird in Hand West signal box on the line from Pontllanffraith HL Station, where a connection was made with the Vale of Neath line to/from Sirhowy Junction for onward connection with Aberdare and other valley lines. R.H. Marrows

triangle for this traffic, all being missing on a drawing for 1900. This chord line was singled in January 1965 and closed in September 1967 with no traffic passing. It was recovered in the November.

Bird in Hand was a very useful place for excursion stock to be reversed and held to work northbound excursions on the Sirhowy line in LNW and LMS days, to such places as Blackpool, Birmingham, Coventry, Manchester, etc, and rugby international excursions to Edinburgh and Heysham for Ireland, so that Pontllanffraith became the starting point for such trains. It was also the route taken between Pontllanffraith and Sirhowy Junction by excursions from the Sirhowy to Barry Island, which ran in up to five parts in the early years of the century but which by the 1950s had become just one from first Nantybwch and then Tredegar, though sometimes with charter specials from such places as Holly Bush. With the closure of the Vale of Neath as a through route in June 1964, use of this once important junction virtually ceased.

However in November 1967, the Cardiff Division of British Rail, in their search to save on track maintenance, decided to close the section of line on Halls Road south of Penar Junction, carrying traffic to and from Oakdale and Markham Collieries and to route

this down the Sirhowy line which was still carrying coal from Wyllie and Nine Mile Point. This involved a reversal of these trains at Penar Junction onto the former Vale of Neath line which was still in position and a short run west to Bird in Hand from where a new link

The Vale of Neath line from Pontllanffraith GWR comes round the bend on the left with the LNWR line from Pontllanffraith LNWR – formerly Tredegar Junction – and both will run south to meet up at Bird in Hand West. R.H. Marrows

line had to be laid to access the Sirhowy line at Tredegar Junction Lower for the Oakdale trains to run to/from Newport.

Sirhowy Junction on the Vale of Neath Taff Vale Extension where coal trains to/from Aberdare diverted to run Tredegar Junction Lower/Gelligroes Junction and via the Sirhowy line to/from Newport. Jeff Stone

Dating from the early part of the twentieth century, a scene at Bird in Hand West with a Coal Tank and what is probably a GW engine shunting in the yard. Gerald Davies Colln

The same view after singling of the line and recovery of sidings. Gerald Davies Colln

The original layout on the GWR left and LNWR/LMS centre and right seen from the bridge carrying the GWR line over the LNW line south of Pontllanffraith. Gerald Davies Colln

However, the Cardiff Division had failed to establish the fact with the NCB that both Wyllie and Nine Mile Point were both to close before the end of the decade, and when this happened, the Sirhowy line was now just carrying the Oakdale and Markham traffic. There were obviously greater savings to be made in closing the Sirhowy line than had accrued from the closure of the southern end of Halls Road, so this was re-opened from 4 May 1970 and the Oakdale/Markham traffic ignominiously transferred back. Some sections of Halls Road had been recovered since closure in 1967 and these had to be replaced.

The other end of the complex, at Tredegar Junction Lower after singling of the Sirhowy line and recovery of the Gelligroes Junction line. Gerald Davies Colln

East of Bird in Hand, the Sirhowy line passed over the Taff Vale Extension and the LNW and GW stations were virtually alongside each other. The LNW station at 11m.7ch. had two facing platforms of equal length with a level crossing and signal box which opened in August 1891 at the south end and, as mentioned, was called Tredegar Junction previous to being Pontllanffraith High Level until 1 July 1911, the GW station being the Low Level.

Pontllanffraith HL was known as Tredegar Junction until 1 July 1911. This view of the level crossing gates during the first decade from alongside the signal box on the down side shows the up platform with the station facilities at the south end. Lens of Sutton

On the evening of Saturday, 26 August 1933, there was a collision at Tredegar Junction Lower involving the 9.5pm ex-Newport running north towards Pontllanffraith. This shows the damage to either the leading or last coach of the three coach train which would have been hauled by a Webb Coal Tank.

A view from the south end of the up platform looking south and showing the level crossing, signal box and double track beyond. At the curve, the Vale of Neath line runs under the Sirhowy to access the Bird in Hand yard and Sirhowy Junction while the Sirhowy line runs on south to Tredegar Junction Lower.
David Lawrence/Hugh Davies Collection

The station on a sunny day in 1949.
E.T.Gill/R.K.Blencowe Colln

An elevated view of the down platform on 28 May 1960, on which there was just a small waiting room and a seat, the main facilities being on the up platform.
E.T. Gill/R.K. Blencowe Collection

A view of the station looking south from the up platform with a few passengers awaiting the next down train. Note the trailing crossover between the up and down lines which might facilitate the release of a banking engine.

An interesting collection of bi-directional LNWR signals south of Pontllanffraith HL on 4 July 1957. The taller arm on the left is for the Sirhowy main line towards Tredegar Junction Lower while the shorter starter and distant signal is for the Bird in Hand West direction leading on to Sirhowy Junction. The up direction signal applied to trains off both routes. T.J. Edgington

Four views of the crossing at Pontllanffraith HL in 1926, by the LMS Publicity Dept., showing cars of that era and pedestrians. Gerald Davies Collection

The Station Master with six of the station staff pose on the seat under the huge station nameboard which unfortunately is not displayed at its best. Gerald Davies Colln

The Station Master, Mr. Forrester, poses outside the Booking Office and Waiting Room on the up platform in the 1920s. Gerald Davies Colln

On to 1951 as Coal Tank 7752, not yet renumbered, waits at the up platform with the 1.10pm service from Newport to Nantybwch on 10 May. Ian L. Wright

Another view of a Coal Tank on a service from Newport, this time seen from the down platform. It was common for trains to be made up of a veteran coach in which workmen were expected to ride and a modern LMS vehicle. Derek Chaplin

The 3.22pm Risca to Nantybwch has former LMS power in the form of Tredegar's Stanier 2-6-2T 40098 as it runs past the signal box into the platform on 3 October 1956. S.Richard/J&J Collection

A 1957 view of the Sunday Nantybwch to Barry Island excursion running into the station on 14 July behind Tredegar's G2 0-8-0 49409. T.J. Edgington

The last 0-8-0 to leave Tredegar, 49064 running with 41204, passes Pontllanffraith HL box as 6641 passes on the up road with the 10.5am Risca to Tredegar, on 8 August 1959. R.O. Tuck/RAS

6641 and its one coach formation as the 10.5am Risca to Tredegar wait at the up platform on 8 August 1959. 6641 was a Barry engine at this time, and may have had overhaul at Ebbw Shops and been allocated to this turn for running in. S. Rickard/J&J Collection

With the end of the service in sight, trains during 1960 were reduced to one coach only. 6412 waits at the up platform with a service from Risca to Tredegar on 4 April 1960. E.T. Gill/R.K. Blencowe Collection

9644 runs south with the 1.40pm Tredegar to Risca on 7 May 1960. R.E. Toop

A 1959 shot of 5727 heading the afternoon miners' train from Nine Mile Point to Nantybwch. Stephenson Locomotive Society

Following the cessation of passenger services on 11 June 1960, the line was singled on 28 May 1961. The up line through the station was retained under the reversible working, the down line being recovered, making a sorry sight in this picture shortly afterwards.

With the disused down platform now marooned, 4643 brings a short train of coal empties southwards through the station in spring 1964.
David Lawrence/Hugh Davies Collection

A view past the signal box along the now singled line is afforded by this picture of 3634 heading a down goods in 1968.

PONTLLANFRAITH HIGH LEVEL STATION

Industry
Gelligroes Colliery

This was located on the railway chord line between Gelligroes Junction and Sirhowy Junction and was linked by a tramroad from the colliery which was away from the railway to a loading point in sidings alongside the chord line. The colliery consisted of two shafts 126ft deep and one level, all accessing the Mynyddislwyn seam. It was owned in 1858-60 by Thomas Powell and in the 1870s by the Gelligroes Colliery Co. It closed in 1887 when owned by Harris & Mitchell but re-opened later and is recorded employing 14 miners in 1901, but was again listed as abandoned in 1902. It probably opened again as it was recorded in the *Colliery Guardian* as closed due to the war. The shafts were finally filled in 1960.

Libanus Colliery

North of Pontllanffraith, this colliery consisted of shallow pits into the Mynyddislwyn seam which in 1870 were owned by the Trustees of the late Thomas Prothero. In May 1879, it was put up for auction and was owned by Bevan & Price in 1880-89, and then by Edmund Matthews in 1922 when it was closed. The No. 1 pit was six feet in diameter and 435ft deep. The pit is shown to have abandoned the Mynyddislwyn seam in 1892 and the plant and machinery to have been again put up for auction. Work however continued in this seam from the Libanus Lower Level (Rose, Plas New or Lower Plas) and the Libanus Upper Level (Blackwood) with a production of 42,358 tons recorded for 1889. In 1900, the Lower Libanus Level was owned by Mathews & Bethel of the Blackwood Gas & Waterworks and employed six men underground and two on the surface, but in 1901, thirty-six miners, in 1902 fifty-three, and in 1905 thirty-nine. The mine apparently closed in 1907. Libanus Colliery was served off a siding alongside the Sirhowy line into which a tramway also fed traffic from the Lower Plas or Plas Bedwellty Colliery.

This was a small mine working the Mynyddislwyn seam at a depth of 279 ft during the nineteenth century. In 1860-5 it was owned by the Prothero Brothers and in 1870 by the Trustees of the late Thomas Prothero.

BLACKWOOD
Railway

An inspection made of the Sirhowy line in 1865, the year of the introduction of full railway passenger services, mentions that Blackwood was then the only station with two platforms. The single line between Holly Bush and Blackwood was doubled on 18 May 1890 and that between Blackwood and Pontllanffraith on 1 September 1891. Prior to this, the single platform at Blackwood station was served by a loop line which enabled two trains to pass at that point. The railway had been built to the north of the original tramroad which ran closer to the Cwm Gelli Collieries. With the doubling of the line and the building of a down platform, the up platform was lengthened though was not as long as the down. The station was hemmed in to the south and north by colliery sidings, the New Rock Colliery to the south and Upper and Lower Cwm Gelli Collieries. Also to the south was Marsh's Siding, closed about 1959 and at the north end Treharne's Rock Foundry Siding. No. 2 signal box at the south end of the up platform was at 9m.60ch. and opened in June 1890, closing in July 1960. Blackwood No. 1 signal box was on the downside at 9m. 27ch. north of the connections into the Cwm Gelli Collieries, opening in February 1914 and closing in May 1961, when reduced to a ground frame.

The station signal box closed just after the withdrawal of the passenger service in June 1960, leaving No. 2 box to control the running lines and most remaining operating sidings, all of which were taken out of use in 1964/5.

North of No. 2 box were sidings serving

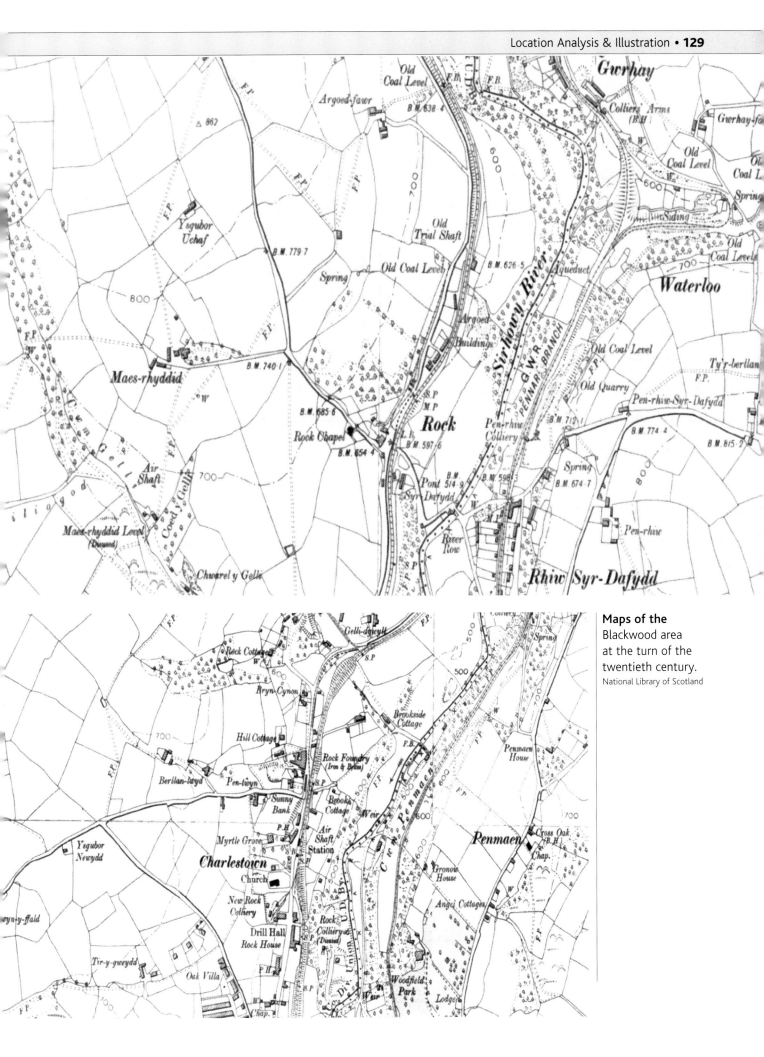

Maps of the Blackwood area at the turn of the twentieth century.
National Library of Scotland

A postcard of the Station Approach at Blackwood with the station Booking Office on the right centre, in the early twentieth century.

The original up platform at Blackwood was designed for only two or three coaches as shown in this 1905 view.
C.H. Forrester

Another view of the up platform c1905 with staff and perhaps passengers waiting for the next northbound train. The signal box is well shown and beyond in the station yard is also the connection into New Rock Colliery.
R.K. Blencowe Collection

In another view along the short original LNW platform looking north c1905, the staff pose, perhaps with the man on the track responsible for the permanent way.
R.K. Blencowe Collection

the Primrose Colliery opened about 1888 by Christopher Pond who owned several small collieries in the area. There was a tramroad bringing in the mined coal for loading in the sidings and extending under the Sirhowy Railway to a tip disposal. Access was controlled by Rock Siding Ground Frame at 8m.77ch., this opening in June 1890 and closing in September 1950.

Industry
Rock Colliery

This colliery was opened as a level and was in operation according to some sources as early as 1820 while others say 1825, when it was sending coal to Tredegar Iron Works. In 1836, it was bought by the Monmouthshire Coal & Iron Co. for £22,000 and on the bankruptcy of this company in 1839 it was sold to the Rock Colliery Co. In 1842 they employed 132 men at the Rock, which then consisted of the Rock Level, New Rock Level, Rock Pit and New Rock Pit. In 1859, the owner was Henry Marsh who had a private siding just south of Blackwood station. Over the years there were many fatal accidents involving roof falls, including one of a man drowned in 1855 due to breaking into old water-logged workings.

The shaft was sunk in the late 1880s but was used only for the raising of coal with its wooden headgear, the miners entering and leaving the pit via the old

The platforms at Blackwood received a wooden extension northwards by 1920, though as can be seen on the extreme right at a higher level than the original platform. The separate office on the left was the new Station Master's Office, and the then incumbent H.W. Forrester in the frock coat is standing outside with Booking Clerk Harry Shaw.

The new extension to the platforms in a 1920 view looking south showing the fence erected between the station and the houses alongside.

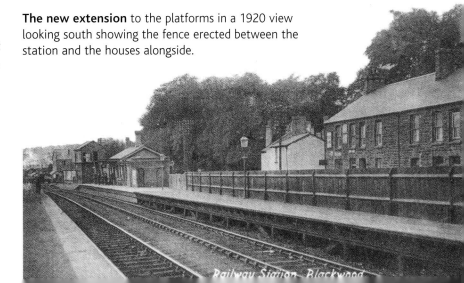

Coal Tank 7712 with the 10.38am Newport to Nantybwch stands at the up platform composed of a close-coupled 4 coach set on 29 July 1935, the lack of passengers on view being representative of the state of the business at that time, with mass migration to the local bus service. W.W. Tasker

In the 1920s and '30s there was a wider range of passenger services on offer, as here with a three coach 3.50pm Blackwood to Abergavenny on Monday, 9 August 1937 with LMS 3F 0-6-0 3656 of Burton depot 17B in charge with an old style Midland Railway tender, presumably borrowed by Abergavenny off an overnight freight working. W.W. Tasker

level. In 1884, the *Western Mail* reported that plans were afoot to re-open the Old Pit to access a large section of the Mynyddislwyn seam, which would involve pumping out the pit and securing it and sinking a new pit. The Old Pit was only about 70ft deep and the New Pit 100ft. The Mynyddislwym had split in this area to form Upper and Lower sections. The Upper seam was 36-48in thick and extensively worked while the Lower seam was 19-36in thick but of inferior quality.

In 1896, the owners were Lewis Lewis & Sons with 46 men employed and by 1908 it had changed hands to Budd & Co. of Dock St., Newport, with 182 men. At its peak in 1916, the colliery employed 182 men working the Mynyddislwyn seams

mainly for house and gas coal. Budd's Blackwood Collieries Ltd. was formed in 1924 to take control of the Rock collieries and in 1927 the company advertised coal from this colliery as follows:-

'Budd and Company, Dowlais Chambers, Cardiff and Newport

First Class Large, Thro' and Thro' and small Bunker Coal (clean burning, durable and of high calorific power). Worked Thro' and Thro' a Speciality .

Proprietors of Aberbeeg, Rock, Plas, Argoed and Gwm-Gelly Collieries.

Celebrated Mynyddislwyn House, Gas, Smithy and Coking Coals, Bunker Coal.

Exporters of all description of Cardiff and Newport Steam, House, Smithy and Anthracite Coals.

Importers of Pitwood.'

On Nationalisation, the Rock Colliery was placed in the No. 6 (Monmouthshire) area, Tredegar Group. By 1954, the colliery employed only 66 men underground and 14 on the surface, in 1956 38 underground, 30 above. Budd's Rock, as it was known, closed in 1957.

Primrose Colliery (also known as New Rock) was located north-east of Budd's Rock Colliery, 30 chains north of Blackwood No. 2 signal box and consisted of two levels driven horizontally into the hillside to work the Mynyddislwyn seam. It was opened about 1888 by Christopher Pond who owned other small mines in the area and produced house, gas, manufacturing and steam coals, employing fourteen men underground and two on the surface in 1896, rising to fifty-five men in 1908. It employed seventy-five when sold to Love & Gittins in 1923 when it was known as Primrose Bridge and was worked with the Rock Level. In 1930 output was 6,000 tons and in 1935 7,000 tons with twenty-one men underground and four on the surface. Similar output was achieved in the early 1940s but in 1945 there were only 10 employed and the mine closed in 1946.

A staff photo from the 1920s at Blackwood with the Station Master H.W. Forrester, Booking Clerks on either side seated, and platform staff.

There was a wider selection of power on the line in the 1920s and '30s as here with 0-6-0 4347 of Abergavenny at Blackwood Yard with a goods train probably from Abergavenny on 29 June 1937. The Goods Yard and Shed were built in 1915. To avoid tender-first working, engines could be turned at Bird in Hand. W.W. Tasker

A half-day excursion to Cardiff leaves Blackwood on 14 March 1936 behind Tredegar 0-8-0 8899, composed of twelve 4wheelers and one 6 wheel compo third. 8899 was often selected for passenger duty of this type so must have been a favoured engine at the depot. W.W. Tasker

A lovely view of Blackwood station from the south end on 11 July 1959. H.C. Casserley

Another view from the south end looking north with an end-on aspect of the No. 2 signal box and a more general view of the platforms on 28 May 1960. Monmouthshire Railway Society.

The service from Risca to Nantybwch was intended to be auto worked and here Ebbw's 6412 heads an auto service northwards on 4 April 1960. E.T. Gill/R.K. Blencowe Collection

Haulage of the Sunday Barry Island excursion has now passed from the Tredegar 0-8-0 to a Radyr 56XX which is seen waiting with its train, headed by a former BPGV coach at the down platform wooden extension on 12 July 1959. H.C. Casserley

The platform staff unload packages from the guard's van of this Tredegar bound service hauled by Ebbw's 7771, with 57XXs having mostly replaced the auto fitted 64XX. David Lawrence/Hugh Davies Collection

The facilities on the down platform are well shown in this view on 28 May 1960 with conventional working, though with an auto coach plus a van.
E.T. Gill/R.K. Blencowe Collection

A Tredegar to Risca service stands at the down platform on 10 July 1958 behind Ebbw Junction's 9644. Note the south end of the down platform received a wooden extension, whereas it was the north end of the up platform, the platforms previously being staggered. H.C. Casserley

Heathfield Bridge, north of Blackwood station, with 3712 on a northbound miners' train in 1959. Gerald Davies

The Station Yard at Blackwood was located at Cwmgelli as on the right of this picture. Note also the railway crossing on the extreme right.

Rock Colliery at Blackwood, owned and operated by Budd & Co.

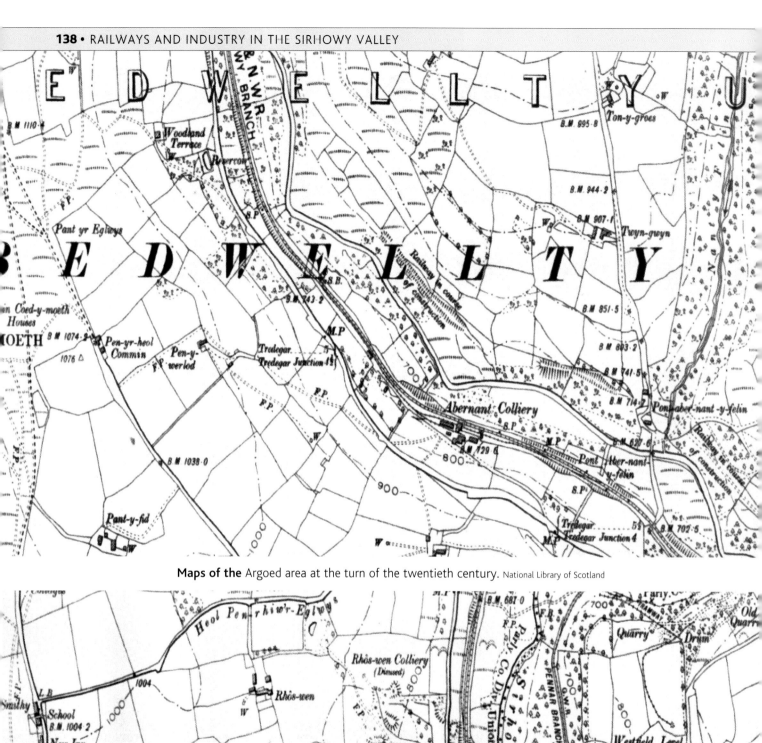

Maps of the Argoed area at the turn of the twentieth century. National Library of Scotland

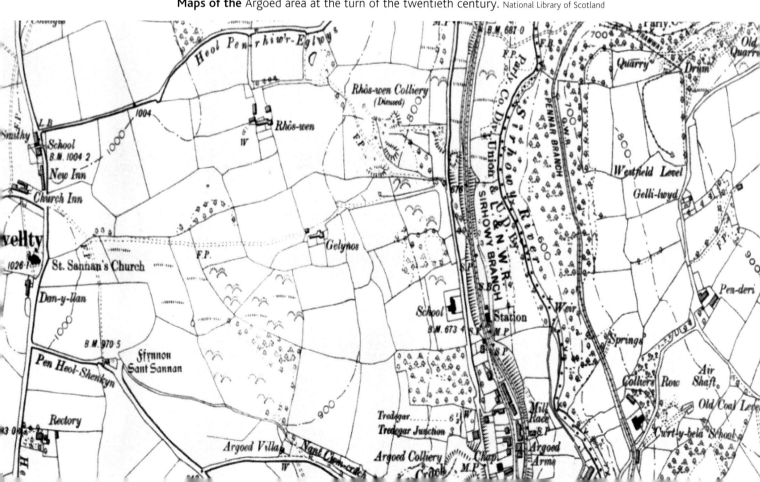

ARGOED
Railway

The original Sirhowy Tramroad ran through the main street of Argoed and this was obviously changed when the tramroad was converted to a railway c1860. The railway was single track at this point but was doubled as from May 1890 when a second staggered platform was added at 8mp and the original one lengthened. By the new century, a Goods shed had been added alongside the up platform. On 29 September 1941, Argoed station was downrated to a halt. A tall signal box to enable the signalmen to see round the bend to the south was built at 7m.75ch. north of the platforms on the up side, opening in June 1890 and lasting until July 1960, after the withdrawal of the passenger service. The line was singled in May 1961.

South of the station were the Argoed or Cwm Creeich Colliery sidings, with a tramroad running west to bring in the coal for loading in the sidings. The original access to these sidings was from north of the station but this was brought south of the station probably in 1890.

North of Argoed were sidings at 7¾mp serving Rhoswen mine, three sidings on the upside fed by a tramroad. By 1912, the siding nearest the up running line had been extended north to between the 7¼ and 7½mp and Rhoswen Siding signal box opened in July 1912, which from December 1945 was open on an as required basis until finally closed in 1960.

Just north of Rhoswen was Abernant Colliery

Industry
Argoed or Cwm Creeich

This was a series of levels producing house coal from the Mynyddislwyn seam as early as 1812 when records show a production of 120 tons per day under the ownership of the Argoed & Newport Coal Co. In 1814, they opened the Argoed Uchaf level. In 1842, the levels were owned by the Tredegar Colliery Co. and employed 141 miners. Records of mine ownership in 1858 and 1870 show Argoed owned by the Tredegar Iron Co., but in 1884 by Morgan & Jones and in 1888 by Morgan & Son, who had problems finding a workable seam. In 1893 the mine was purchased by J.H. Lloyd & Co., but his costs in trying to make the

High Street, Argoed.

The Sirhowy Tramroad ran through the main street at Argoed before the railway was built along a separate trajectory. This is one of several postcards available showing the tramroad running along High Street, Argoed, as it would have been until the 1860s.

4399. The Railway Station & High Street, Argoed. Ernest I

A view from high ground of the staggered platforms, goods yard and High Street at Argoed c1910.

The 10.38am Newport to Nantybwch departs from Argoed on 30 September 1935, the first day of use of vestibule and corridor stock on the Sirhowy line. W.W. Tasker

mine into a profitable business led him to bankruptcy in April 1894. In May 1895, the mine was put up for auction as:

'The mines, veins or seams of coal and other materials belonging thereto, the rights and privileges of working thereof, and also the plant and machinery…and to be sold as a going concern.'

The mine was bought by Happerfield & Willans of Newport who employed fourteen men underground and three on the surface, but by 1901 this had risen to thirty-six. In 1908, ownership passed to Budd & Co. who by 1913 employed fifty men.

Budds owned the mine until 1923 when it employed eighteen and then it was bought by W. Harrhy who ran it as the New Argoed Level. In 1935, the Upper Argoed Level was owned by W.G. Price who by 1937 employed thirty-one. The Mynyddislwyn seam in this area had split into two sections, generally separated by 25ft of stone. The top section was the more profitable varying between 36-48in in thickness, the lower section being generally of poor quality with a thickness of 19-26in. The level closed by the end of the 1930s.

A selection of prints from the 1930s, all by W.W. Tasker, Courtesy Gerald Davies

Between Argoed and Markham Village Halt, a Coal Tank with a 3 coach train, the first coach a modern LMS coach with two veteran vehicles following, the later standard formation on many trains to/from Newport. W.W. Tasker

Tredegar was a dream depot for those interested in passenger vehicles, with LNW and L&Y coaches in everyday use. Here three such vehicles for a train to Newport are seen approaching Argoed from Markham Village Halt. W.W. Tasker

A southbound train to Newport passes a northbound train of coal empties approaching Argoed. W.W. Tasker

Between Abernant and Argoed, a Beames 0-8-4T runs south with a train of coal on duty 50 in the 1930s. W.W. Tasker

Argoed station lay on a tight curve and had staggered platforms with water columns at the end of each and the signal box built into the upside bank. The siding running into the goods yard can be seen from centre to left. SLS

Looking south from the south end of the down platform. Note the water columns at the end of both up, the down staggered platforms and the siding behind the up platform.

A 1960 view of the southbound platform at Argoed with the station facilities as this platform was used by people travelling to Newport. The substantial awning provided much needed shelter from the valley rains. The trailing crossover from the Goods Yard siding through to the Down Main can be seen in front of the signal box. E.T. Gill/R.K. Blencowe Collection

A Coal Tank waits at the up platform as the photographer takes a view from the train window with the down starter off. Note the steep climb from the station to the road in the centre. Alastair Warrington Collection

A scene of peace and tranquillity as the sole occupant of the up platform watches 8766 run into the up platform with a train from Risca to Nantybwch in 1959 with the home signal visible left of centre. The small waiting room was the only facility afforded to passengers travelling north. SLS

A Tredegar to Risca service calls at Argoed at 2.5pm on 7 May 1960, by when one coach sufficed for the number of passengers travelling, the engine 9644. The siding serving the goods yard is on the left. R.E. Toop

The signal box was built on stilts and rested against the bank. It was built high to afford the signalman a good view of trains approaching, especially in the up direction which was on a tight bend.

Rhoswen

A small level near Argoed owned in 1860 by Marshalls and working the Mynyddislwyn seam for house coal. In 1868, ownership had passed to Bevan & Price and in 1889, still under the same ownership, produced 3,087 tons of coal. In 1900, it was owned by Thomas Williams of Argoed who in 1902 employed just three men underground. In 1907 Price & Smith were owners and in 1910 employed ten men. They remained owners throughout the 1920s and into the 1930s but still with only a few workers. The level probably closed before the war. The expansive siding facilities provided by the LNWR seem quite disproportionate to the likely output with so few workers.

There were several other small mines and levels in the Argoed area, many of

which operated only in the nineteenth century. No information is available to me on the location of these and some may well have been on Halls Road, especially those owned by Christopher Pond.

ABERNANT
Railway

Abernant lay between Argoed and Holly Bush and consisted of a colliery and a colliers' platform. There were two sidings under the screens which continued down to the outlet at Abernant No. 2 signal box at 7m.8ch. which opened in June 1890 and was reduced to a ground frame in August 1930. The inlet at the north end was controlled by Abernant No. 1 which opened in March 1890 and closed in July 1915 from when the colliery was served from the south end. Between the north inlet and the screens there were a further four sidings. The colliery, owned by the Bargoed Coal Co., opened in 1888 and closed in 1932, the site being cleared in April 1936.

Industry

Two shafts were sunk to the Brithdir seam in the 1880s by the Bargoed Coal Co. and the pit was linked underground to Llanover Colliery on the other side of the Sirhowy River, which was served initially

A map of Abernant Colliery.

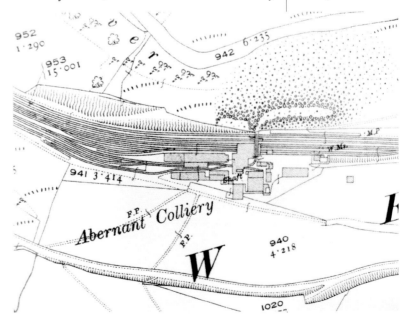

Abernant Colliery was at Argoed and was a prolific colliery. A rake of empty Bargoed wagons are in the forefront with others placed under the screens for loading.

off the Halls Road Tramway, taken over by the GWR from 1877. The Argoed West pit was 489ft deep and elliptical in shape while the East pit was 495ft deep. In 1889 it produced 10,000 tons of coal which had risen in 1894 to 92,800 and in 1896 employed 279 men underground and 44 on the surface. By 1913, this had risen to a combined team of 483 men. The manpower level decreased at the end of the 1920s and in 1930 was down to 330/85, 1931 only a combined 200, only 100 in 1932 when production stopped and the colliery closed. The Brithdir seam which was worked by Argoed was also known as the Tillery, Red Ash and Pontygwaith and lay approx. 230 yards beneath the Mynyddislwyn. It was

extensively worked in a band 3-4 miles wide with work carried out in a north-easterly direction until closure.

MARKHAM VILLAGE HALT
Railway

With the opening of Markham Colliery, served off Halls Road , in 1910-13, a miners' village was built across the river in the Sirhowy Valley and a colliers' platform was provided on the upside of the LNWR line, following which a station with two facing platforms was opened on 1 February 1917 at the 6½mp., when the colliers' platform ceased to be used. Abernant No. 1 signal box was opened at the south end of the up platform at 6m.39ch. in July 1915 and closed in May 1961, having been renamed to Markham Village signal box in the early 1930s.

North of the platforms were two sidings on the upside called Markham's Sidings dating from 1913 when the colliery across the river was opened and which were probably used to receive materials during its construction, all outwards traffic being conveyed over Halls Road. Though it is difficult to see what use they had in the meantime, other than the usual engineering traffic, they remained until taken out of use in May 1961 when the running lines were singled.

A two coach Newport to Nantybwch train pulls away from the staggered up Argoed platform with power to spare in the form of Fowler 2-6-2T No. 70 in the 1930s.
W.W. Tasker

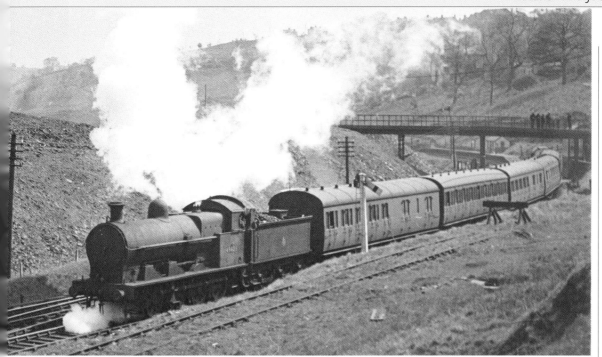

Markham Village Halt was built to serve miners working at Markham Colliery across the valley on Halls Road. The miners' trains starting and terminating at this station were for Markham Colliery miners. Here are two view of a northbound miners' train provided to take home the morning shift leaving the station behind 0-8-0 49409 on 27 April 1957, formed of veteran GW non-corridor stock which had replaced veteran LMS stock.
S. Rickard/J&J Collection & R.O. Tuck/RAS

Another miners' train, this time of 3 coaches behind Stanier 2-6-2T 40098, heading north past Markham Village in the 1950s. Originally the LNWR/LMS provided the stock for these miners' trains, producing some veteran stock of great interest drawn from several pre-Grouping companies but during the later 1950s most stock was provided by the WR.
S. Rickard/J&J Collection

Ebbw's 8766, working the branch in conventional mode, waits for the guard's signal at the up platform and then passes the signal box with a Risca to Nantybwch service in 1960. SLS

A pleasing shot of Ebbw's 6426 running into Markham Village Halt working with auto stock on 28 May 1960. E.T. Gill/R.K. Blencowe Collection

Ebbw's 6426 working a one-coach service on 4 April 1960. The train is seen waiting to leave, with a good view afforded of the signal box. E.T. Gill/R.K. Blencowe Collection

A down auto service, propelled by a 64XX, leaves the down platform and passes the up in 1959.

A view from the 1920s with a Nantybwch to Newport train rounding a bend opposite Oakdale Colliery on Halls Road. W.W. Tasker

A close-up view of Markham Village signal box in 1959.

HOLLY BUSH
Railway

The line between Holly Bush and Blackwood, originally single, was doubled on 18 May 1890 and that from Holly Bush to Bedwellty Pits by October 1891. The original single line station was located at 5m.15ch. but when the line was doubled, a new station was built at 5m.46ch, south of Holly Bush colliery, the screens for which were at 5m.31ch. with three tracks passing under for varying types of coal and two tracks on either side of the screens for inwards empties and outwards loaded. Holly Bush signal box was located at the north end of the up platform (south end of the colliery) and opened in June 1890 with the doubling of the line and closed in September 1938.

The colliery sidings ran from 5m.13ch. at the north inlet to 5m.40ch.at the south outlet and were taken out in March 1935 and September 1938 respectively.

Industry
Holly Bush Colliery

This consisted of four levels and a shaft to the Brithdir seam. The first of the levels was driven in c1870 by E.D. Williams of Blackwood and in 1882 was shown as run by his executors. The New Holly Bush Level was driven in 1889. In 1896, the Old Level is shown as employing fifty-one men underground and twenty-five on the surface, with the New Level forty-nine men underground. In 1900 the totals employed were forty-nine and twenty-four at the Old Level and ninety-three and one at the New. In 1916, the total employed at both levels was 120, and in 1919, one hundred. The Holly Bush

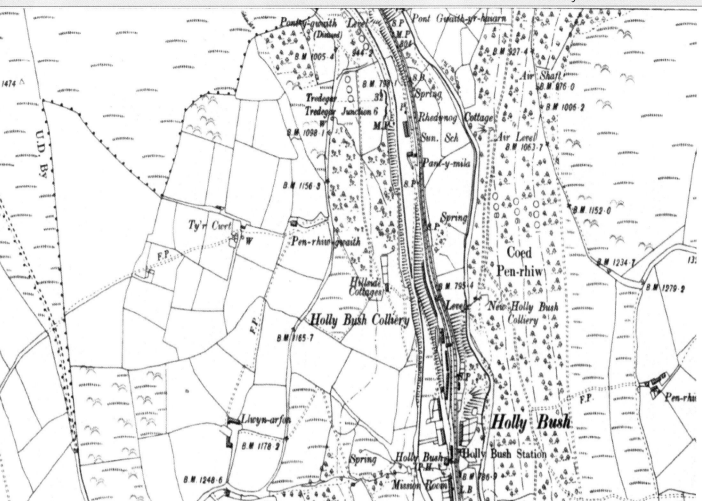

A **map** of Holly Bush at the turn of the 20 C.

A **northbound** 5 coach train c1910 at Holly Bush platform hauled by a Webb Coal Tank. The 5 coach sets were in use until 1st class was withdrawn on the Sirhowy, when the formation was reduced to 4 close-coupled coaches. Lens of Sutton

The staff pose on the up platform in what is probably a 1920s view, showing the station nameboard and the up passenger waiting shelter, the main facilities being on the down platform for the benefit of the larger numbers travelling to Newport.

A 1908 view of the northern section of the station with the signal off for a northbound train, though all the passengers are on the southbound platform suggesting that a train to Newport is due. The signal box is just beyond the up signal and the colliery is behind the signal box.

A not unusual wet day at Holly Bush with the up platform seen from a down train on 13 September 1951. H.C. Casserley

Levels were not a prolific mine and in March 1921 both pits abandoned work on the Brithdir seam.

In July 1929, the Tredegar Iron & Coal Co. reopened the Old Level for a distance of 700 yards to install low-lift centrifugal pumps to protect Markham and Oakdale pits from flooding. By that time, all work on the Brithdir seam to the north of this level had stopped and the company were becoming increasingly worried at the accumulation of water breaking into the Oakdale workings. The pumps were dealing with 25,000 gallons per hour out of a totality of 525,000 gallons per hour pumped out of Oakdale, Llanover and Abernant.

Snow comes most years to the upper Sirhowy Valley and with no passengers in evidence a 57XX makes its call at Holly Bush in less than pleasant conditions in January 1960. Alan Jarvis

A one-coach auto service from Nantybwch to Risca with a 64XX in charge on a dull day in 1960.

One sole passenger leaves the northbound auto train, the engine of which stands alongside the water tower which was a feature of Holly Bush station. A. Pym Collection

A full view of the station with a down train with a 57XX and probably one coach making the service on this day in 1960. SLS

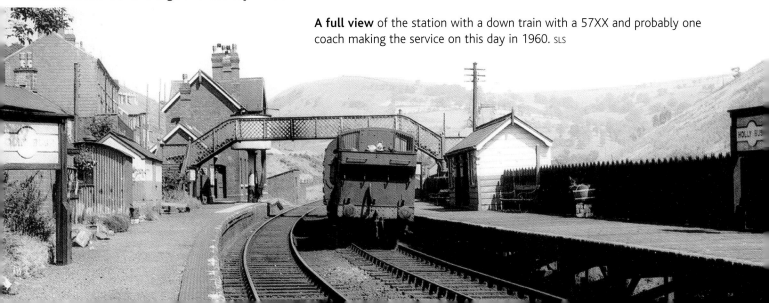

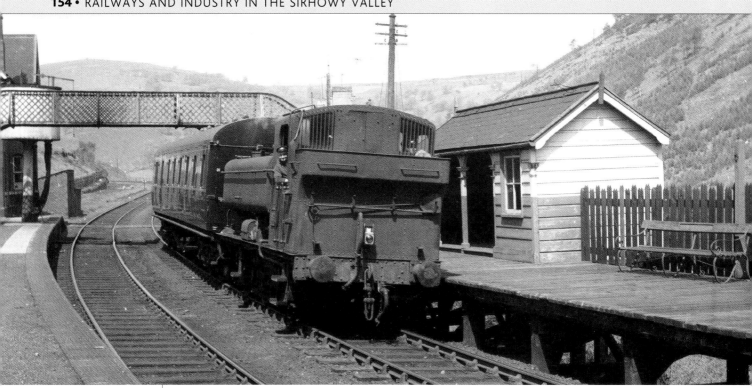

Another conventional train made up of 9644 and one coach make the 1.55pm departure to Risca on 7 May 1960. R.E. Toop

Looking along the down platform a one coach auto service runs into Holly Bush with a service to Risca on 28 May 1960. E.T. Gill/R.K. Blencowe Collection

On the last day of service, Saturday, 11 June 1960, 3634 works the 3.37pm Risca to Nantybwch with one auto coach in conventional mode. E. Wilmshurst

Following the withdrawal of the passenger service in June 1960, the line was singled in 1961. Here are two pictures of 3691 running south EBV over the up line which then became reversible until the branch was closed following the closure of the last two collieries at Wyllie and Nine Mile Point in 1969. The first is taken approaching the station and the second passing through the station in 1964. Gerald Davies

Holly Bush looking south.
M. Vrettos Collection

Holly Bush Colliery was located north of the station on the upside of the line. The down home signal can be seen on the extreme left and houses in the village beyond.

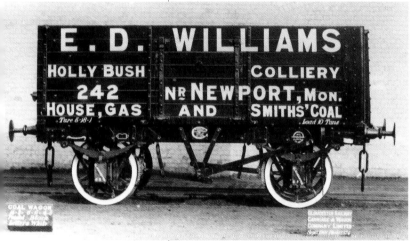

Two new coal wagons in the name of E.D. Williams Holly Bush Colliery, which produced House, Gas and Smith's Coal, the first wagon built, as so many were, by Gloucester Carriage & Wagon.

A wagon label in use from Holly Bush Colliery to Lyonshall via Abergavenny Junction in 1901.
Alastair Warrington Collection

POCHIN PITS

Railway

Located at the 4¾mp, about three miles south of Tredegar, Pochin Pits were sunk in 1876. There was a TIC link line running from Pochin to Bedwellty Pits, a distance of just over a mile, and this ran on to Tredegar Iron Works, via Ty Trist and Whitworth Collieries, which meant that for these flows of coal to the works, they paid no carriage charges to the railway, the trains being worked by their own engines and wagons. The screens, located near the 4¾mp, were fed by three tracks which opened out to the south into three longer sidings down to the outlet at Pochin Pits signal box at 5m. 5ch., opened in September 1891 and converted into a ground frame in May 1961.

There were staggered platforms alongside the screens at 4m.56ch. named Pochin Pits Colliery Halt, used by the public until October 1922 and then by colliers only until the colliery closure.

Industry

Pochin Pits were named after Henry Davis Pochin, a director of TICC, and were sunk in 1876-80 with a mineral take of 3,200 yards north to south and 2,000 yards east to west. The sinking was completed in ten months in 1880 to a depth of 340 yards, the first coal being raised in 1881 from the Yard seam which was in full production at 80in thick in 1883. In 1888, the colliery was working the Big Vein (Four-Feet) and Yard seams. The South or No. 1 Pit had

Map of the Pochin Pits area at the turn of the twentieth century.
National Library of Scotland

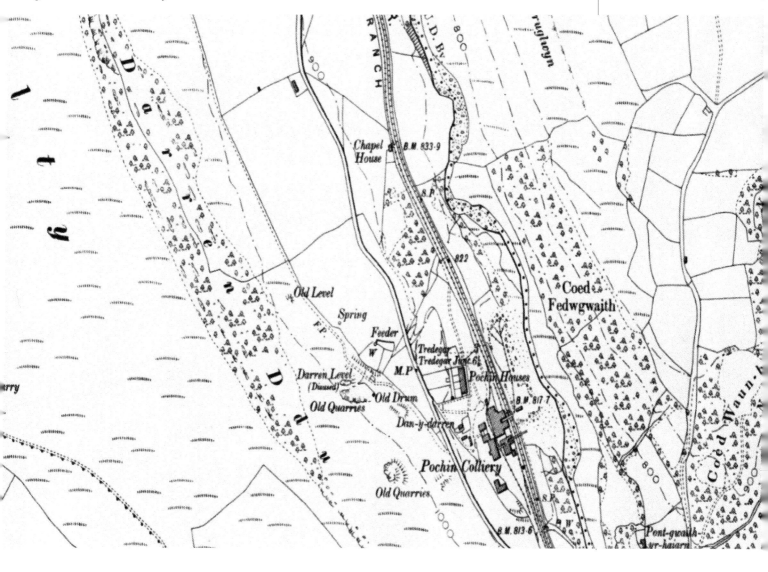

Pochin Pits Halt was closed to the public in 1922 but remained in use for colliers until closure of the colliery. There were staggered platforms, the up platform being to the north of the down, with the colliery sidings running alongside the up line, as can be seen from this very good view taken from the south end of the down platform with the tall up home signal located for best viewing on the end of the down platform.

a winding depth of 437 yards to the Old Coal seam, taking only a minute to wind two trams of coal. The North or No. 2 Pit was the downcast ventilation shaft with the winding depth 316 yards to the Yard seam, also carrying two trams per wind. The wooden head frame was replaced in 1920 with a lattice steel construction. In 1897 a surface washing plant was installed.

In June 1911, it was announced that the Upper Rhas Las seam had been developed at Pochin with a satisfactory output. Both the Upper and Lower Rhas seams underlay the whole of the Pochin

The small Pochin Pits signal box was located on the down side of the line at 5m.5ch. from Nine Mile Point. It was opened in September 1891 and was reduced to a ground frame in May 1961.
Gerald Davies Collection

POCHIN PITS

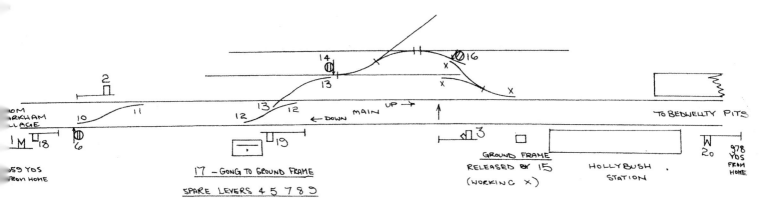

17 – GONG TO GROUND FRAME

SPARE LEVERS 4 5 7 8 9

GROUND FRAME
RELEASED BY 15
(WORKING X)

HOLLYBUSH
STATION

TO BEDWELLTY PITS

FROM
MARKHAM
VILLAGE

59 YDS
FROM HOME

978 YDS
FROM HOME

Pochin Pits Signal
Box diagram.

take area and this bode well for the future. In 1913, the colliery employed 1,693 men and the company advertised as follows:-

'Tredegar, Mclaren Merthyr, Tredare Merthyr, Best Welsh Steam Coal of Great Efficiency. Large Size. Thoroughly Screened and Cleaned. Supplied to British Admiralty and Foreign Governments
Used for Trial Runs of H.M. Battleships *Tredegar* – A Locomotive Coal of Highest Quality
Speciality for Bunkers – Washed Nuts & Peas

Shipping Ports: Cardiff, Barry, Newport and Penarth
Tredegar Iron & Coal Company Ltd., London – 60 Fenchurch Street, Cardiff – The Exchange.'

In 1935, Pochin was the largest of the TIC's collieries, employing 1,409 men underground and 166 on the surface, with an output of 42,000 tons that year. In 1937, the capacity of the washery was increased to 100 tons per hour. In the 1940s, the screening plant consisted of three coal tumblers which tipped the coal onto three 'picking' belts that were fitted with Jigging screens. The full trams gravitated

Miners' trains
were a feature of the Sirhowy Valley with the Pochin train probably the most famous. The train was composed of some twenty coaches in the early part of the century of 4 and 6 wheel variety and would have needed banking to assist the coal tank in charge.
Gerald Davies Collection

Coal Tank 1005 is in charge with colliers still joining the train as others lean out of the windows as the train prepares to leave, the front section of the train being all close-coupled 4 wheelers.
Gerald Davies Collection

A group of colliers, including one woman centre right, pose for the camera at the end of their shift at Pochin. As can be seen, many are boys who did menial tasks both under and above ground.
Gerald Davies Collection

from both the pits to the 'creepers', were weighed at the top of the creepers and passed on to the tumblers. They then gravitated back to the pit top.

The inlet sidings had a capacity of 220 empty wagons with the outlet sidings holding 120 loaded. The underground pumps dealt with some 61,000 gallons of water per day.

In 1943, the number of miners

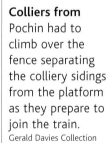

Colliers from Pochin had to climb over the fence separating the colliery sidings from the platform as they prepare to join the train.
Gerald Davies Collection

Another view of the colliers, this time apparently leaving the train just arrived prior to going on duty for their shift.
Gerald Davies Collection

Tredegar Co. Travel Disc Blackwood to Pochin Pits.
Gerald Davies Collection

employed had fallen to 732/162 working five seams, viz. the Meadow Vein, Big Vein, Old Coal, Lower and Upper Rhas

Las. At Nationalisation, Pochin was placed in the Tredegar group of the No. 6 (Monmouthshire) area and at that time employed 711/181 and was working all the seams above except the Big Vein. In 1950, the NCB estimated there were some 2.8mtons of reserves at this colliery. Pochin coal mainly consisted of Type 301A prime coking coal with all the seams in the Lower and Middle Coal Measures readily accessible, general mining conditions being good. Output had fallen badly from the 1930s when it was 420,000 in 1935 to normally less than 200,000 after Nationalisation and by 1960/1 it was down to 92,000. In May 1964, the NUM pressed the NCB to explore the Garw seam at the colliery which was 29in thick, but they disagreed on whether it was workable or not. The NCB announced the closure of the colliery would be on 25 July 1964 with those men still employed there, a total of 411, transferred to the nearby Markham and Oakdale.

3691 arrives with a low loader and brake van in tow to clear the colliery in the mid-1960s. Gerald Davies

3691 forms up the train to clear the colliery output on the day to Rogerstone. Gerald Davies

3691 heads away from Pochin Pits with the loaded wagons from the day's output, bound for Rogerstone Yard in the mid-1960s. Gerald Davies

Four views of Pochin Pits in full production.

BEDWELLTY PITS
Railway

These were just under a mile north of Pochin and the TIC had a link line running between the two collieries on the up side of the running line. The original single running line was doubled in February 1875. Approaching Bedwellty Pits Halt there was an accommodation crossing at the 4mp with Bedwellty Pits signal box on the down side at 3m.74ch. The Halt was at 3m.62ch. and had two facing platforms of equal length. There were crossovers between the two running lines and the TIC line just south of the platforms.

The original signal box was at the end of the down platform and opened in February 1875, closing in December 1877 when it was moved south to 3m.74ch. to be closer to a crossover between the two lines, and to the private TIC line. The running lines were singled from May 1961 with realignment of the other track.

Bedwellty Pits were north of the halt with two batches of coke ovens shown on a plan for 1880. By 1900, the siding layout had been much altered with long inlet sidings stretching back to almost the 3mp and the outlet sidings to the 3¾mp. There were five sidings entering the screens but only four emerging, these feeding into three outlet sidings. There were also five sidings coming off the inlet and running to other parts of the colliery. Following the closure of No. 1 Pit in 1941, the connections into the Bedwellty Pits complex were taken out in 1945, access to the running line having been controlled by a ground frame since the closure of Upper Bedwellty Sidings signal box at 3m.8ch. in 1905.

Industry

Bedwellty Pits were opened by the TICC in the mid-1800s. The mine consisted of Nos. 1 and 2 Pits and Bedwellty Nos. 1 and 2 Levels. The shafts were one upcast and the other downcast ventilation. They were only some 12 yards apart and descended to the Big Vein seam about 230 yards deep. No. 2 Pit accessed the Four-feet seam at about 210 yards. The Polka or Upper Black Vein seam was 47in thick but was divided from the 33in thick Lower Black Vein or Rhas Las by 22ft of rock. The Big Vein group of seams consisted of excellent sections but interspersed

A map of the Bedwellty Pits area at the turn of the twentieth century.
National Library of Scotland

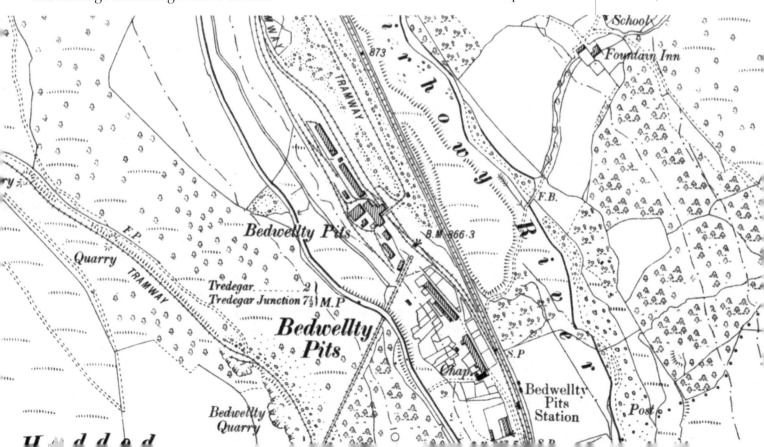

The 1.10pm Newport to Nantybwch departs effortlessly from Bedwellty Pits Halt with Coal Tank 58933 in charge of its three coach train.
P.B. Whitehouse/M. Whitehouse Collection

with clod e.g. Four-Feet 65in, Clod 36in, Yard seam 39in, clod 36in, Three-quarter seam 72in. The Old Coal seam was 27in thick, then 8in clod, then coal 24in, while the Elled consisted of 72in of coal. The Ty Tryst Colliery had two similar shafts connected to the Bedwellty shafts. In November 1869 coal was being raised in Nos. 1 and 2 Bedwellty Pits at an average of 540 tons a day.

There were 26 horses employed at the coalface, though the trams were brought out by a steam-driven haulage engine. The Brithdir seam was worked by a Level 800 yards above the pit and the coal came down an incline to the railway sidings below, about 150 tons a day being produced, equal to about 20 wagons.

In 1878, the Pits were working the Big Vein, Yard, and Nos. 1 and 2 seams. The No. 1 Level worked the Brithdir as above, and the No. 2 Level the Old Man's Coal. The difference between the two operations is illustrated by the fact that in 1896 the Pits employed 560 men underground and 102 on the surface whereas the Levels employed twenty and eight.

In July 1898, the Pits were linked to the newly opened McLaren Colliery in the Upper Rhymney Valley. The Brithdir (or Pontygwaith) seam was abandoned in October 1900, the Pits then working the Big and Yard seams. Bedwellty coals were generally classed as type 301A Prime Coking Coals for use as foundry and blast furnace coke.

The new century saw the workforce strengthened considerably, the 1908 figures being 1,060/117, with a total of 1,251 in 1913/5, 1,066 in 1916, 918/157 in 1918 and 1,053 in 1919. By the depression years of the early 1930s, there had been a dramatic fall in the number employed and in production. In 1932 there were only 540 employed in total, but by 1934 output was only 10,000 tons with 46/10 men employed, and though this rose to 80/18 in 1938, production was soon to cease, No. 2 Pit closing in 1939 and No. 1 in 1941.

The same train waiting at Bedwellty Pits up platform and a rear view departing. Note the veteran leading coach 22242, provided for miners' use if travelling other than on the special miners' trains.
P.B. Whitehouse/M. Whitehouse Collection

A well soaked up platform on 13 September 1951.
H.C. Casserley

There were two shelters for passengers joining but generally the platforms offered little protection from the often wet, windy and snowy weather, as these views show. Gerald Davies

Now in the snow... A northbound auto service calls with no sign of passengers in January 1960. Alan Jarvis

And just to prove that the sun does shine...The up platform again in full sunshine and a view up the track towards Tredegar. Malcolm James

In the later 1950s, an Ebbw 57XX calls at the station with a service for either Risca or Newport, consisting of two vans and a passenger coach. The vans would have been off the early morning service from Newport. SLS

Just a single coach forms this lunchtime service from Nantybwch to Risca at 1.45pm with power provided by 9644 on 7 May 1960. R.E. Toop

BEDWELLTY PITS

Bedwellty Pits Signal Box Diagram.

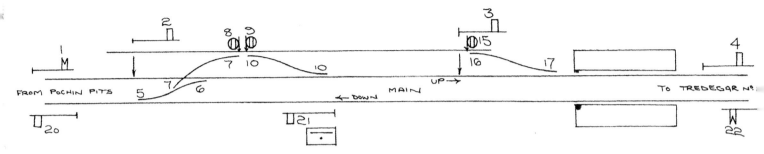

Bedwellty Pits colliery.

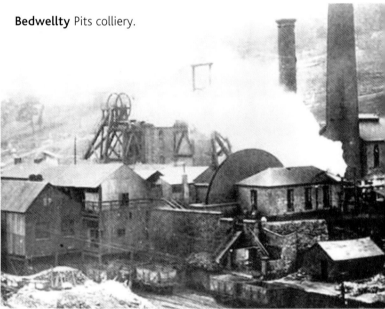

Bedwellty Pits signal box after closure. The box lay north of the station at 3m.74ch. from Nantybwch. Gerald Davies

The Tredegar Iron & Coal Co. had their own line between Pochin Pits and Tredegar Ironworks, seen in the centre with the main line on the left, singled in May 1961.

TY TRIST
Railway

The line from south of Tredegar was doubled as far as Bedwellty Pits in February 1875. The Ty Trist colliery complex was all on the up side with nothing on the downside other than the Tredegar Co.'s line on the other side of the Sirhowy River, well removed from the LNW railway, until the line crossed the river north of the level crossing at the north end of the station and connected into a siding.

Two sidings owned by the Alexandra Dock Co. were installed alongside the down line by 1909 between the 2¾ and 3mp, for holding formed trains. These were constructed when Newport Docks were being reconstructed and were probably in connection with the filling in of the original Town Dock. The Alexandra Dock Co. had identified a source of cheap infill material from the slag tips at Tredegar. The former Quarry Sidings behind the Ty Trist signal box had been re-laid and used for the loading of the slag, for which a crusher was installed. To provide space for the forming up of

trains to Newport, the two additional loop sidings were constructed on the down side, leading out of the former shunting spur. The cost of the works, put at £500, was covered by the Alexandra Dock Co. and was approved by Colonel Yorke on behalf of the Board of Trade in September 1909. Though the sidings were owned by the ADCo., none of their engines were ever concerned with their operation, which was conducted in full by the LNWR which conveyed the trains to Nine Mile Point where it was taken over by the GWR. The slag traffic lasted for a few years while the disused dock was being filled and the installation was taken out of use probably around 1920. The two sidings next to the main line were afterwards put to good use by the LNWR and then LMS and used to hold traffic to and from Ty Trist Colliery.

The original Quarry Siding at the 2¾mp, controlled by Ty Trist signal box, was closed and removed by 1930. It was on the down side of the line opposite the

Approaching Ty Trist from Bedwellty Pits, the 3.27pm Risca to Nantyubwch two coach train approaches Tredegar and Ty Trist with 7781 on 14 August 1957. S. Rickard/J&J Collection

Ty-Trist Siding
Signal Box located at the southern exit from Ty Trist colliery.

the withdrawal of the passenger service. There were three sidings passing under the screens at Ty Trist, north of which were two sets of Coke Ovens (on a plan for 1900) one of which was shared with coal from Whitworth Colliery.

Following the closure of first Whitworth and then Ty Trist collieries, all the trackwork on the up side was recovered leaving only that serving the engine shed on the up side south of the station, this lasting until the closure of the engine shed in June 1960. In August 1961, the running lines south of Tredegar were singled, following the withdrawal of the passenger service officially on the 13th but actually on 11 June.

Industry
Ty Trist

Nos. 1 and 2 Pits were sunk in 1834 to the Elled (Two-Feet-Nine) seam, with the Upper Ty Trist sunk in 1841 and the No. 3 Pit in 1868. The No. 1 was 217 yards deep and was further deepened to the Old Coal (Five-Feet/Gellideg) seam in 1868. No. 2 Pit was 221 yards deep and later deepened to the Rhas Las seam. There was also a batch of 64 coke ovens. The original wooden headgear was replaced by a steel construction in 1933. The No. 3 Pit was the upcast ventilation shaft, also 221 yards deep, originally sunk to the Yard seam and then deepened to the Old Coal seam.

Records for this colliery show that around 1850 miners there earned between 18-21/- a week. Children under seven were still employed underground to get where grown men could not, and earned 1/6d. to 2/- per week. Dragger girls could earn 3/6d. to 6/6d a week while women earned 12/- to 14/6d. Women were still employed at Ty Trist as late as 1878.

The local newspaper in July 1876 gave an interesting insight into the process of screening and washing of coal as follows:-
'The coal won is very clean and all is sent up (the shaft). When the coal is tipped over the screen, the large goes at once into the trucks, and the small

connections into the sidings serving Ty Trist and Whitworth Collieries.

Ty Trist signal box controlling entrance to the colliery was just over a quarter mile north of the northern entrance into Bedwellty Pits, with the TICC private line alongside the up running line, running right through to the TICC Works north of Tredegar station. This connection to/from the running lines accessed Ty Trist and the nearby Whitworth Colliery, running through into sidings behind the Tredegar Engine Shed. Lower Ty Trist Siding signal box on the down side of the running lines, opened in 1876 and closed probably in 1883 when a new box was provided, the running lines having been doubled in March 1875. Another new box was opened on the same site at 2m.62ch. (from Nantybwch) in February 1936, closing in July 1960 after

Two excellent views of Ty Trist Colliery, the first showing the main running lines in the foreground and with Tredegar and TICC branded wagons.

falls though to the centre of a bunker. At the bottom of this bunker are valves which are opened by trams running underneath. When the tram is full, it empties itself into another bunker placed over washing troughs, and when the slack (i.e. small coal) falls into these it is carried by the water a distance of 75 yards. During this transit, the rubbish sinks to the bottom of the trough, and girls are employed to manipulate the mixture so as to let the coal float off. The latter eventually finds its way into another large bunker and thence into false bottomed trams to the (coke) ovens. About 150tons per day are washed in this manner.'

In 1892, a modern coal washing plant was constructed at surface level, with a capacity of 75tons per hour.

The TICC advertised coal from Ty Trist exactly as was listed under Pochin. Ty Trist generally produced type 301A

Prime Coking Coals for use in foundries and blast furnaces, and as such most of its produce was used by the Tredegar Iron Works and then Whiteheads.

In 1935, Ty Trist employed 821 men working underground and 99 on the surface and produced 260,000 tons of coal. The coke ovens which had by now become dilapidated were closed down in March 1945.

At Nationalisation, Ty Trist was placed (naturally) in the Tredegar group of the No. 6 Monmouthshire area. But by then the workforce was down to 404 men underground and 144 on the surface with production down to 120,000 tons. The Meadow Vein and Old Coal seams were the only seams being worked. By 1950, all coal seams at Ty Trist except the Meadow Vein had been exhausted, and reserves in this seam were put at 1.7m tons. From 1953 onwards the workforce was only in the 300s. with production a maximum of 72,000 but as low as 47,000 in 1958.

Working conditions were also poor with a weak structure overhead and 18-36in of clod often fell when the 24-30in seam was cut into. Under such difficult conditions, the colliery closed on 31 January 1959.

The *Coal News* of September 1950 reported on Alice James, aged 74, the last surviving woman who had worked on the surface of a colliery in the South Wales coalfield, and the first woman member of the South Wales Miners Federation. She had worked on the screens at Ty Trist Colliery.

WHITWORTH COLLIERY
Railway

The sidings feeding Whitworth Colliery were an extension of those into Ty Trist, these running on behind the Engine Shed and Station to the Tredegar Iron Co. north of the station and level crossing. Whitworth Colliery had two sidings running under the screens, another two running through between Ty Trist and Tredegar Works. South of the screens, a batch of Coke Ovens is shown on a plan for 1900, probably shared with Ty Trist, who also had a batch of their own. There were also several other sidings in the colliery yard.

Alongside the up running line was Tredegar South End Colliers' Halt at 2m.27ch. built for miners at Ty Trist and Whitworth Collieries and those travelling to work at other collieries from Tredegar. Tredegar No. 2 signal box was located on this platform to control crossovers between the up and down running lines and the entrance into the engine shed and station yard. This box was the previous Tredegar Yard South End signal box, opened in February 1875 and closed in January 1897. The new box was located at 2m.26ch. and was opened in January 1897.

The Tredegar Co. also had a line running well east of the River Sirhowy which originally served Tredegar Gas Works, this connection being removed by 1920. This line ran to/from their Works north of the level crossing, bridging the river to do so.

Industry

Whitworth Colliery was sunk in 1876 by TICC and was only 100 yards north of Ty Trist. In 1888 it was working the Old Coal and Bydelog seams while in the same year, Whitworth Drift Mine was working the Elled, Big Vein and Yard seams. In 1896, the Pits employed 442 men underground and 56 on the surface and were now working the Little Yard seam also, while the Drift had 224/29. Comparable figures for 1900 show the Pits with 391/80 and the Drift 107/41. Production was Type 301A Prime Coking Coal.

A plan of Whitworth Colliery.

Three views of Whitworth Colliery, located to the north alongside Ty Trist and also served by the through TICC line from Pochin Pits to Tredegar Ironworks.

The Company prospectus for June 1912 stated that Whitworth was losing money due to the high cost of working the coal. However, the Elled seam had recently been brought into use and it was hoped that the development of that seam would improve the financial results and working conditions. The Tredegar Co. advertised Whitworth coal exactly as Bedwellty and Ty Trist. Manpower dropped to 251 in 1916 and 217 in 1919 and in July 1921, the press reported that due to the post-war trade recession, the Tredegar Company had been forced to stop production at Whitworth permanently. Whitworth Colliery was then absorbed into Ty Trist until the latter closed in 1959.

TREDEGAR MOTIVE POWER DEPOT
(See Chapter 3)
TREDEGAR STATION

There was only ever a single platform at Tredegar station, double track starting southwards from 1875 at Tredegar South (No. 2 signal box). There were however three running roads through the station, the Platform Road, Middle Road and Goods Loop, plus another loop, enabling trains to pass, though empty passenger stock could be held on each road except the platform road, as can be seen in the supporting photographs. There was a level crossing at the north end controlled by the original Tredegar Signal Box opened in February 1886. This closed in December 1902, when a new box was provided which became No. 1 signal box when No. 2 opened in 1897 at the south end of the station complex.

Tredegar Station and Yard occupied a confined area which was required for stabling of stock and this may account for the fact that Goods Traffic (Sundries and Full Loads) for Tredegar were later handled at Sirhowy where there was abundant space for a Full Loads Yard with roads between, north of the station and for a large goods shed at the south end of the station complex. Whether there was originally any facility at Tredegar itself is a matter of conjecture as a drawing for 1880 shows two buildings with no description which might have been used as Goods Sheds, one on the east side of the yard with a line passing through the shed, and one on the west side of the complex behind the platform. Neither was shown on a plan of the same area for 1900.

In order to provide separate facilities for miners, including at the nearby Ty Trist and Whitworth collieries, a separate platform (with no facilities) was provided at the south end of the complex named Tredegar South End Collieries Halt at 2m.27ch. which was used by any colliers' trains conveying miners for Tredegar. Southbound trains using the platform then used a crossover at the south end to access the down running line, while northbound trains ran through Tredegar

A view looking south along the Miners' Platform with the signal box and signal beyond. The signal on the left marks the start of the two track section to the south.
Allan Pym Collection

A view of the miners' platform from the south end of Tredegar passenger platform. Ty Trist colliery can be seen at the south end of the miners' platform and there is a good view of the connections into the engine shed and the south end of Tredegar Station Yard.

Station platform, or if this was occupied, crossed onto the Middle Road and back onto the single line north of the LC., at No. 1 signal box.

Though Ty Trist and Whitworth collieries closed in 1959, Pochin Pits carried on until 1964, so miners' trains were still required on a lesser basis between Nantybwch, Tredegar, Pochin, Wyllie and Nine Mile Point but with the withdrawal of the public passenger service in June 1960, the miners' trains were also withdrawn. This removed most of the reason for the existence of Tredegar shed and this was closed at the same time, with Ebbw Junction taking over the provision of power for the remaining requirement, with a train per day from Rogerstone Yard. As the only traffic between Nantybwch and Sirhowy was the passenger service, this section of line closed as from 11 June 1960.

The line was singled throughout southwards from Tredegar No. 1 signal box, the previous down line being

retained in use. During 1961, all track in the engine shed was removed, as was that through the platform, the only running tracks left being the Middle Road and the Goods Loop, the sidings in the station yard also being taken out of use. There was still house coal passing to the NCB Landsale and Concessionary depot at Sirhowy but the NCB undertook to convey this by road and from 4 November 1963, there was no further

A view of the Miners' Platform probably taken from the coal stage in the engine shed in the 1930s. An 0-8-4T is running south light on the left and a Coal Tank with two coaches is running along the miners' platform to access the passenger station.

58899 runs through the South End Miners' Platform with a departing service for Newport on 24 March 1951.
J.J. Smith/Bluebell Railway Archive

rail movement between Tredegar and Sirhowy. Tredegar station remained open for freight traffic throughout the decade but closed on 30 April 1969 when no further services ran north of Pontllanffraith (Tredegar Junction Lower), leaving only the Oakdale coal trains diverted from Halls Road, running between there and Newport. Both Wyllie and Nine Mile Point had also closed by the end of the decade and with the transfer of the Oakdale services back to the southern end of Halls Road in May 1970, the remainder of the Sirhowy line from Tredegar Junction Lower to Risca closed on 4 May 1970.

Tredegar No. 2 signal box located at the south end of the miners' platform.

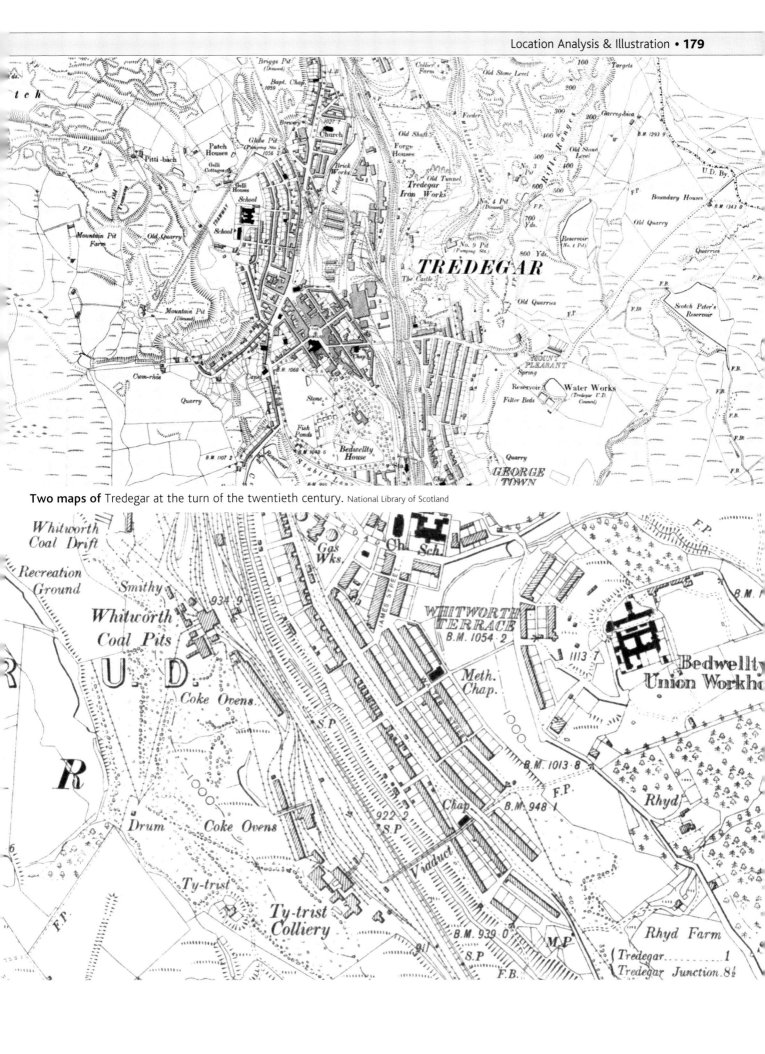

Two maps of Tredegar at the turn of the twentieth century. National Library of Scotland

A high level view over the south end of the Tredegar railway complex, some time between 1910-14, showing wagons in Whitworth Colliery at the bottom of the picture, the engine shed centre, with just a few Coal Tanks visible, indicating a weekday view, the yard behind, and the Georgetown residential area of the town.
Lens of Sutton

A view of the level crossing at the north end of the station and yard in the early years of the new century showing the substantial footbridge under which are a group with a horse and trap.
Gerald Davies Collection

Another view of the north end of the station with the No. 1 signal box and signalman, and gates closed to the road, with a group of station staff all eager to be photographed in about 1905.
Gerald Davies Collection

Two Coal Tanks with footplate and shunting staff pose outside the No. 1 box at the north end of the station about 1905.
Gerald Davies Collection

A posed picture of station and footplate staff in 1909 with Coal Tank 429 and a 5 coach train at the platform. Olivia Ashton/Gerald Davies Collection

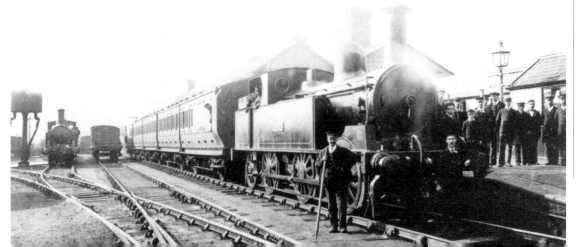

A 1905 posed picture of a well-presented Coal Tank at the head of a five coach set at Tredegar platform, with another Coal Tank in the yard.
Gerald Davies Collection

The area later to become the station yard was previously covered in greenery, as seen in this view of the south end of the station in the early twentieth century. A Coal Tank is approaching the station EBV, with empty coaches at the South platform and also in the yard.

A 1920s view of the south end of the main station platform with part of the yard in which empty 4 wheel passenger stock and two Coal Tanks can be identified with the water tower and empty coal wagons on the far left.

Tredegar Station, from Railway Bridge. 1313.

Another view of the yard and platform from the 1920s, with an interesting 3 route signal in the yard, with LMS vans, other empty coaching stock and the water tower. The tall chimneys of Ty Trist and Whitworth collieries can be seen across the centre of the photograph with the engine shed and coaling plant.

Alastair Warrington Collection

A view from the centre of the station platform looking north in 1939 with two coaches to form a northbound train at the platform and a Coal Tank in the yard siding with coach 27984, which may be in the process of being added to the train at the platform, though the engine is bunker-first when all northbound workings were engine-first.

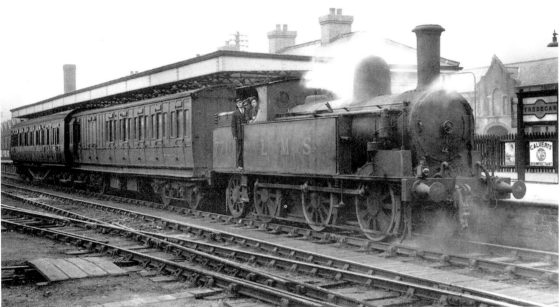

Coal Tank 7710 with the 7.22am from Newport two coach train on 29 March 1948. W.A. Camwell/SLS

The early morning sun lights the scene well as 7782 stands at the head of the 7.22am from Newport on 26 April 1948. W.A. Camwell/SLS

58899 pulls out of the yard either with ECS for Nantybwch or to set back into the platform on the wet 13 September 1951. H.C. Casserley

With snow on the ground on 29 December 1956, 40098 marshals empty stock in the sidings north of the station. John Hodge

On a rainy day, 3747 with a single auto coach train from Risca on 29 December 1956. John Hodge

A view north from the north end of the single platform on 13 July 1958. There are still four sidings on the up side but the cattle pens have gone from just north of the signal box. The long siding alongside the running line terminates north of the bracket signal, all of which refers to the running line.
H.C. Casserley

The late 1950s when news of the impending closure of the passenger service brought more interest in photography. Little activity is evident in this view of the station looking north along the single platform with an auto coach and a coach of a miners' train visible in the yard sidings on 14 July 1959.
R.F. Roberts/SLS Collection

The 11am Nantybwch to Risca is propelled into Tredegar by 6412 in auto mode on 28 July 1959. R.O. Tuck/RAS

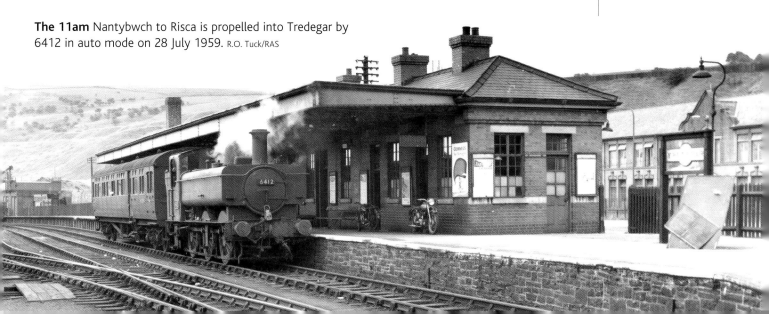

A view of the station and yard from the shed coaling stage in 1959 with a 57XX on shed and an empty five coach miners' train in the yard including two of the former BPGV flat roof coaches displaced from that line when the passenger service was withdrawn. These coaches continued to work from several South-East Wales depots as they were still in good condition, though aesthetically it might have been better if they had been kept in sets rather than mixed with other stock. SLS

Tredegar station yard on 8 August 1959 looking towards the single platform from the south of the yard. The coaches from a miners' train on the left are being cleaned and 5727 is approaching with a van from the north end of the yard. An auto coach and two non corridor coaches plus two brake vans are also visible. S. Rickard/J&J Collection

A few inches of snow were on the ground in January 1960 to set off this view of the north end of the station complex, with the LNW signal at danger, the level crossing gates closed and No. 1 signal box standing stoically beyond. Two sets of two-way signals can be seen beyond, the bracket down home signal left of centre being an interesting combination of up and down arms. Alan Jarvis

Tokens in Tredegar No. 1 box for the section on to Sirhowy as in January 1960. Alan Jarvis

Veteran stock was used on the main service to Newport, especially as the coach for miners to travel in. Here is low-roofed M6521 in the yard in 1950.

Until the end of the LMS era, Tredegar was home to a large selection of veteran LNW and L&Y coaches and vans. For the miners' trains, use was made of ageing passenger stock which had been displaced by new vehicles and this built up into a wonderful collection. One of the early prizes was the Pochin Pits train of up to twenty 6 wheelers which operated in the 1920s. This has been shown in the section dealing with Pochin Pits but here is the train standing in the yard at Tredegar in about 1920.

Former Lancashire & Yorkshire open third M27990 in the yard with other vintage stock in 1950.

A former LNWR 6 wheeled van 284680 retained as part of the Tredegar Breakdown Train until the 1960s. Gerald Davies

A view from the footbridge at the north end of the station with 6412 standing below at the platform with a Railmotor arrival from Risca on 4 April 1960. There is only one BSK, some vans and brake vans in the station sidings which means that all the miners' trains are out. E.T. Gill/R.K. Blencowe Collection

Even when stock provision passed to the Western Region, interesting examples turned up in the form of two former Burry Port & Gwendraeth Valley coaches displaced when the passenger service on that line closed. Here W1327W stands in the yard, having been detached from its normal set on 13 July 1958. The BSKs were useful vehicles and were often used on the Sunday Barry Island excursions. H.C. Casserley

Following the decision to introduce a new service from Risca to Nanytbwch with Railmotors, Ebbw Junction auto fitted 64XXs were provided with either one or two auto coaches, as here with 6412 on a one coach train at Tredegar platform in 1958. Lens of Sutton

Auto coach W173 with a 77XX forming a train to Risca.
M.Vrettos Collection

Many services were covered by one coach trains in conventional mode with non-auto engines which meant that they had to run round at the end of each journey. Here 3700 stands at the platform with the 1.40pm service to Risca and then departs on 14 July 1959.
Both R.F. Roberts/SLS Collection

The 10.25am to Nantybwch stands at the platform with 8766 while 9662 heads a miners' train in the yard on 14 July 1959. R.F. Roberts/SLS Collection

The memory that will last forever of Tredegar is surely of a Coal Tank standing at the single platform with its two coach train from Newport with a veteran coach for miners' use and a quality LMS coach. Here 7829 has arrived with the 7.22am from Newport in the early 1950s.

The 1.40pm to Risca one coach train is ready to depart on 7 May 1960 in the bright sunshine. R.E. Toop

7787 waits to depart southwards with empty stock for a miners' train, with a former BPGV coach in the formation, as 9644 waits to leave with the 1.40pm service to Newport on 7 May 1960. R.E. Toop

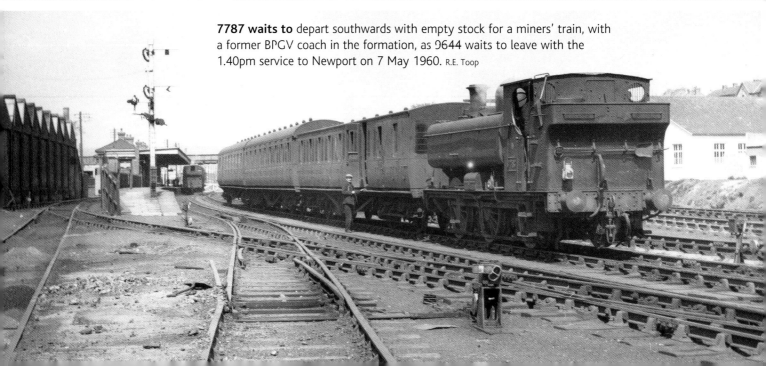

9644 runs round its train at the north end of the station prior to working the 1.40pm to Risca on 7 May 1960. R.E. Toop

5727 brings a short down goods into the station yard across the level crossing on 8 August 1959.
S. Rickard/J&J Collection

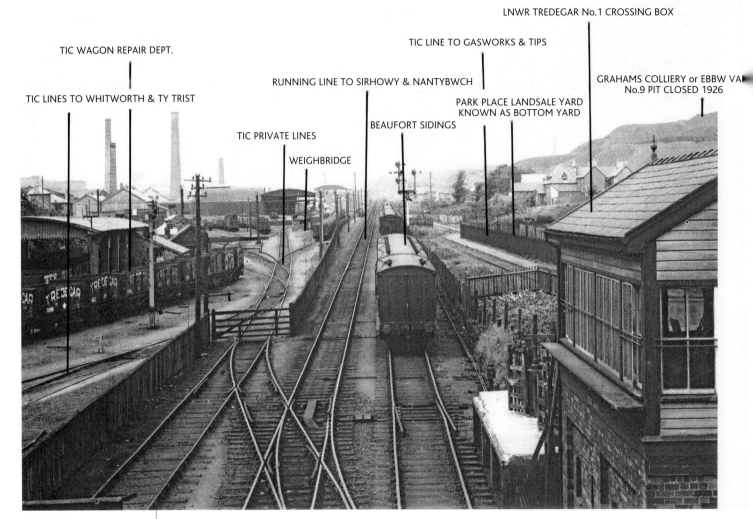

TIC WAGON REPAIR DEPT.

TIC LINES TO WHITWORTH & TY TRIST

TIC PRIVATE LINES

WEIGHBRIDGE

RUNNING LINE TO SIRHOWY & NANTYBWCH

BEAUFORT SIDINGS

TIC LINE TO GASWORKS & TIPS

PARK PLACE LANDSALE YARD
KNOWN AS BOTTOM YARD

LNWR TREDEGAR No.1 CROSSING BOX

GRAHAMS COLLIERY or EBBW VA
No.9 PIT CLOSED 1926

A view up the line
from the bridge
with details of all
the lines involved.
Gerald Davies Colln

An LNWR Gas Tank
at Tredegar.
Alastair Warrington
Collection

The Trevil
Tramroad Engine
Shed on 14 June
1949.
Alastair Warrington
Collection

A group of station
managers and
workers possibly in
1905. The Station
Manager and
Goods Manager are
probably those in
the centre.
Gerald Davies Collection

Another staff
group from the
1920s with the
Station Master
middle second row
and one of the 5
coach trainsets in
the background.
Gerald Davies Collection

Two groups
of station staff
probably from the
1920s, possibly
passenger and
goods.
Gerald Davies Collection

TREDEGAR IRONWORKS
Location

North of the level crossing and No. 1 signal box on the up side of the single running line was Tredegar Iron Works, the original owners of which (with the Sirhowy Ironworks) were the developers of the Sirhowy Tramroad from which the railway was developed. A copy of the 1920 railway plan of the works is attached from which it will be seen that approaching the works from the LC, there

A **view of** the works when in full production with its many chimney stacks, of which at least ten are in this picture.

A **view from** the footbridge at the north of the station probably in the 1920s, showing the works on the left, which had passed to Whiteheads in 1903. Ten wagons are in the works inwards siding which may have come from either Ty Trist or Whitworth Colliery located to the south. R.K. Blencowe Collection

Whiteheads Rolling Mills. The works were at this site from 1903 to 1920 when they moved to Newport.

A **view of** part of the Whiteheads works with a variety of empty open wagons awaiting loading.

The General Offices of the Tredegar Iron & Coal Co. with a section of Whitworth Colliery and the through lines to the Works.

Some of the products of the Tredegar Iron & Coal Co.

A south end section of the plant as at May 1969.
Alastair Warrington

A **line-up** of Tredegar Iron & Coal Co. engines and staff in their yard in the early years of the century. Six engines are included in the scene.

were a dozen or so reception sidings for inwards and outwards traffic, which was worked to/from the respective sections of the works by Tredegar company engines. The works predate the building of the Sirhowy Tramroad, but obviously developed in the course of time especially when the railway provided vastly improved transport facilities.

History

The works were founded in 1799 by the owners of the nearby Sirhowy Ironworks, Samuel Homfray, Richard Fothergill and Matthew Monkhouse, keen to increase iron making capacity in the area and make use of available resources. Land was leased from Lord Tredegar, Sir Charles Morgan, at an annual rent of £300 for the first five years and then £500 for the rest of a 99-year lease. The developers invested £40,000 in the works and three furnaces were built in 1800-1 but were not put in blast until 1802, each producing 30-50 tons of pig iron per week. The new works had a radical effect on the area; in 1801 the parish of Bedwellty had a population of 619; within ten years, it was 4,590.

Puddling and rolling mills were in operation by 1807, when No. 4 furnace went on blast increasing output to 4,000 tons per annum. By 1817, a No.5 furnace had been commissioned raising output

An early engine built for use at the Tredegar Works, No. 194, built in 1873 to a 2ft 11½in gauge with 10x18in cylinders.

to 10,000 tons per annum, all from locally available resources of iron ore, coal and limestone, with movement of raw materials into the works (including limestone from Trefil) by tramroad which also conveyed the iron produced either direct to Newport or to the canal at Crumlin, probably via Beaufort.

Richard Fothergill, who had invented a procedure for trams to pass each other en route, which foresaw the railway points system, retired in 1818, causing big problems for the Sirhowy Works. His son Rowland Fothergill took charge and in 1829 bought a steam locomotive for the works, designed by George Stephenson and named *Britannia*. There were many

0-4-0 *Graham* at the works in the 1920s. This was doubtless named after the owner of Graham Navigation Colliery east of the works.

0-6-0 *Hercules* still at work on the site of the old works in 1952. The NCB line to Sirhowy is in the background. SLS

Sir John with wagons of recovered coal from Ty Trist Colliery, some of which will go to Sirhowy Coal Yard, at the weighbridge at Tredegar Iron Works. Gerald Davies

teething problems at its introduction, the heavy and rigid engine breaking many of the iron tram plates, which needed to be replaced by wooden ones, derailing and striking trees as it passed by. However, it was soon running along the tramroad to Newport and back twice a week hauling a load of 80 tons at 6mph. By 1830, the five furnaces at the works were producing some 18,500 tons of iron per annum.

The works were enjoying an excellent reputation for the quality of their product and in 1836 a group of American industrialists decided to make their own rails for the rapidly expanding American rail network and hired staff from the works to go to Richmond, Virginia, and set up a new works there, also called Tredegar.

In April 1855 a notice appeared in the *Daily News* that Tredegar Works had manufactured a Monster Rail 86ft 2in long and weighing 1,902lb, one of the longest, heaviest and most perfect double-headed rails ever made. This had been produced with huge support from the workers who had volunteered to make it without pay. The rail was sent off by rail to Newport en route to exhibition at the Palais de l'Industrie, Paris. In September 1860, another event of great magnitude for the works occurred with the commissioning of a huge blowing engine to increase the volume of air blowing through the blast furnaces. The steam cylinder was 57in diameter, with a 13ft stroke; the blowing cylinder 144in with a 12ft stroke. The beam connecting these cylinders was more than 50ft in length and 6ft wide at its centre point, the weight of each side of the beam being more than 25 tons. The whole machine weighed more than 70 tons and was cast by a Newport company. The machine was remarkable for its quietness of operation and received great praise from the owners for the all-round improvement it made to the operation of the plant.

In 1868, the involvement of the Homfray family in the Tredegar works

The Tredegar Iron & Coal Co. owned a large fleet of wagons of various types, mostly mineral carrying, such as this 12 ton coal wagon 3410, built in March 1912 by the Gloucester Railway Carriage & Wagon Co. Ltd. in slate colour with white lettering. It had a tare weight of 6 tons 15cwt 1qr.
Alastair Warrington Colln.

There were many agents attached to the Tredegar Co.'s collieries as shown on this 10 ton Badman Bros. wagon No. 80, advertising the company's Gas, Steam, Anthracite and House Coals. The wagon was built in March 1914 by the Gloucester Railway Carriage & Wagon Co. Ltd. and was painted red with white lettering. It had a tare weight of 6 tons 9cwt 2qr.
Alastair Warrington Colln.

ended when they sold their shares to the Fothergill and Forman families, their co-partners. The coal now being produced by the pits owned by the company was now a hugely important part of the business and was in great demand, so much so that in 1873 the then owners of the works and collieries formed the Tredegar Iron & Coal Co. and abandoned iron making on a large scale, retaining the mills for manufacture of material for their works and colliery use only. In 1882, the works rolled its first steel rails but in the face of the huge competition from the giant Ebbw Vale Steelworks, the Tredegar Works ceased all steel production in 1901.

Whiteheads

In 1903, the redundant works was purchased at scrap value by L.D. Whitehead and the new works began by re-rolling axles into iron bars. In 1906, the works imported and set up at Tredegar one of the few existing continuous rolling mills from the USA. In the face of much scepticism in the field of activity, the new plant began operations in 1907 but progress was slow with many teething

The NCB set up a Shed and Central Workshops at Tredegar Iron Works where *Sir John Wyndham Beynon* of 1920 is seen alongside *Ulysses*, also of 1920, in July 1952. Alastair Warrington

problems. A new company, Whiteheads Iron & Steel Co., was formed to take over the business of the re-rolling of steel, the previous company having run out of cash to finalise the development. By 1910,

the new mill was operating successfully and in 1914 the company announced that they intended moving their operations to Newport where they had already purchased a tract of land on the western edge of the town. The war years precluded progress but in 1920 the new mill was installed at Courtybella, near the site of the original passenger station, fronting Mendalgief Road, and operations at Tredegar were terminated.

Coal Mining

There were a multitude of small coal mines developed from a very early era in the Tredegar and Sirhowy areas to feed the two ironworks. The only collieries to develop into sizeable proportions were those at Tredegar – Ty Trist and Whitworth – and further down the Valley at Pochin and Bedwellty. The small developments were almost all away from the railway, though many were served by tramroads which fed into the Tredegar Ironworks Private Line and were all

Another view of the depot in July 1952 with the same two engines and *Ulysses* now on the left. Alastair Warrington

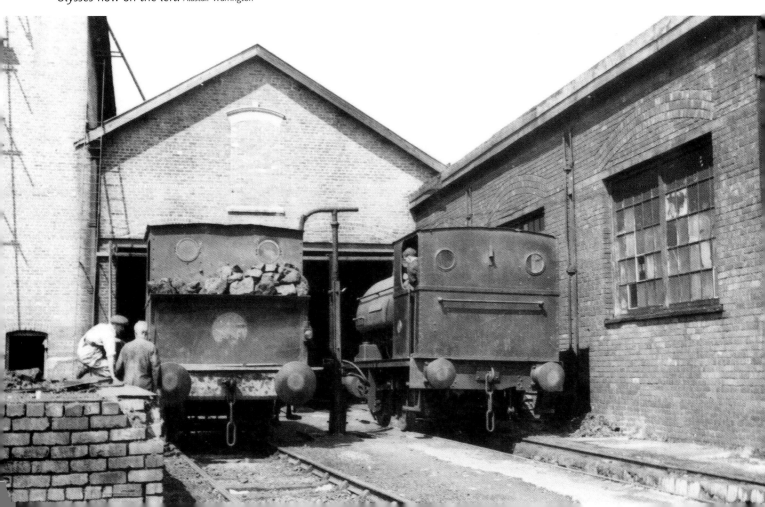

Condemned GW
850 Class 0-6-0s were always popular with the collieries due to their short wheelbase, and here 1966, withdrawn from Whitland shed in 1939, is seen at the Central Workshops in August 1955.
Alastair Warrington

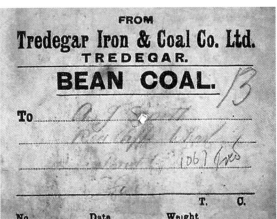

A Tredegar Iron & Coal Co. Ltd. Wagon Label for bean coal consigned to the Radcliffe Wharf, Bristol.

owned by the Tredegar Iron Co. and later Tredegar Iron & Coal Co. Most started as water balance pits and were worked on the 'contractor' system (see below under TICC).

The earliest levels worked harked back to the early years of the Sirhowy Tramroad and were connected to the Tredegar Ironworks as part of this development.

Cwm Rhos Mine was one of the earliest levels in the area and was driven into the hillside in 1802, before becoming part of the developing works site.

Jack Edwards Mine was a small level near the northern outcrop of the Lower and Middle coal measures about 1802 and was probably worked by him as contractor.

Nantybwch Mine was another early

level, driven in 1802 into the outcropping seams of the Lower and Middle coal measures and working both coal and iron ore. The closure date is uncertain.

Hard Level, which opened in 1804, was at Sirhowy but fed into the Tredegar Works being at the end of the Tredegar Company's private tramroad and subsequent railway line.

Forge Level was driven in 1804 and closed pre-1878.

Shop Level was another of the small levels that dates from 1804 and like Cwm Rhos was enveloped in the workings of the Ironworks in the course of time.

Tramroad Level was likewise driven in 1812 but its closure date is uncertain. Most of the closure dates for these levels will have been due to exhaustion.

Bron Heulog Level was driven into the Garw seam and was owned by E .Bufton. It employed twelve men and was abandoned in 1912.

The following pits were all under the same management:- **Ash Tree Pit**, also known as **Pwll Mary Isaac,** opened in 1826 and filled in 1897, **Water Wheel Pit** opened in 1830, **Upper Ty Trist** opened in 1841, **Yard Level** located at Sirhowy at the end of the Tredegar Ironworks private line from their works, and operated between 1802 and 1823. All were phased out by TICC before the end of the nineteenth century, after its formation in

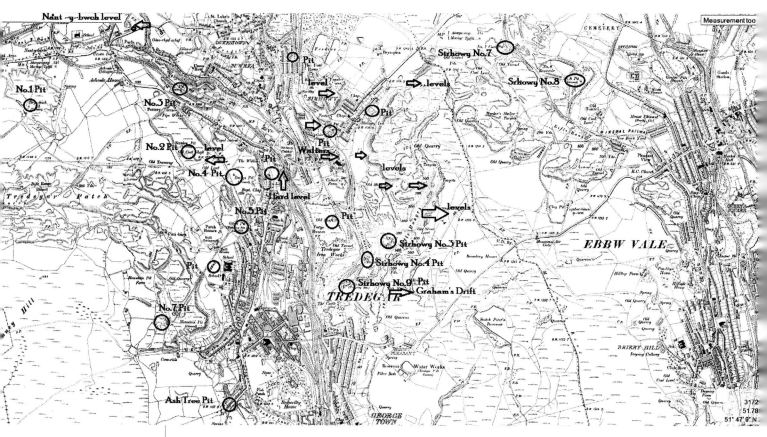

A map showing the location of the pits owned by the Tredegar Iron & Coal Co. in the Tredegar and Sirhowy areas.
Gerald Davies Colln

1873 when the impetus changed from iron making to coal production from deeper and larger pits.

Duke's Pit was reputed to be the first pit in South Wales to use the water balance method of coal mining and was the first pit to be sunk in the Tredegar area in 1806. It was located near the northern outcrop of the coking coal seams of the Middle and Lower coal measures and consisted of one shaft 8ft in diameter and 100ft deep. Its closure date is uncertain.

There were also twelve pits which were named as numbers i.e. No. 9 Pit, but most also had names, often after the contractor. Small amounts of information are available on them as follows:-

No. 1 Pit or Bryn Bach, opened in 1818, still working in 1878 though possibly closed in 1879.

No. 2 Pit or Evan Davies Pit, also called Stanley's Pit, opened in 1820 and shown as abandoning the Little Yard seam in 1893.

No. 3 Pit or Quick's Pit opened in 1834, still working in 1878, abandoned the Old

Coal seam in 1880. The Old Coal (Five-Feet Gellideg) seam consisted of (from the top) Yard Coal 40ins., clod 4ins., Gilwich coal 16ins., clod 46in, coal 20in, clod 33in, fireclay 29in, clod 9in and Old Coal seam 54in.

No. 4 Pit or Briggs Pit opened in 1830 and abandoned the Old Coal seam in 1889.

No. 5 Pit or Globe Pit opened in 1840 and was not filled in until 1948.

No. 6 Pit or Doctors Pit opened in 1832 and closed in 1888.

No. 7 Pit or Mountain Pit. More is known about this pit. It opened in 1841 to a depth of 210 yards and was claimed to be the deepest water balance pit in the world. It produced 52,800 tons in 1889 and 39,500 tons in 1894, and closed in 1896. Details of the seam sections in this pit are available as follows:- Engine Coal 45in, Meadow Vein top coal 28in, clod 4in, coal 14in, Old Coal 37in, Upper Rhas Las 12in, Lower Rhas Las 25in. The Big Vein group of seams measured from the top Big Vein 72in, clod 36in, Yard seam

36in, clod 8in, Three-Quarter seam 76in. In 1888 it worked the Little Yard and Old Coal seams and probably closed in 1897.

No. 8 Pit or Steven Charles Pit opened in 1838 but was amalgamated into the Whitworth Drift mine in 1888 and was filled in 1897.

No. 9 Pit was opened in 1839.

No. 10 Pit or Yard Pit was sunk in 1838 to 111 yards with seam sections being Elled 48in, Big Vein 72in, Three-Quarter 72in, Rhas Las 33in, Bute 14in. It was filled in 1957.

No. 11 Pit or Evan Evans Pit opened in 1839 and was filled in 1897.

No. 12 Pit or David Jervis Pit opened in 1840 and was filled in 1897.

Some pits and levels were opened in the early twentieth century. Gelli Colliery was a small level that was producing coal in 1902, employing six men, and owned by the Gelly Colliery Co. No previous record of its existence has been found for 1888 or later in 1913.

Plantation Colliery consisted of two pits and is shown as owned and managed in 1918 by D. Williams of Nantybwch and employing sixteen men. In 1921 this changed to D. Williams & Sons who employed 6/2 men working the Yard seam. Ownership changed several times during the 1930s; in 1930 it was owned by A. Harris with seven men employed still working the Yard seam, and in 1932 by Ben Williams. In 1935, it was owned by Williams Plantation Colliery Co. Ltd., employing 20/4 and produced 5,000 tons of house coal from the Old Coal (Five-Feet Gellideg) seam. In 1937, it employed eight men but was listed as temporarily closed but was shown working again in 1938-47 owned by Mrs. F. Williams of Tredegar, employing 4/2 men. The No. 1 Pit was abandoned in 1944 and in 1943-45 No. 2 employed four men working the Old Coal seam. The Yard seam was abandoned in 1945, the Brithdir Rider seam in 1948 and the Old Coal seam in March 1949 when it still employed four men.

I am indebted to Ray Lawrence for these details.

SIRHOWY
Railway

The sidings of the Tredegar Iron Works stretched from just north of the level crossing at Tredegar right up to beyond the station at Sirhowy. The building of an ironworks at Sirhowy had predated that at Tredegar and had given its name to the Tramroad to Newport and indeed the Valley itself. Beyond Tredegar the running line was single to Nantybwch but, unlike at Tredegar, there were up and down platforms at Sirhowy with a loop running line giving access. On the up side there was a large goods yard and goods shed from where all goods traffic for Tredegar was handled, the area possessing the one feature missing at Tredegar, namely space for developemt. The goods yard and shed are shown on a plan for 1880, but whether these facilities were first available at Tredegar is debateable. It would appear that between 1880-1900 the goods facilities at Sirhowy were considerably extended, using the area of the sidings that originally accessed the Ironworks, to create a yard for full loads and extending the goods shed. The Sirhowy River ran right through the railway facility at Sirhowy and bridges over it were necessary south of the platform and within the area of the TICC sidings. The Rassa Railway also ran into

Sirhowy Station looking south with posed staff, possibly in 1905.

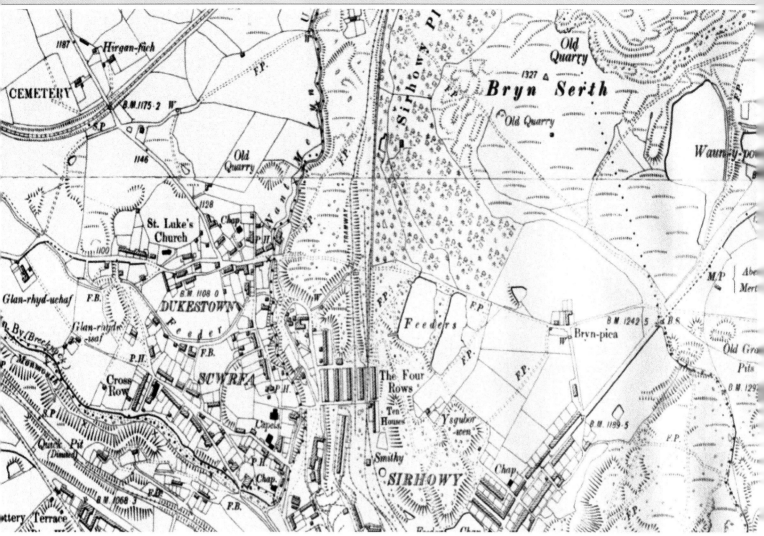

A **map** of the Sirhowy area at the turn of the twentieth century.

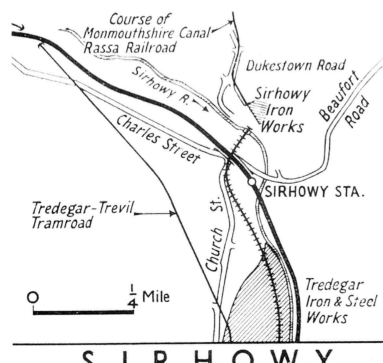

Sirhowy Ironworks in the 1870s.

Sirhowy Ironworks conveying limestone from Trefil.

The high level of use of domestic coal in the area into the 1960s and the number of miners entitled to concessionary coal supplies created a need for the NCB to maintain a landsale and concessionary coal depot at Sirhowy and this remained in use serviced by NCB engines using BR wagons, many of which came in from collieries still producing domestic coal in other parts of South Wales (e.g. Maesteg and Garw), this forming the majority of the inwards traffic to the Sirhowy Valley line. The fact that this was virtually the only traffic left on the line made the working uneconomic and the arrangement came to an end in November 1963 when the line between

Sirhowy Station in 1905, a posed picture with the station staff and engine 88.

Tredegar and Sirhowy was closed. This seemed a strange decision when it still left freight facilities, traffic being very sparse, in existence south of Tredegar, until the closure of the Tredegar to Pontllanffraith section in April 1969.

The Goods Shed and Yard staff on 16 January 1923.

A view of Sirhowy Station from the north end with the Goods Shed and Yard on the left. Goods traffic for Tredegar was processed through Sirhowy due to lack of space at Tredegar.
H.C. Casserley

Another view of Sirhowy Station from the north end from ground level, showing the track curvature approaching the station, the goods shed, the station footbridge and the signal box on the right.
E.T. Gill/R.K. Blencowe Collection

Looking up the platforms towards Nantybwch on 11 April 1960.
Alastair Warrington

The view south from Sirhowy Station with the connection into the Goods Yard in the centre. The tracks became single beyond Sirhowy as can be seen.
R.M. Casserley

8766 with the single coach 10.25am Tredegar to Nantybwch in July 1959. SLS

6426 heads a single coach auto service from Risca to Nantybwch at 4.36pm on 28 May 1960. The Abergavenny photographer John Beardsmore is standing alongside the station nameboard also recording this photograph. E.T. Gill/R.K. Blencowe Collection

A pannier runs north through Sirhowy with an empty miners' service to Nantybwch on 28 May 1960. This position affords a good view of the connections into the south end of the Goods Shed. E.T. Gill/R.K. Blencowe Collection

Sirhowy Bridge, (The Death Trap) Tredegar. MON.

Sirhowy Bridge carrying the railway north of the station, the roads beneath known locally as the Death Trap.

On 12 July 1952 the bridge was replaced, these two pictures showing the work in progress.

Alastair Warrington

This type of scene was typical at Sirhowy Valley stations when a school or church party was leaving on a charter service. This is Sirhowy in the 1950s when the destination could well have been Barry Island.

An elevated view of the Goods Yard at Sirhowy with coal merchants traffic accounting for much of the business, a situation common to very many yards.

A return miners' train to Nantybwch calls at Sirhowy with one of the former BPGV low-roofed brake seconds leading. The connection into the Coal yard can be clearly seen and the other trackwork at the north end of the station. Transport Treasury

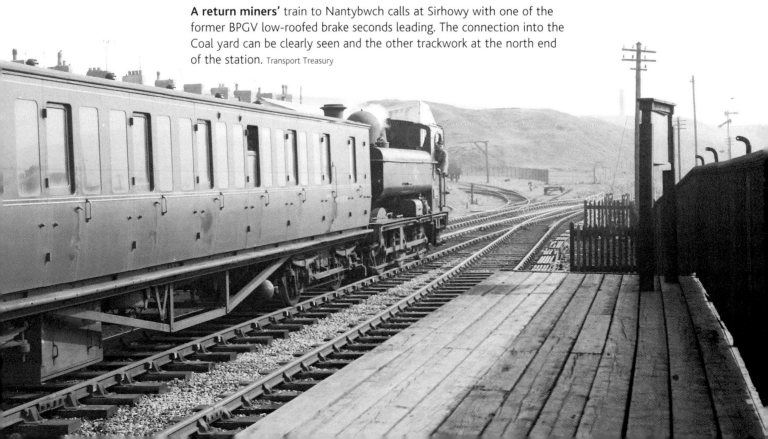

Entering the single line section to Nantybwch, 40098 heads a miners' train in the mid-1950s.

With snow on the ground in January 1960, a pannier tank takes water from the LNW type water column before departing for Nantybwch. A. Jarvis

An NCB 0-6-0 between Tredegar and Sirhowy with a load of coal for the yard at Sirhowy in 1969.
Alastair Warrington

Where once there was a railway ...The tracks have been taken up and the station buildings and signal box taken down. The former Goods Shed has been taken over by a local concern whose cars are parked around the previous northern entrance.

Sirhowy Ironworks

(NB There are several potted history accounts of Sirhowy Ironworks, containing contradictory data regarding production tonnages and dates. I have studied several of these and my account attempts to interpret them to produce a logical position.)

The Sirhowy Ironworks dates from 1778 when Thomas Atkinson, William Barrow, Bolton Hudson and John Sealey leased land at Sirhowy on which to build a coke furnace for the production of pig iron, using the locally available resources of iron ore, coal and limestone. The contract ran for forty years at an annual rental of £134, this becoming the first furnace fired by coke rather than charcoal in Monmouthshire. A square furnace was initially built of stone from the Sirhowy river with a hand-operated bellows until a water wheel was set up in the river, this doubling the weekly production to about 10 tons of pig iron. By 1790, fifty men were employed but a slump in the demand for pig iron saw the plant sold.

In 1794, the works were bought by William Barrow and Matthew Monkhouse who were joined by Richard Fothergill, later to be much involved with the building of the Sirhowy Tramroad. By 1799, the plant had been significantly developed and in that year they installed a 20HP Boulton & Watt steam blowing engine to provide a hot blast, required for when a second blast furnace was constructed in 1801-2, increasing production to 100 tons per month. Also in 1799, the nearby Tredegar Ironworks was founded by Fothergill, Monkhouse and Samuel Homfray, all eager to make use of the abundance of locally available resources. Initially, most of the pig iron made at Sirhowy appears to have been sold to the Merthyr ironworks but by 1803 Sirhowy pig iron was being sent to the new Tredegar Works for conversion into finished products from where it needed to be transported to Newport Docks. Transport of their produce was a huge problem and they were involved with others in the plans for the original Sirhowy Tramroad through to Newport, the Monmouthshire Canal being an awkward distance away in the Ebbw Valley at Crumlin. The supply of pig iron to Tredegar continued until 1818 when everything changed at Sirhowy.

In 1818, the original 40-year lease, taken out in 1778, expired and Sirhowy Works was put up for sale. It was bought by the Ebbw Vale Works owners and as the new lease owners they raised the annual rental of the land from the original £134 to £2,500 which Fothergill refused to pay, removing or destroying all the equipment

Sirhowy Ironworks in the 1870s.

Part of the Blast Furnaces at Sirhowy Ironworks.

at the works before it could be taken over by the new owners. An ensuing lawsuit saw Fothergill fined £6,000, in retaliation for which he refused to carry any of the Sirhowy Works' produce on the Sirhowy Tramroad, so that it had to be conveyed by the Rassa Railway across to the Ebbw Vale Works until in 1832 a tunnel 1½ miles long was driven through the mountain to link the two works.

By 1826, there were three furnaces in operation at Sirhowy of which two were in blast producing 7,800 tons of pig iron during the year. By 1839-40 there were four furnaces in operation and a new high pressure steam blowing engine was installed from the Neath Abbey Iron Co., with the works still operating in a subordinate role to Ebbw Vale, under which they supplied Ebbw Vale with pig iron where it was worked into wrought iron and later into steel. In 1844 Abraham Darby and Partners bought both the Ebbw Vale and Sirhowy works, five furnaces now being operative at Sirhowy, of which four used the hot blast technique, producing up to 500 tons of pig iron a week. A series of

A preserved section of the Blast Furnaces of Sirhowy Ironworks.

An early example of an 0-6-0 locomotive in use on the Sirhowy Railway in the 1860s, working where the railway was still being made.
Courtesy T.N. Charles

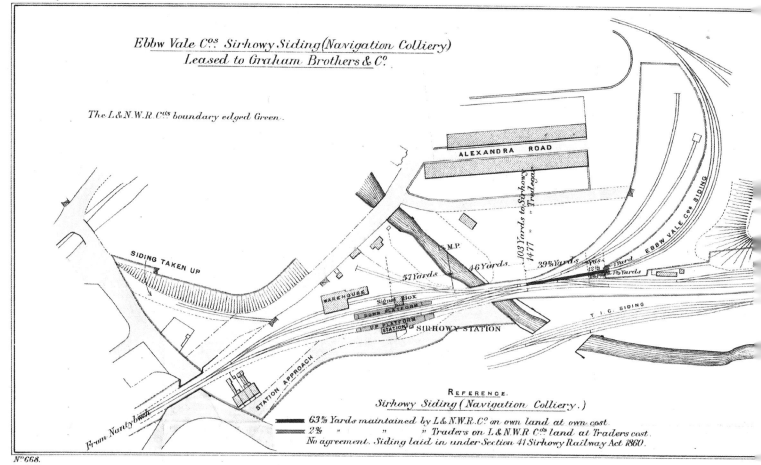

*Ebbw Vale Cos Sirhowy Siding (Navigation Colliery)
Leased to Graham Brothers & Co.*

The L.&N.W.R.Cos boundary edged Green.

REFERENCE.
Sirhowy Siding (Navigation Colliery.)

63⅞ Yards maintained by L.&N.W.R.Co on own land at own cost.
2⅜ " " " Traders on L.&N.W.R.Cos land at Traders cost.
No agreement. Siding laid in under Section 41 Sirhowy Railway Act 1860.

Nº668.

improvements in operations followed under Darby's management, the most important being the perfection of the hot blast technique developed at Ebbw Vale, the benefits of which were passed on to Sirhowy, open top furnaces now being capped and the previously escaping hot gasses now piped down to increase the heat of the blast in the furnace. The 60in beam blowing engine worked in unison with the 52in pumping engine, provided with steam by nine boilers. The works were now reported to include 'four refineries, cast houses, bridge houses, four mine kilns, coke yards, two lime kilns, a clay mill and two winding engines'. The pig iron produced was transported to the rolling mills at Ebbw Vale Works through two tunnels.

By the 1850s, there were five blast furnaces in operation at Sirhowy but this proved too great a capacity for the state of the iron trade at that time and by the 1870s, this had been cut back to three. By 1877, the amount of cast iron produced was greater than could be contained in the cast houses and they were partly demolished. In 1879, all three operating furnaces were closed down and iron production ceased, 300 workers being made unemployed. The works reopened shortly afterwards but closed again finally in 1882. The plant however continued to produce coke for Ebbw Vale until this ceased also and the works were closed in 1905.

Graham's Navigation Colliery

There were various small levels and mines in production in the Sirhowy area sunk to feed the Ironworks and all started life as water balance pits. The main rail-connected pit loading to wagons was Graham's, served off a siding east of the running lines, which had a direct connection into Sirhowy Ironworks. Originally called Sirhowy No.9, or First Class, Pit, it was the last of nine pits sunk to feed the Ironworks. It was sunk in 1843 as a water-balance winding pit, owned by the Sirhowy Iron Co. which came under the Ebbw Vale Co. in 1818. In 1888, it was working the Old Coal (Five-Feet/Gellideg) seam and in 1896 employed 229/136 men working the Meadow Vein, Black Vein and Ganister seams. In 1902, it was leased by Graham's Navigation (Merthyr) Co. Ltd., who changed its name to Graham's Navigation. That year it employed 450 men. In 1907, it employed 174 men underground and 34 on the surface, with the nearby level having 47/4. By 1911, the combined employment was 282 miners. By 1913 it was owned by Graham's Navigation (Merthyr) Co. Ltd. and had expanded to employ 450 men and 650 in 1915/6. At this time, the colliery was also working the Meadow Vein, Black Vein and Elled seams. Employment and production then declined markedly so that in 1918, the totals employed were only 190/15.

In 1919, the ash content of coal produced at the colliery was only 3.21 per cent, one of the best in the coalfield. In 1923 production was 140,000 tons. The colliery was then owned by T.C. Graham of Mount Stuart Square, Cardiff, who changed the name of the colliery and its production to Graham's Navigation, or the Sirhowy Pit, advertising its Admiralty Coal as:

> 'Graham's Navigation (Merthyr) Steam Coal'
> Fixed Carbon………..78.63%
> Volatile Matter………17.16%
> Ash…………………… 3.21%
> Moisture……………..... 1.00%
> Sulphur……………….… 0.68%'

It now employed 700 men but in December 1924 the Yard and Big Seams were abandoned and the pit closed.

The Levels worked alongside the Pit. The last levels in production were Nos. 3 and 4 which worked the Engine Coal

A new 12ton wagon for coal use for Graham's Navigation, No. 892 tare 6 tons 14cwt, built by Ince Waggon & Ironworks, for returning empty to Tredegar.

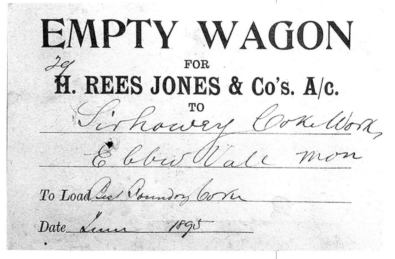

H. Rees Jones were Agents for the Sirhowy Coke Works and used this wagon label for their Best Foundry Coke in June 1895.

seam and closed in 1924. However, the mine was re-opened by Williams Bros. as Sirhowy Navigation and in 1930 employed 230 miners, producing 50,000 tons. Records show that by 1937 only 32 men were left employed there, the mine closing shortly afterwards.

The **Sirhowy Colliery** was a small level near the northern outcrop of the coalfield, also called the Black Vein Level. It was shown as owned in 1917 by J.C. Jenkins, and producing coking, house and steam coals. In 1918 it was working the Sirhowy Elled and Big Vein seams with seventeen men. In 1928, twenty-nine men were employed, but the site was abandoned in 1929. However in 1932 it was back in production, owned by M. Walters & Sons of Tredegar and in 1935 by D.C. Jenkins of Newport but with only three men underground and one on the surface, working the Elled seam.

The **Elled Colliery** was a small level owned by Phillips & Williams, working the Two-Feet-Nine Elled seam. In 1903/5 it is shown as only employing five men, in 1908 6 and only four in 1910. Elled mines were also at Tredegar with Nos. 3, 4 and 9 shown as abandoning the Yard seam in 1913, with J.C. Jenkins shown as owning an Elled mine in 1917.

The **Ganister Colliery** was shown in 1888 as owned by the EVISC Co. working the Rock Vein and Ganister seams. In 1896 it was shown as working for stone only. In 1908 it employed 16/2 men, and in 1911 employed 14 men, owned by D. Morris of Ebbw Vale. Between 1923-41 it employed less than ten men and appears to have closed in 1941, coal having finally been worked from the Old Coal and Ganister seams.

The **Glanhowy Colliery** is shown as working in 1921, owned by D.C. Jenkins & Co. of Newport, in 1923 employing 17/3 men, and 32 in 1929. In 1930 the owning company was shown as Jenkins & Co., the mine working on the Elled, Big and Black Vein seams. By 1934 only a few were employed working the Elled seam for house and steam coal and the mine was abandoned in 1943.

Mines working on this basis supplying Sirhowy Ironworks were:

No. 1 or Company Pit, sunk pre-1840 to 63 yards, closed by 1878.

No. 2 or Hollybush Pit, sunk pre-1840 to 46 yards. Also known as David Protheroe's, recorded as working in 1878 but closed by 1888.

No. 3 or Donkey Pit, sunk pre-1840 to 35 yards, closed by 1878.

No. 4 Pit shown as being worked by the EVISC Co. in 1878, working the Three-Quarter (Upper-Six-Feet) seam in 1888, and not listed after that date.

No. 5 or Joe Gibbs Pit, sunk about 1840 to 50 yards and closed by 1878. The Meadow Vein seam was worked containing coal and fireclay.

No. 6 or David Thomas Pit opened c1840 and closed by 1878.

No. 7 or Mathusalem Jones Pit opened c1840 and closed by 1888, an elliptical pit 80 yards deep. In 1893 it produced 53,700 tons of coal from the Gwar-y-cae seam and in 1899 employed 331 men. In 1900 the pit employed 199 men underground and 124 on the surface, working the Gwar-y-cae, Bydelog Fireclay and Ganister seams. In 1902, 299 men were employed but in 1907 this was down to only 12/2, the pit probably closing after this date.

No. 8 or Edwards Jones Pit opened c1840 and shown as working in 1878 but not 1888.

No. 9 or First Class Pit became Graham's Navigation and is dealt with above.

I am again indebted to Ray Lawrence for these details.

NCB Yard

Following the closure of mines, levels and collieries in the Sirhowy Valley, a requirement still existed on the part of the NCB to offer Landsale facilities for coal merchants in the area, to replace what was normally offered through station yards, and to provide facilities for coal merchants to deliver concessionary coal to miners and retired miners in the area, an important ongoing requirement. For this purpose, the large Sirhowy Yard was used as a distribution centre, operated by NCB engines, with coal being brought in from other collieries still producing household coal. The yard was closed towards the end of 1963 enabling the line between Tredegar and Sirhowy to be closed in November 1963.

NANTYBWCH
Railway

A mere 1¼ miles north of Sirhowy was

A view of the down platform at Sirhowy on the last day of service, 11 June 1960, from an up train into Nantybwch. E.T. Gill/R.K. Blencowe

the end of the Sirhowy Valley line at Nantybwch where the line converged with the MT&A line just north-east of the station. Shortly after leaving Sirhowy the line crossed the 3ft 6in Brinore (Bryn Oer) Tramroad which ran for eight miles from Talybont-on-Usk to Trefil, and was a product of the Brecknock & Abergavenny Canal Act of 1793 which authorised the building of tramroad connection into the canal from an 8 mile radius. Built in 1814, it was operational between 1815-65, as a horse-worked plateway serving the Bryn Oer coal patches and Trefil limestone quarries, a single track with thirteen passing places. The tramroad was used to convey coal, mainly from the Rhymney Valley to the canal (a branch having been opened by Benjamin Hall), limestone from Trefil to the Tredegar Ironworks and products from the Tredegar Ironworks to the Monmouth & Brecon Canal at Talybont. It also carried coal from the Nantybwch Level (located just north of the MT&A line, north-east of Nantybwch station) to the

Tredegar Ironworks. It was overtaken by the conversion of the Sirhowy Tramroad to a railway, and the upgrading of the tramroad from Trefil to serve Tredegar and Ebbw Vale into a railway. One of the chief sponsors of the tramroad was Benjamin Hall, and the engineer responsible for its construction was George Overton (1775-1827). The finance required for its construction was raised by public subscription at a cost of £12,800.

In order to make the necessary connection with the MT&A, the Sirhowy line swept around in a half circle between Sirhowy and Nantybwch, before arriving at a triangular shaped platform with an additional separate eastbound MT&A platform shown on a plan for 1870, on which the Sirhowy single platform was shorter than the MT&A westbound. The layout was changed, probably in 1891, to provide an additional down Sirhowy platform, the arrival platform having been extended to the length of the MT&A westbound platform. The Sirhowy branch track was doubled into a loop through the station to permit trains off the MT&A to pass trains standing in the terminating platform. Little operational use appears to have been made of the down platform, other than as a passing loop.

West of the platforms on the MT&A route were three long sidings which were often used to store the longer miners' trains to relieve accommodation problems at Tredegar. These ceased to be used for MT&A purposes following the closure of that route from 6 January 1958 and until May 1960 were used for Sirhowy purposes.

Station operations were under the control of Nantybwch No. 1 signal box located on the triangle platform. Opened in August 1891, MT&A responsibilities were removed in January 1958 and control over Sirhowy line movements were withdrawn earlier than June 1960, probably by November 1959. Following closure of the passenger services on 11 June 1960, the section of line between Nantybwch and Sirhowy

was closed on the 13th, and the line was recovered in May 1961.

Until the end of 1928, there was a small Control Office at Nantybwch which controlled the Sirhowy line and probably the whole of the MT&A. As part of the remodelling of the District Traffic Supt.,'s Office at Abergavenny, the Nantybwch Control was closed and transferred to Abergavenny. This was at an estimated cost of £3,900. The reason given was that the Nantybwch Office was 'inconveniently situated for the Control of the old LNW lines in South Wales and is not provided with satisfactory telephonic communication'. The move enabled an immediate staff cost saving of £500 pa. Though the improvement in telephonic arrangements was probably worthwhile with the old bus circuits very unreliable, Nantybwch was far more central to the LNW lines in the area than was Abergavenny, though much of the marshalling and traction activity centred on that location.

A Map of the Nantybwch area showing both the Sirhowy and MT&A lines at the turn of the twentieth century.
National Library of Scotland

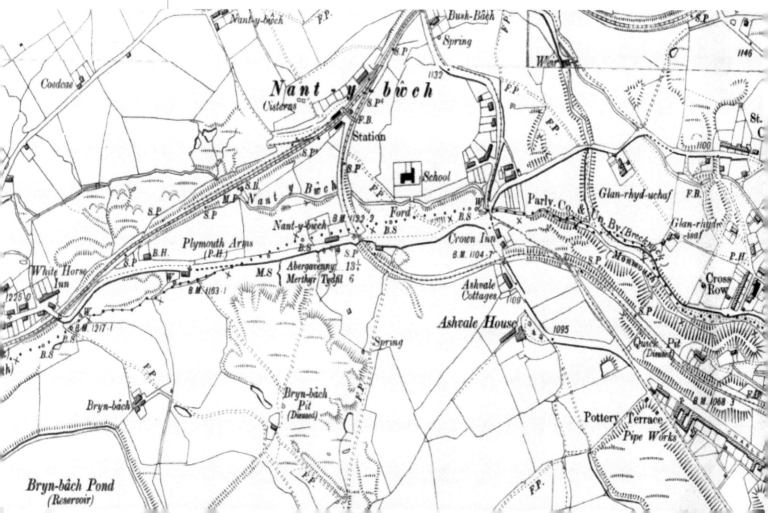

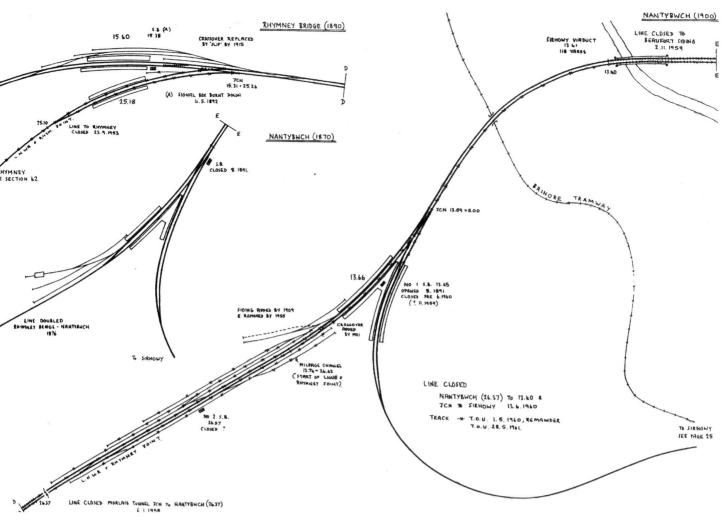

A plan of Nantybwch in 1900, updated to the 1960s. Courtesy R.A. Cooke

7752 arrives from Newport as 58933 carries on to Abergavenny perhaps for some repair to be undertaken at the main depot. P.W. Whitehouse/M. Whitehouse Collection

Such awesome sights as this, showing both the Sirhowy and MT&A platforms, were an everyday occurrence at Nantybwch until the early 1950s when the Coal Tanks were withdrawn. The 9.5am from Newport is double headed from Tredegar by 7710 and 27654 with two coaches, one a veteran vehicle for miners' use, with an Ivatt 2-6-2T on a Merthyr to Abergavenny train at the MT&A platform. SLS

Two coach auto working with a Tredegar based 64XX was intended to be the pattern of working, but this soon changed to an Ebbw 64XX, then only one coach and finally to a 57XX with one ordinary coach. This very pleasing view of Nantybwch shows most of the station with 6426 on the Risca auto that day, 28 May 1960. Monmouthshire Railway Society.

Coal Tank 27663 approaches Nantybwch with the three coach 8.50am from Newport on 2 June 1947, when these engines worked the majority of the passenger service. W.A. Camwell/SLS

Coal Tanks 7710 and 27654 make a striking sight as they stand at Nantybwch with the 9.5am from Newport on 26 April 1948. 27654 would return with the 11.10am service to Newport while 7710 would pick up another working.
W.A. Camwell/SLS

Two Coal Tanks, 7710 and 27654, arrive at Nantybwch with the 9.5am from Newport on 26 April 1948. W.A. Camwell/SLS

27654 stands at the head of the two coach 11.10am to Newport on 26 April 1948, the rear veteran vehicle being for miners en route. W.A. Camwell/SLS

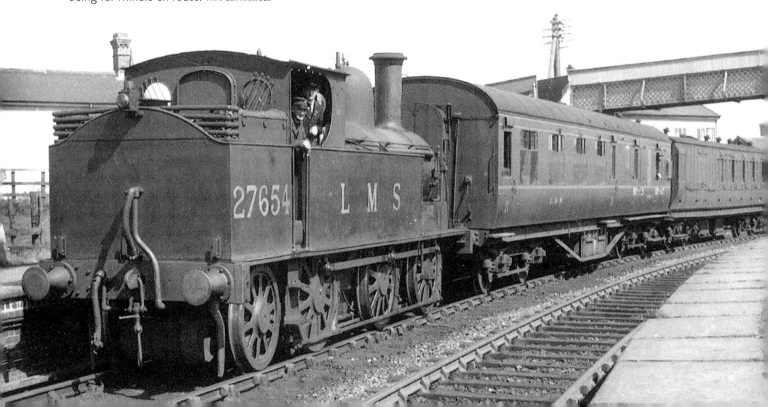

Following Nationalisation in 1948, the remaining tanks were renumbered into the 589XX series. Here 58925 heads a three coach Newport service on 19 August 1950. The coaches were typical of the genre of vehicles used with the rear ex-LNW coach for miners' use. P.W. Whitehouse/M. Whitehouse Collection

Another view of 58925, from the platform side, waiting to depart to Newport on 19 August 1950.
P.W. Whitehouse/M. Whitehouse Collection

Still not renumbered after Nationalisation, 7833 approaches Nantybwch with the 3.50pm from Newport at 5.15pm on 19 August 1950. No miners' coach was needed at this time of day.
P.W. Whitehouse/M. Whitehouse Collection

The early morning sun lights this scene of 7721 with the 8.50am train to Tredegar on 26 April 1948, conveying the van off the first train up from Newport at 4.20am.
W.A. Camwell/SLS

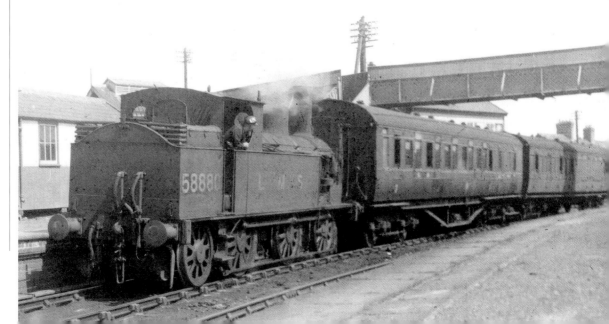

58880 with two veteran coaches to form a service to Newport on 14 June 1949.
C.H.A. Townley/IRS

The incoming train from Newport has been diverted into the down Sirhowy platform with 7752 and two coaches so that 49146 can run light through the other platform road on 19 August 1950. P.B. Whitehouse/M. Whitehouse Collection

A grimy 58933 runs into Nantybwch with the 1.10pm train from Newport, with a miners' coach on the front at this time of shift changeover. P.B. Whitehouse/M. Whitehouse Collection

Another excellent view of the north-east end of the platforms with unidentified Coal Tanks on a Sirhowy service with engines on both ends of one coach, and on the MT&A service to Abergavenny. SLS

On a dull 10 May 1951, 7752, still not renumbered after 2½ years, with the 9.5am ex-Newport on 10 May 1951. The usual LNW coach for miners' use is on the front. Ian L. Wright

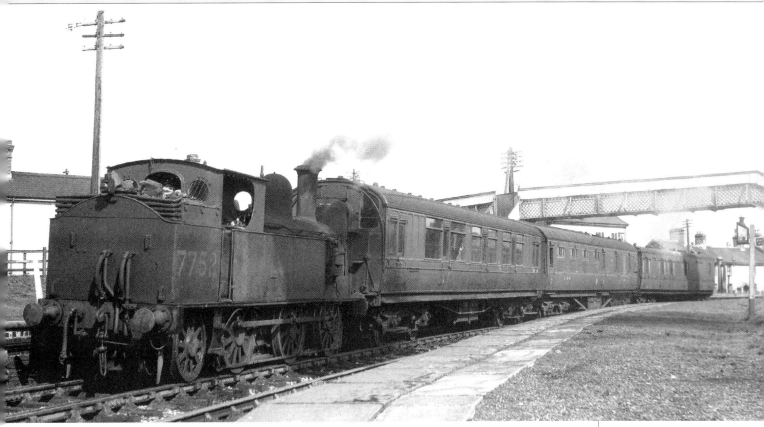

Three views of 7752 waiting to leave with the 11.10am to Newport, with three coaches including a miners' coach on 24 March 1951, the third view showing the platforms in wide aspect.
J.J. Smith/Bluebell Railway Archive

Super D 0-8-0s were a common sight at Nantybwch on freight and passenger, especially on heavy excursions. 49409 brings a miners' train around the last bend into Nantybwch on 13 April 1957, then leaves the empty stock in the MT&A sidings before returning LE to Tredega.
All by Ian L. Wright

49064 banked by another Super D works a train of coal probably bound for the Midlands via Abergavenny on 19 August.
P.B. Whitehouse/M. Whitehouse Collection

49064, working from Abergavenny shed, just ex-works and still carrying a 3A shedplate, heads a Merthyr to Abergavenny service as a Coal Tank arrives with a Sirhowy service at the other platform on 19 August 1950.
P.B. Whitehouse/M. Whitehouse Collection

Something of a new look to the Newport service on 13 May 1954 with Stanier 2-6-2T 40097 and two brake seconds, one former LMS, the other former GWR, but no miners' coach. T.J. Edgington

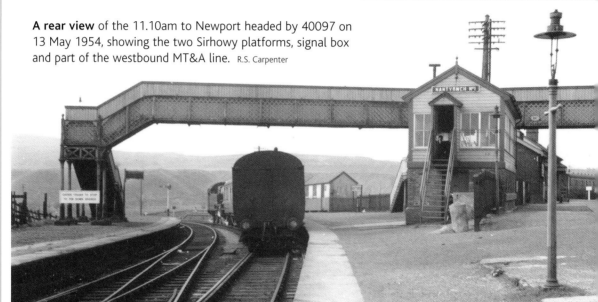

A wide angle view of the Sirhowy platforms from the south with Ivatt 2-6-2T 41204 on the three coach 11.10am to Newport on 11 July 1953.
J.J. Smith/Bluebell Railway Archive

A rear view of the 11.10am to Newport headed by 40097 on 13 May 1954, showing the two Sirhowy platforms, signal box and part of the westbound MT&A line. R.S. Carpenter

The Ivatt 2-6-2Ts were initially more frequently used on the Merthyr and Abergavenny service. Here 1203 has not yet been renumbered, working an eastbound service on 26 April 1948. W.A. Camwell/SLS

A three coach miners' train from Markham Village runs into Nantybwch with 41204 on 14 August 1957.
S. Rickard/J&J Collection

...and ends its journey at the east end of Nantybwch station. R.O. Tuck/Rail Archive Stephenson

An afternoon miners' train from Nine Mile Point of 6 ex-GWR coaches has been banked by Stanier 2-6-2T 40171 on 14 August 1957. S. Rickard/J&J Collection

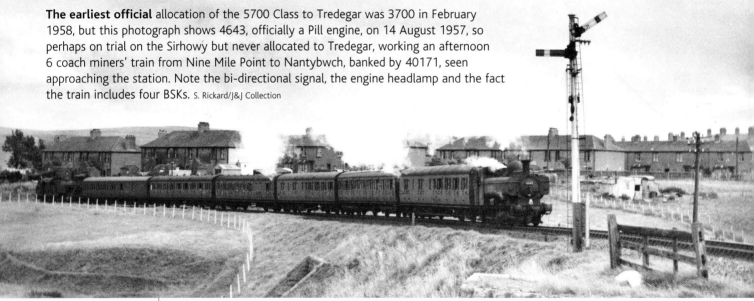

The earliest official allocation of the 5700 Class to Tredegar was 3700 in February 1958, but this photograph shows 4643, officially a Pill engine, on 14 August 1957, so perhaps on trial on the Sirhowy but never allocated to Tredegar, working an afternoon 6 coach miners' train from Nine Mile Point to Nantybwch, banked by 40171, seen approaching the station. Note the bi-directional signal, the engine headlamp and the fact the train includes four BSKs. S. Rickard/J&J Collection

3700 sits at Nantybwch waiting to return with the 4.50pm to Risca with its challenging one coach load downhill on 14 July 1959. R.F. Roberts/SLS

8766 was another pannier that spent time at Tredegar, though the official allocation ledgers do not record it as such, only at Ebbw Junction which suggests that this main depot sent engines to Tredegar as required, especially to replace the intended auto engines. Here it is with the 10.25am to Risca, at an unspecified date. SLS

A 57XX of the later series with the rounded cab roof has banked this miners' train into Nantybwch containing in the formation two of the former BPGV coaches now allocated to Tredegar, in April 1960. The engine will now work the empty coaches back to Tredegar Station Sidings.
E.T. Gill/R.K. Blencowe Collection

6426 is on auto duty on 28 May 1960 and waits at Nantybwch with the 6.30pm from Risca. At this time 64XX engines were provided from Ebbw Junction on a daily basis and if none was available, the service would be covered by a non-auto fitted pannier. D. Lewis

A final look at the view down the Valley on 11 April 1960 as the two starting signals keep guard over departures from both platforms, the two lines merging before passing over the bridge across the Sirhowy River. Alastair Warrington

And a final look back at Nantybwch as the single incoming track splits into two for the platforms, where a 64XX is waiting with a single auto coach for Risca on 3 January 1959. Alastair Warrington

In characteristically snowy winter weather in January 1960, a miners' train approaches the station banked by a 57XX. Alan Jarvis

CHAPTER SIX

THE LAST DAY –
11 JUNE 1960

THE FINAL DAY of passenger services on the Sirhowy Valley was a cloudy day with the usual Valley drizzle on occasions, so by the evening when a special train ran as the 6.32pm ex-Risca, conditions for photography were not particularly good, especially for colour. The ordinary service of engine and one auto coach operated but in non-auto mode, with engine 3634 which had to run round at the end of each journey.

Photographer Mark Warburton of Bristol travelled on the last train and recorded the scene at several places along the line. All those 13 photographs with no other credit are those taken by Mark on

The 3.37pm to Nantybwch stands at Risca behind 3634 in conventional mode on the last day of service. E. Wilmshurst

Here the train is at Holly Bush with only a couple of people to record the scene.

The train has now arrived at Tredegar and is photographed from the track, ready for its next duty. E. Wilmshurst

3634 at Nantybwch with the one coach 3.37pm service from Risca, from which several passengers have alighted, and which will return with the 4.42pm to Risca. E. Wilmshurst

the evening. Ever optimistic, Mark used colour film but the evening was so gloomy that colour film made little impact and we have reproduced the photos in black and white.

The special final train stands ready to depart from Risca with 8711 and three coaches and a van. Passengers take their final photographs with the signal off for departure.

THE LAST TRAIN

The 6.32pm from Risca to Tredegar (due 7.27pm), which should have been formed off the 4.50pm from Nantybwch with one coach, worked up specially from Ebbw

One of the few photographs of a
train at Ynysddu was provided on
the evening of the special.

The special at Pontllanffraith beneath the splitting
bracket signal for the Sirhowy and Bird in Hand routes.

Conditions at Blackwood for photography were poor with the light fading.

Junction and was formed of three coaches and a van, worked by 8711 and was extended on to Nantybwch and return before forming its booked return, the 7.52pm ex-Tredegar, which would be the last passenger train on the line. For some reason, Ebbw included a parcel van at the rear of the northbound formation, with an

The train at Argoed with time-keeping slipping probably due to the travelling photographers.

Now at Markham Village Halt with the down signal pulled off.

auto coach front followed by two seconds, one of which was a brake.

For a last train, it was a rather disappointing affair. For the photographers, a departure time of just short of 8pm needed some sunshine to brighten the potential, but the day was dull with rain and there was no sunshine. No attempt had been made by Ebbw Junction to present a cleaned-up engine and 8711, which was provided for the up run at 6.32pm from Risca, had not been cleaned for some time. Neither had 3634, the other engine working

the branch that day.

The 6.32pm from Risca was formed of three coaches and a van. Just why the van was needed is a mystery, perhaps for bicycles. Despite the amount of photography by travelling photographers, the up train arrived at Tredegar only 2 minutes late.

The 6.32pm from Risca normally terminated at Tredegar at 7.27pm to return at 7.52pm, but as this was the last train, it was extended specially to Nantybwch. At Tredegar, 8711 ran round the train and banked it to Nantybwch with 3634 as train engine. Departure from Tredegar was at 7.38pm and arrival at Nantybwch at 7.50pm. This put 8711 in the right position to work back after a hopefully quick turnround, with 3634 returning light to Tredegar in advance. The train departed Nantybwch at 7.50pm with the bunker of 8711 chalked 'Last Train From Sirhowy Valley', but when 3634 came on the front at Tredegar, this became obscured. Arrival at Tredegar was at 8.05pm and by the time 3634 had

been attached, departure was at 8.15pm, 23mins after the normal departure of the last train of 7.52pm. The train arrived at Risca at 9pm, having taken only 45mins for the journey from Tredegar instead of the 7.52pm's booked 52mins.

On arrival at Risca, 3634 was quickly detached and ran to shed at Ebbw, suggesting the crew were by then well over time. 8711 then worked the train forward to Newport, leaving Risca at 9.10pm.

The classic view at Holly Bush with the round water tower alongside the footbridge where a few photographers are recording the scene.

The train at Tredegar now with 3634 as train engine, 8711 being in the course of running round to bank the train to Nantybwch. The number of onlookers is building up on the platform.

Another view of the train at Tredegar now with 8711 attached rear.

The special at Nantybwch with a goodly crowd of onlookers to record the event, which was not accompanied by such a crowd-puller as the closure of the MT&A, now standing closed on the other platforms.

The last train stands at Nantybwch with 'Last Train From Sirhowy Valley' chalked on the bunker. 8711 worked the train to Sirhowy where 3634 was attached as pilot and the chalked title on 8711 then became obscured. D.K. Jones Collection

The doubleheaded final train stands at Tredegar in the gloom of the evening around 8pm.

The train at Risca with 8711 now in sole charge, 3634 having quickly been uncoupled and departed. 8711 now worked the train on to Newport.
R.K. Blencowe Collection

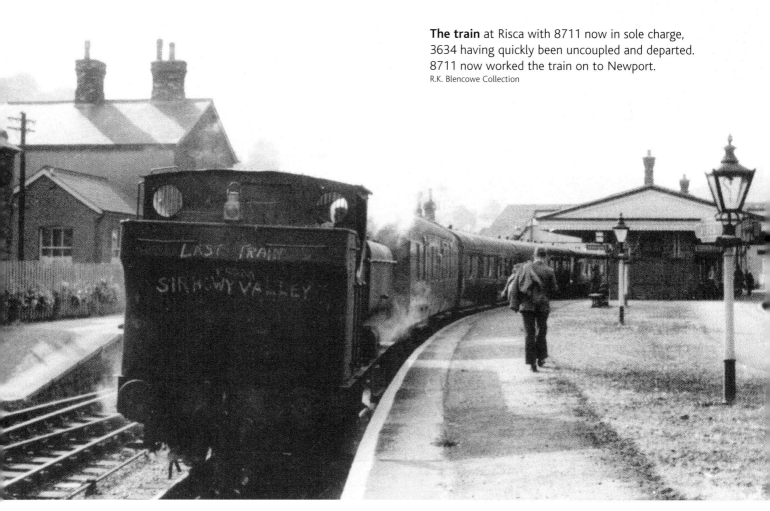

CHAPTER SEVEN

TREDEGAR IRON & COAL CO. (TICC)

THE ORIGINAL TREDEGAR Iron Company (TIC) was formed in 1799, and out of this, the Tredegar Iron & Coal Company (TICC) was formed in 1873 to recognise the fact that the company was now concentrating on coal production and was reducing its involvement in iron and steel.

The Tredegar Iron Company was formed in 1799 by Samuel Homfray, Richard Fothergill and Matthew Monkhouse, having secured a lease from Sir Charles Morgan (Lord Tredegar) for 3k. acres for 99 years at a rental of 2s.6d. per acre per annum, on which they would set up an iron works to make use of the indigenous resources of iron ore, coal for coke and limestone, using the soft water from the River Sirhowy. Levels driven into the outcropping seams produced the ore and coal but underground mining was necessary to produce the volumes required. Their first pit was Duke's Pit, sunk in 1806, the second the No. 1 Pit or Bryn Bach in 1818 and the third the No. 2 in 1820. Others followed but when No. 7 or Mountain Pit was sunk in 1841, at a depth of 210 yards, it became the deepest water balance pit in the world. The company went on to sink about twelve pits and to develop scores of levels.

Most were worked on the contractor system, based on an agreement made between the iron company, contractor and a group of workers to produce coal or iron ore from a particular mine. The company would lease out the mine and the contractor had to find the equipment and manpower to work it, agreeing a stipulated amount of coal or iron ore to be delivered to the ironworks at a fixed price, payment being made quarterly. Contractors had to borrow money from Bristol financiers to start up in business, purchase tools and pay their workmen until a quarterly payment was made by the ironmaster. This meant that the contractors and workmen were almost always in debt and this was the origin of the hated truck system operated by the ironmasters.

Tredegar Ironworks gained a very good reputation for the quality of their finished iron product, especially rails, as detailed previously, and for a while used the whole of their production to satisfy their own demands. Demand for quality steam coal was expanding at a huge rate and the company decided to switch their business largely from iron and steel to coal production and sale. The Tredegar Iron & Coal Company was formed out of the original company by Isaac Lowthian Bell, William Menelaus, Henry Davies Pochin, William Newmarch, Sidney Carr Glyn, Benjamin Whitworth and Edward Williams who were later joined by James Wyllie and Charles Markham, the new company then concentrating on coal production and marketing, so that the last steel made at Tredegar was in 1901. A perhaps unique trait of the new company was to name their collieries after directors of the company e.g. Whitworth, Pochin, Markham, Wyllie and McLaren.

The first major sinking of the TICC was Whitworth Colliery at Tredegar which produced its first coal in 1876, followed by Pochin Pits the same year. By 1878, the company operated Ash Tree Pit (opened in 1826 and closed in 1897, also known as Pwll Mary Isaac), Bedwellty Pits and Levels, Darran Levels, Tredegar Pits Nos. 1,3,6,7 and 8. Ty Trist, Whitworth Pit and Drift and numerous Patches. Coal production reached almost 0.75m. tons in 1885, increasing to almost 0.9m. by 1895, with over 3,000 men, women and children employed underground and on the surface. McLaren Colliery was sunk in 1897, the only TICC pit outside the Sirhowy Valley.

In 1896, the Company owned eight collieries/mines, all located in Tredegar and all managed by W.H. Routledge, as follows:-

Name of Mine	Employees	
	Underground	Above Ground
Bedwellty Levels	20	8
Bedwellty Pits	560	102
Pochin Pits	896	133
Stanley -	4	
Tredegar No. 7 - -	Stopped	
Ty Trist	526	92
Whitworth Drift	224	29
Whitworth Pits	442	56
TOTAL	2668	424
	3092	

In 1903, the company controlled the mineral rights to 4,600 acres but by this time many of the smaller workings in the Tredegar area were becoming exhausted. In 1906, the company acquired the mineral rights for Lord Tredegar's lands further down the valley between Holly Bush and Ynysddu. This had stunning results and produced three new collieries at Markham, Oakdale and Wyllie. Subsidiary companies were formed to manage the new sinkings. The Oakdale Navigation Colliery Co. managing and operating Oakdale and Waterloo, which started production in 1912, and the Markham Coal Co. which sank Markham

in 1913 further up the valley. It was originally intended that the Tredegar (Southern) Collieries Ltd. should sink the third colliery at Gelligroes near Ynysddu, but severe flooding experienced during the sinking and the First World War combined to delay the project and Wyllie Colliery at a new site was developed in 1925, the last deep mine to be sunk in Monmouthshire. In each case, the TICC built model villages to house the workers at the new pits, though many of those working at Oakdale lived at Blackwood.

Between 1873 and 1923, the annual output of the company's mines rose from 600,000 to almost 3m., employing 11,745 workers in 1923 with an annual wage bill of £1.5m. About 400,000 tons were exported annually through Newport Docks. The depression of the late 1920s and early '30s hit the company badly and output was down to 1.9m. tons and manpower halved to 5,900.

Details of the Company for **1923** show:-
Registered Office:- Tredegar Mon.
Class of Coal:- Coking, Steam
Other Minerals Worked:- Ironstone
Company Directors:-
Chairman Rt. Hon. Lord Aberconway P.C., 43 Belgrave Sq., SW1
Managing Director A.S. Tallis J.P., Llwyn Celyn, Caerleon, Mon.
Directors Major E.A. Johnson-Ferguson, Luckington Court, Chippenham
Arthur Lawrence J.P., 6 Park Place, Cardiff
The Hon. H.D. McLaren CBE MP, 38 South Street, Mayfair W1
Evan Williams JP, Glyndwr, Pontardulais
Col. A.K. Wyllie C.B., 39 Prince's Gate SW 7
General Manager W.D. Woolley Secretary H.O. Monkley Agent W. Stephen Davies

Collieries/Mines Owned

Name	Locality	Manager	Employees	
			UG	AG
Bedwellty	Tredegar	Evan Rees	103	44
McLaren Merthyr	Abertysswg	David Kendrick	1317	243
Pochin	Holly Bush	T. Reynolds	1928	175
Proedrhiwgaer	Tredegar	Evan Rees	72	12
Ty Trist	Tredegar	W.H. Warburton	1659	304
TOTAL			5079	778
			5857	

Details for **1933** show more information on the physical side of the business:-
Registered Office 60 Fenchurch Street, London EC3
Seams Worked Big Vein, Yard, Rhas Las, Polka, Elled, Three Quarter, Red Ash, Old Coal, Little Yard
Power Used Electric: Voltage 6,600 and 550 AC, 40 Cycles.
Annual Output 1,250,000 tons
Class of Coal Coking, Steam
Other Minerals Worked Ironstone

Chairman Rt. Hon. Lord Aberconway P.C., 43 Belgrave Sq., SW1
Deputy Chairman The Hon. H.D. McLaren CBE MP, 38 South Street, Mayfair W1
Directors Sir Edward Johnson-Ferguson, Luckington Court, Chippenham
N.J. McNeil, Claremont, Lake Road East, Cardiff
Evan Williams JP, Glyndwr, Pontardulais
W.D. Woolley, Rhyd Hall, Tredegar
General Manager W.D. Woolley
Manager David Evans Secretary H.O. Monkley Agent G.E. Golding

Collieries / Mines Owned

Name	Locality	Manager	Employees	
			UG	AG
Bedwellty	Tredegar	A.F. Williams -	12	
McLaren	Abertysswg	J.R. Tallis	900	140
Pochin Pits	Holly Bush	H. Evans	1325	155
Ty Trist	Tredegar	A.F. Williams	795	98
TOTAL			3020	405
			3425	

Details for 1940 show that there were now
two Managing Directors:-
 Sir Holberry Mensforth, The Red House,
St.John's Road, Hazelmere, Bucks
 W.D. Woolley, Rhyd Hall, Tredegar
And that the General Manager was now
Daniel Morgan
With the Agent now J.R. Tallis
Annual Output was now down to 1m.tons

Collieries/Mines Owned

Name	Locality	Manager	Employees	
			UG	AG
Bedwellty	Tredegar	B.L. Phillips	110	20
McLaren	Abertysswg	K.D. Woolley	600	110
Pochin Pits	Holly Bush	A.F. Williams	1180	162
Ty Trist	Tredegar	B.L. Phillips	415	90
TOTAL			2305	382
			2687	

By 1945, output had recovered to just
over 2.3m. tons with manpower 6,500.
   With Nationalisation in 1947, by
when Bedwellty Pits had closed, the
mining interests of the company came
under the control of the NCB. At this
time, the former General Manager had
become Deputy Chairman and Managing
Director, Daniel Morgan was General
Manager and the Board of Directors had
been joined by Charles M. McLaren and
Sir Holberry Mensforth at the expense of
Evan Williams and N.J. McNeil.

Collieries/Mines Owned

Name	Locality	Manager	Employees	
			UG	AG
McLaren	Abertysswg	G.H. Goulding	592	147
Pochin Pits	Holly Bush	B.L. Phillips	739	167
Ty Trist	Tredegar	A.F. Williams	428	139
TOTAL			1759	453
			2212	

   In June 1953, an EGM of the company
voted to wind up the company and all
its subsidiaries voluntarily, appointing
Alexander Grieve as Liquidator.

CHAPTER EIGHT

REFLECTIONS ON TY TRIST COLLIERY

(BY AN UNKNOWN AUTHOR)

WITH THE ADVENT of the Industrial Revolution, enterprising Englishmen learned of the potential mineral wealth existing in South Wales. They arrived in the northern region of Glamorgan and Monmouthshire to discover the extensive untapped coalfields lying below the surface. They had come upon the rich wealth hidden away in the basin of the valleys, and so alighting upon the upper reaches of the Sirhowy Valley were among the formative pioneers in founding the town of Tredegar. No doubt they found a luxuriant wooded valley with an abundant supply of water, the then perfect setting for many a poet's eulogies. But industrialisation was soon to blacken and smear this idyllic landscape, and so it was in the adjoining valleys. These energetic newcomers were ironfounders, their initial objective the mining of iron ore which lay near to the surface. Their fuel was charcoal, obtained from the plentiful supply of wood available. When the supply of wood diminished, it was discovered that coal was abundantly available alongside the previously sought iron ore. Thus was born the coal mining industry with ever burgeoning markets in Britain and overseas.

Amongst the newly formed ironmasters was Samuel Homfray who sagaciously selected a sheltered plot of land, abounding with trees, to establish his residence, thus in the centre of the expanding town of Tredegar. This locality we know today as Bedwellty Park. On the hillside to the west of the town were sunk a series of shallow pits, primarily for iron ore. The lowest of these was later used to develop the renowned Elled coal seam. It was sunk near a farm called Ty Trist – house of sorrow or sadness. Legend would have us believe it was haunted. Up until relatively recent years, the crumbling remains of this old homestead were still to be seen. Today there is no trace of the mine buildings that were situated nearby. The ruined farmhouse stood in a hollow completely surrounded by shale mounds.

It is easy to imagine that the inhabitants of that farmstead vigorously resisted the encroachment of what to them was an unnatural industry. The whole area from the original outcrop workings downward in a southerly direction had by this time become riddled with shafts, tunnels and drifts sunk to the various coal seams. As these extended southwards, they became gradually deeper. In the course of time, operations moved from the area local to Ty Trist farm to a more convenient site on the valley floor, close to the River Howy. The newly constructed Sirhowy Valley Railway [from 1860] afforded excellent facilities for transporting the envisaged production of coal to Newport and the coal exporting ports. The new mine undertaking retained the same name as the first exploratory shaft – Ty Trist Colliery.

There two shafts were duly sunk, somewhat enterprising for those early days of the coal industry, but insignificant compared with the shafts excavated in modern times. They were oval in shape, brick-lined, designed to accommodate two cages, each carrying one wooden tram, probably of one ton capacity. The owners of the colliery were the Tredegar Iron & Coal Company, and the colliery 'take' or area to be worked was ambitiously extensive. The first coal seam to be reached, the Elled vein, was developed in conjunction with the original shaft on the adjoining hillside. This seam, marketed under various names, was renowned throughout the eastern region of the coalfield for its steam raising qualities. It is distressing to note that in the lean times between the two World Wars, supplies of this high quality coal were loaded on coal ships at Cardiff Docks at the ridiculously low price of 17/- a ton, free on board. Thus was the mineral wealth of South Wales shamelessly expended. There is good reason to believe that Italian trains, during the Mussolini era, were powered by the Elled coal from Ty Trist Colliery. As time passed, the shafts were deepened to engage other seams, namely the Big Vein, the Yard Vein, the Upper and Lower Rhas Vein and others. These were all worked more or less extensively subject to the limitations of faulting, thickness, quality, water and other complications encountered in the exploitation of coal. The colliery had its ups and downs in the 19th century as did many other industrial undertakings. Yet there is no record of its having been closed, except during the occasion of strikes or disputes. One such conflict occurred in 1898 when there was a six month lockout, when there was general unrest throughout the coalfield. In 1868 Ty Trist Shaft No. 1 was deepened to reach the Old Coal seam at a depth of 221 yards. It was later to be worked extensively and proved to be of comparable merit to the Upper Elled seam. A third shaft of similar dimensions was put down to the same seam to serve for ventilation and to pump out water that was to become an ever increasing problem. This area, stretching north of the colliery, to the outcrop range had, during the years, become honeycombed with mine workings throughout all the coal seams, the inevitable outcome being that surface water seeping into the old roadways and galleries found its way to the lowest point. This naturally meant that Ty Trist Colliery had a serious pumping problem. At the lowest end of the take, a substantial amount of coal was left unworked, so as to prevent this water from becoming a formidable dilemma to collieries that had by this time been established lower down the valley. Thus a permanent pumping station was constructed and early in the 1900s a battery of centrifugal pumps was installed by the Swiss company Sulzer. Near the shaft bottom an extensive sump was excavated to catch the water from the upper side of the shaft. The water in this catch basin was raised to the surface by the powerful Sulzer pumps at the pit bottom. This pumping system effectively solved the water problem during the life of the colliery. On its closure, it was replaced by an automatic, remotely controlled system suspended in the pumping shaft.

The development of the Old Coal seam proved to be the most productive era of the colliery's life. The upper seams continued to be worked from the second shaft. As the years passed, technical advancements were introduced in line with more informed management. Electric power was installed followed by compressed air; roadways were enlarged, steel supports brought into use and more robust tracks laid. The horseshoe type of steel arching was designed and manufactured at the company's ironworks and, having proved to be sturdy and functional, eventually replaced timber in all the main roadways. A washer continued in use almost up to the time of the colliery's closure, but an extensive battery of coke ovens was not replaced when it became obsolete.

The original wooden headframe was replaced by one constructed of steel and so with the march of time wooden trams gave way to those fabricated in steel. The colliery workshops were modernised and the extensive steam generating plant gradually contracted with the increasing use of electric power. Yet the steam winding engines remained efficient and were never converted to electric power. Machine coal cutting equipment was introduced rather slowly, but progress is inevitably triumphant and as mechanisation evolved, so the number of horses used was gradually decreased. It is believed that, at one time, more than a hundred horses were stabled below ground.

No records exist of the colliery's overall coal production in the course of its long life [a questionable statement, as annual figures were produced for all collieries]. It surely must have amounted to many millions of tons. The peak was probably reached in the period prior to the Second World War. Both shafts were then winding coal for two shifts a day, the number of men employed being well over a thousand. Output on occasions reached 10,000 tons a week.

The colliery workforce was drawn mainly from Tredegar, and many of the rows of terraced houses were built by the colliery company to house the miners and their families. Those miners living in outlying areas were conveyed to Ty Trist Halt [Tredegar South End] by train. Those living closer to the colliery simply walked to work. Ty Trist had no pithead baths, presumably because so many of the miners lived close to the colliery and the lack of this facility might have been an additional contention for the eventual closure of the colliery.

Mercifully the mine suffered no major disaster throughout its long working life, though mining accidents took their toll in deaths and serious injury, while the general adverse working conditions inevitably impaired the overall health of every miner. In the early days, poor ventilation, naked lights, the emission of methane gas and crude methods of blasting brought serious risk of burning. Old timers recall hearing tales of burned men being rushed to their homes for treatment and of seared body parts smothered with rags. The breathing of foul air gave rise to colliers' lung, when the miner coughed his heart up, crouched over his fireside. Improved mining methods and increased safety reduced many of the early perils, but mechanisation brought new hazards. Until the introduction of dust suppression equipment, dust diseases were extremely injurious. Stone dust produced by blasting was the cause of silicosis. Coal dust created by machine mining was responsible for pneumoconiosis. Ty Trist had its share of sufferers as did every other colliery. The number of those killed, maimed or otherwise disabled can only be a matter of conjecture, as there are no records available. The mining of South Wales coal assuredly extracted a severe toll in blood, a sacrifice so readily forgotten by many, especially politicians. It is still possible to find on some headstones in Cefn Golau and Dukestown cemeteries the foreboding words 'Killed at Ty Trist Colliery'.

When Nationalisation arrived in 1947, the colliery was already on the decline. The production seams were largely exhausted. This does not mean that all the available coal had been mined; it is quite possible that similar amounts remain unworked. This is contained in seams that are too thin, too dirty, of poor quality, or where conditions are geologically unsound. In the mine's early years, the coal supply must have seemed inexhaustible. Many areas were bypassed for various reasons. Coal that was then considered too hard, too soft, too thick, too thin, or perhaps waterlogged could now be mined by mechanical means. Yet to work these isolated areas today would be an almost impossible, and certainly uneconomic, proposition.

Only the Meadow Vein remained in any workable measure towards the close of the pit's lifespan, and was a poor proposition commercially. The Meadow Vein was mechanised, but nevertheless it was obvious that the underlying policy was for an early closure. Borings had been formally put down at various points in the take to a seam thought to be present approx. 30 yards below the Old Coal seam. No immediate plans were envisaged for this seam, and it became evident that closure was imminent. Opposition was loud and prolonged and eventually, presumably as a sop, it was announced that the possibility of working the Garw Vein seam would be investigated. Although thin, little more than two feet thick, it was of high quality. It was decided to explore the potential and mechanical faces were opened up. If it had proved profitable, an immense area was available for exploitation, which would have meant an extension to the life of the colliery. Unfortunately, these hopes were not realised, despite the expenditure of much time, money and effort. The colliery was now regarded as being uneconomic. Uneconomic it may have been, but due regard must be paid to its highly productive past. It must certainly have rewarded the past owners for their original speculation to the amount of many millions of pounds during its long duration of more than 100 years.

And so in 1959 the long prophesied closure of Ty Trist Colliery came to pass. With its demise, the people of Tredegar witnessed the passing of a productive industry synonymous with the very name of Tredegar, which touched the life in some way or other of every man, woman and child of the community.

At the close of this short review of Ty Trist Colliery, it would not be amiss to briefly recapitulate on some facts and figures relating to the mine. The year 1826 witnessed the excavation of Upper Ty Trist, which was the lower of one of a group of shallow pits on the hillside adjoining the Recreation Ground, sunk principally to mine iron ore. It was deepened in 1841 to exploit the Elled Vein seam in conjunction with Ty Trist Nos. 1 and 2. It was duly filled in, some time in the year 1897. In 1834 Ty Trist shaft No. 1 (Downcast) was sunk. The shaft was elliptical in form, having a 15ft. major axis and a 10ft. minor axis. It was dug to a depth of about 60 yards to the Elled Vein seam. In 1868 it was deepened to 221 yards to the Old Coal seam. Also in 1834, Ty Trist Shaft No. 2 (Downcast) was sunk. It too had an elliptical shaped shaft 15ft. x 10ft. and correspondingly was sunk to a depth of approx. 60 yards to engage the Elled Vein seam. It was eventually deepened to 138 yards to the Rhas Las seam. Both Nos. 1 and 2 shafts were drained by a waterwheel pumping system.

As the colliery prospered it was decided in 1868 to sink Shaft No. 3, the Fan Pit Upcast. This shaft was 14ft. in diameter and reached down to the Yard seam, and was later deepened to 221 yards to reach the Old seam. Underground workings employed the Longwall method of headings and stalls in the Old Coal seam, and intensive machine mining in the Meadow Vein. In 1910, the colliery employed 1,220 men. Coal production in 1954 reached 66k. tons and in 1959, the year of closure, the recorded output was 65,723 tons.

CHAPTER NINE

HALL'S ROAD – THE PENAR BRANCH

HISTORY OF HALL'S TRAMROAD (GWR PENAR BRANCH)

Hall's Tramroad, which became the Penar Branch of the GWR, ran from Markham Colliery to Hall's Road Junction on the Western Valley line, just south of Crosskeys. The original Hall's Road ran mainly from Hall's collieries at Mamnoel (or Manmole), south past Waterloo Colliery and through his Pen(n)ar Tunnel to the Crumlin to Newport Canal at Abercarn, where Hall built a basin alongside the Canal of some 500 yards where his coal and iron traffic could be loaded from tramroad wagons onto the canal barges.

The main significant event that begins the history of Hall's Tramroad dates from 1808, when the whole of the Abercarn(e) Estate, including the Ironworks and the Lordship of the Estate, was taken over by the partners in the Cyfarthfa Works of Merthyr Tydfil, namely Richard Crawshay, Joseph Bailey (his nephew) and Benjamin Hall (son-in-law). When Richard Crawshay died in 1810, his son William bought out the other two partners, the partnership finally being dissolved in October 1811 and with the money, Joseph Bailey bought the Nantyglo Ironworks and Benjamin Hall purchased the whole of the Abercarn Estate with the Ironworks and the Lordship of the Manor, giving him ownership of much of the area through which the Monmouthshire Canal (MCC) ran and with powers to develop the situation for his own benefit. Under the terms for the development of the canal,

the MCC agreed to build tramroads (or whatever was needed) to bring traffic to the main canal over a distance of 8 miles, with the rider that if the MCC did not agree to build such connections, they could be built by the traders. As might be expected, the MCC never agreed to spend money building such tramroads, leaving them to be provided and financed by the traders, so relations with the MCC didn't start on good terms. Thus Hall was always intent on outdoing the MCC, though he had another rival in the neighbouring mine owner Sir Thomas Protheroe of Newport, a ruthless businessman who would do anything to outdo his rivals.

One of Hall's first moves was to build a 500 yard long basin serving the main canal alongside the ironworks, where he loaded his traffic brought in by tramroad, either from the ironworks or his collieries into barges to be conveyed to Newport. Protheroe owned the Hafodyrisclawdd Colliery, near to Manmoel, and had made application to the company for a tramroad to be built to link this with the canal, which as usual they had rejected but had agreed to him building it himself, though this would have to be along land already earmarked for Hall's Tramroad from Manmoel. Though there was bitter rivalry between the two, the matter was finally settled by Protheroe agreeing to use Hall's line and paying the necessary charges. It would appear that Hall's line may well have started north of Protheroe's colliery at a quarry under Hall's ownership.

Hall also constructed tramroads to link the various parts of Abercarn Ironworks which were well spaced from each other, with the basin for loading to the canal. Also, a separate section of tramroad was built northwards from 1810 to bring coal from the Cefn Coch and Kendon Collieries in the Newbridge/Crumlin area, with a branch from Cwmdows, down to his basin, so long as favourable terms on charges could be agreed, though this did not form part of the ultimate tramroad taken over by the GWR. The Kendon Colliery had been seeking their own tramroad link to the canal head at Crumlin but were constrained to use Hall's line down to his basin at Abercarn. At the same time, the main trunk route was also extended from Pentwynmawr to Hafodyrisclawdd (completed by 1814) to continue the line from Abercarn, which pre-supposes that Penar Tunnel had also been built by that time.

Though work on his tramroad and commercial activities were proceeding apace, Hall died in 1817, and as his son and successor was still a minor, the business was carried on by his executors but mostly by John Llewellin, agent to the Hall family. A difficult matter that needed resolving related to two brothers, Evan and Lewis Lewis, to whom Hall had leased a small colliery two years before he died. In 1825, they decided to avoid paying the costs of transhipment at Hall's basin and then the MCC charges on the canal, by contriving to use the Penllwyn Tramroad which had recently been built from Pont Syr Dafydd to Nine Mile Point from where the Sirhowy Tramroad could be joined, giving them tramroad conveyance through to Newport. To do this, they had to tunnel under Hall's Tramroad to come up alongside the Penllwyn. When John Jones of Llanarth, the owner of the Penllwyn Tramroad, found out about this, he informed the Halls' agent who immediately instructed the brothers to return to the agreed mode of transport or face penalty of £5,000,

which of course they did; such were some of the ruses and schemes resorted to by the traders to circumvent the high charges being levied at the time.

One of the main problems with the Crumlin Canal was with the water supply which was often insufficient and at other times in winter froze, bringing activities to a stop. In order to allow for these matters, Hall Jnr., who had now taken over the reins, put a resolution to the MCC Committee in October 1826, following a long hot summer that had seen water supply to the canal at a very low level, that he should be allowed to extend his tramroad from Abercarn to join the Sirhowy Tramroad at Risca and thus create an alternative access to Newport when the canal was out of action. This was quickly passed as the inability of the canal to cope at times in summer and winter did nothing to enhance the good relations with the traders, and this alternative would be well received. The MCC in their acceptance made no mention of the problems with the canal, but said that the need was down to the increase in the level of trade on the canal. The MCC were themselves to construct a tramroad from Crumlin to Risca and to allow Hall to join it at a point one mile from the North Wall of Risca Bridge (the Sirhowy Tramroad's Risca Viaduct). This was signed by Sir Charles Morgan (Lord Tredegar) as chairman of the MCC and also by Hall, who stated that he accepted the terms but that if the MCC failed to provide, it would be open to him to provide the necessary at his discretion, which was within the 8 mile clause of the original Act. The tender of Thomas Davies of Eglwysian of 4s10d. per yard (the MCC to provide the rails) was accepted and it is probable that the work was completed to the satisfaction of the MCC and Hall as Davies was then given the contract to construct a further three miles of the Crumlin Tramroad.

The date of completion of Hall's southern section of his tramroad is

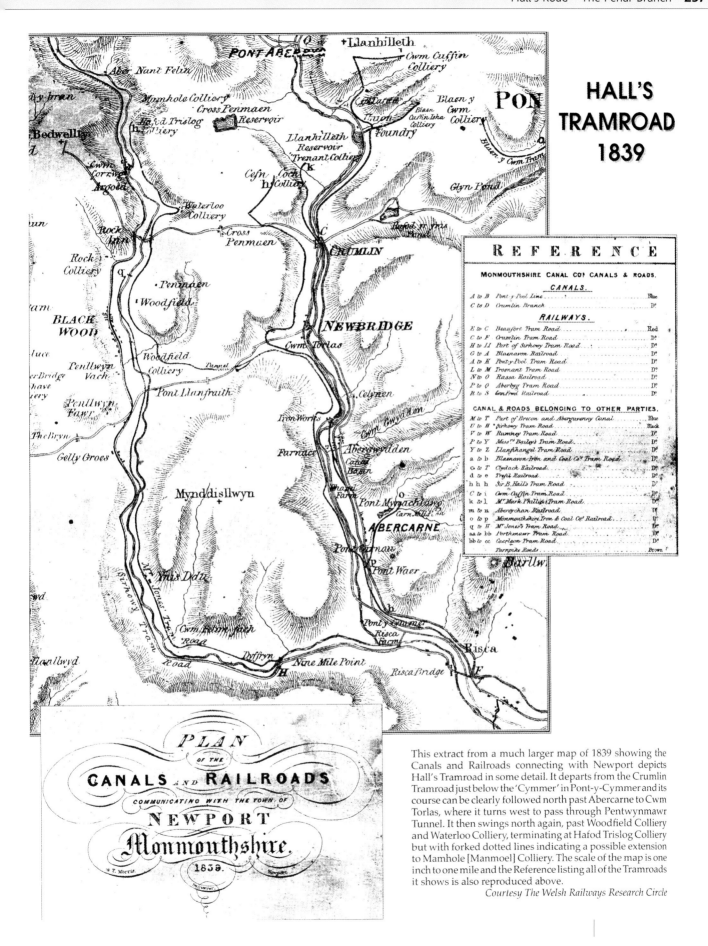

HALL'S TRAMROAD 1839

REFERENCE

MONMOUTHSHIRE CANAL C.º CANALS & ROADS.

CANALS.

A to B	Pont y Pool Line		Blue
C to D	Crumlin Branch		D.º

RAILWAYS.

E to C	Beaufort Tram Road		Red
C to F	Crumlin Tram Road		D.º
H to LL	Part of Sirhowy Tram Road		D.º
G to A	Blaenavon Railroad		D.º
A to K	Pont-y-Pool Tram Road		D.º
L to M	Trosnant Tram Road		D.º
N to O	Rassa Railroad		D.º
P to Q	Aberbeg Tram Road		D.º
R to S	Canford Railroad		D.º

CANAL & ROADS BELONGING TO OTHER PARTIES.

M to T	Part of Brecon and Abergavenny Canal		Blue
U to H	Sirhowy Tram Road		Black
V to W	Rumney Tram Road		D.º
P to Y	Mess.ʳˢ Bailey's Tram Road		D.º
Y to Z	Llanfihangel Tram Road		D.º
a to b	Blaenavon Iron and Coal C.º Tram Road		D.º
C to T	Clydach Railroad		D.º
d to e	Trefil Railroad		D.º
h h h	Sir B. Hall's Tram Road		D.º
C to i	Cwm Cuffin Tram Road		D.º
k to l	M.ʳ Mark Phillips Tram Road		D.º
m to n	Abercarn Railroad		D.º
o to p	Monmouthshire Iron & Coal C.º Railroad		D.º
q to H	M.ʳ Jones's Tram Road		D.º
aa to bb	Porthmawr Tram Road		D.º
bb to cc	Caerleon Tram Road		D.º
	Turnpike Roads		Brown

This extract from a much larger map of 1839 showing the Canals and Railroads connecting with Newport depicts Hall's Tramroad in some detail. It departs from the Crumlin Tramroad just below the 'Cymmer' in Pont-y-Cymmer and its course can be clearly followed north past Abercarne to Cwm Torlas, where it turns west to pass through Pentwynmawr Tunnel. It then swings north again, past Woodfield Colliery and Waterloo Colliery, terminating at Hafod Trislog Colliery but with forked dotted lines indicating a possible extension to Mamhole [Manmoel] Colliery. The scale of the map is one inch to one mile and the Reference listing all of the Tramroads it shows is also reproduced above.

Courtesy The Welsh Railways Research Circle

Hall's Road in 1843 showing Collieries served and Connecting Lines.

HALL'S TRAMROAD 1843

Shewing collieries served and connecting lines

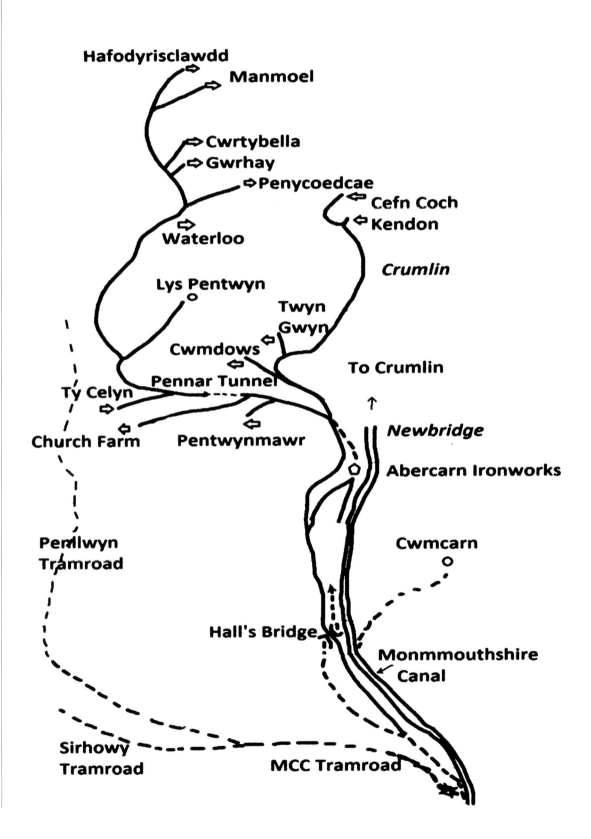

unsure, but is probably 1828 which was when an agreement was dated for the junction between the two lines. There were, however, two problems facing Hall, firstly the fact that his tramroad was at a much higher level than that of the MCC in the area of intersection at Pontywaun and secondly that the gauges of his tramroad and the MCC tramroad which would convey his wagons to Newport were different. How this problem was resolved is not clear but resolved it was. With the alternative means of transport to Newport now provided, use of the canal at Abercarn fell rapidly with most of the traffic using the new and improved tramroad now equipped with larger wagons.

Though use of the canal did doubtless suffer at this time, evidence of its continued use by Hall via his basin occurs in 1833 when the Abercarn Works was let to Daniells & Co., when Hall reserved to himself the right to use the tramroad through the works to reach the canal basin, indicating that the tramroad from Newbridge to Abercarn was still in use. Plans for 1834 and 1839 show the line from Kendon Colliery to be separate from the new tramroad down to Risca and still to be connected to the canal at Abercarn. However, the John Prujean map of 1843 shows the Kendon line having a junction with the line down to Risca, whereas the Mynyddislwyn Tithe Map of 1845 shows the Kendon line abandoned.

The MCC's tramroad from Risca to Crumlin was completed about the end of July 1828, providing unbroken tramroad communication from Newport to the top of the Western Valley. In 1829, it was realised that it would be quite possible for Hall to extend his Kendon branch northwards on the opposite side of the valley to their line and thus compete with them, so in July 1829, the canal committee contacted the owner of the land over which Hall would have to pass in order to build any extension, offering him £300 a year over 20 years if he refused Hall

permission to pass over his land, an offer he readily accepted.

In May 1830, Hall applied to the MCC for permission to cross their new tramroad to provide a new connection between his extended tramroad and the Abercarn Works. Though this was considered to be an attack on potential trade onto their (MCC) new tramroad, this was eventually agreed.

In 1836, Hall let the Abercarn Colliery (adjacent to the basin) and a colliery at Cwmcarn to the new Monmouthshire Iron & Coal Co.(MICC Co.), who created their own tramroad connection into the latter colliery from the canal at Pontywaun Bridge. Hall's Tramroad ran parallel with the canal at this point but well above the MCC tramroad. In August 1838, the MICC Co. asked the MCC for permission to build a bridge over the canal to enable them to load coal onto Hall's line rather than onto the canal. This the MCC agreed to only at such times that the canal was out of action, but the matter was never resolved as the MICC Co. went bankrupt within a year of the request.

Though a locomotive had run down the Sirhowy Tramroad to Newport at the end of 1829 and been put into successful usage on the line thereafter, it was not until May 1840 that the MCC decided it was time to introduce locomotive haulage onto its tramroads. After due deliberation of the implications, it was decided that the whole tramroad would need to be relaid with stronger platerails to bear the increased weight of the locomotives. In 1845, the MCC obtained an Act empowering it to use only its own locomotives on the line, thus avoiding damage and problems with machines over which they had no control. In order to capitalise on this, the Act empowered them to purchase or lease any private tramroads connecting into theirs. The three years allowed by the Act had passed before any progress was made and they needed to return to Parliament for a renewal of their powers in 1848, when they also changed the title of the company to the Monmouthshire Railway & Canal Co. (MRCC).

In November 1848, the MRCC gave notice to all the freighters and other tramroad owners that as from 1 August 1849, all wagons running on their line would need to comply with an improved specification, a copy of which was served with the notice. This caused great consternation among the freighters who were using a large variety of different wagon types, many of their own design, not fitted with buffers and not suitable for locomotive haulage, even at the low speed of 10mph allowed. The new wagons needed to be fitted with a form of wheel designed by the Ebbw Vale Works and capable of running either on a plateway or on a line of standard gauge edge-rails, a design which had been available for some time. The MRCC gave further notice that after the same deadline, only locomotive haulage would be allowed on any part of the line, meaning an end to horse haulage, a massive change.

The implications of these notices were sent to the Commissioners of Railways who sent Capt. J.L.A. Simmonds to examine the whole question of locomotive haulage on a plateway. He reported that in 1828, 96,230tons of coal had been brought onto the MRCC line from Hall's Tramroad and that the main freighters on that line – Thomas Powell of Hafod-yr-Isclawdd, Martin Morrison of Cwm Dows and W.S. Cartwright of Waterloo Colliery – had in use 560, 240 and 210 non-standard wagons which would have to be taken out of use to comply with the MRCC directive. The MRCC were forced to withdraw their directive because of the massive effect on the freighters' wagon fleets, and also because they did not have sufficient locomotives to do the work involved themselves. This situation did not last long and in January 1850, the MRCC were able to renew the directive, much to the consternation of the Hall's

Road users who had been slow to take the necessary steps to upgrade their fleet of wagons.

At the point where Hall's Tramroad passed over the MRCC line at Pontywaun, the MRCC had insisted that they should have the responsibility for constructing the actual arch over their track, though Hall would be paying for the bridge structure, At the time of that decision, the MRCC line was only intended to be single but under the new proposals to lay double track all the way from Newport to Beaufort, the arch under Hall's track needed to be widened for which his permission needed to be obtained. This was not without problems as there were some 300 loaded wagons passing down the valley with an equal number returning empty each day and the delays incurred while the necessary building work was carried on were substantial. The matter was finally settled by laying double track to both sides of the bridge but retaining only single track under the bridge with a policeman (signalman) stationed at the bridge to control the sets of points necessary for the passage of trains over the single section while it obtained.

Following the terms of the 1845 Act, under which the MRCC now had powers to purchase or lease connecting lines into their line, in September 1852, a sub-committee examined Hall's line with a view to leasing it, but found that to bring it up to the necessary standard would cost some £20,000, an untenable position which caused the whole idea to be dropped. A proposal to allow Hall to construct his own plateway alongside the MRCC line through to Newport was also dropped.

At a special meeting called on 1 June 1853, the MRCC announced their intention to convert their plateways into standard gauge railways as soon as the wheel arrangements on the traders' wagons could be altered. Thomas Brown, resident engineer of the Ebbw

Vale Works, now taken over by the Coalbrookdale Company of Shropshire, announced that his company was about to take over Hall's Tramroad on lease and gave an assurance that all wagons would be fitted with suitable wheels and the tramroad upgraded to railway standards. Hall's Tramroad was effectively leased to the Ebbw Vale Iron Co. on 29 July 1853, the lease to run for 20 years at an annual rental of £30, the low rent reflecting the high level of expenditure necessary to upgrade the line. Also within the terms of the lease was a clause binding the Ebbw Vale Co. to charge the same rates as applicable on the MRCC line.

Despite Thomas Brown's assurance that all the wagons running over Hall's Tramroad would be converted by the prescribed date, there were considerable problems in financing this with the traders and in November 1854, an agreement was obtained with the MRCC for a siding to be constructed at the south end of Hall's Road long enough to accommodate all the wagons coming down the tramroad so that their contents could be tipped from the higher level into the newer MRCC wagons on the parallel track below. Large sections of Hall's Road remained unaltered by the Ebbw Vale Co., though the northern section was probably upgraded for the opening of the Taff Vale Extension of the Newport, Abergavenny and Hereford Railway at Penar Junction in 1858, which afforded a new connection with Newport Docks via Pontypool, while Ebbw Vale Works also became better connected via the Crumlin Jn. to Llanhilleth link line into the Western Valley line through Aberbeeg.

In May 1860, the MRCC announced that as from 1 October that year, it would be upgrading its line to a full standard gauge railway, and completely withdrawing the use of combined wheel arrangements, thus forcing any connecting line, such as the Sirhowy and Rumney railways, to do likewise. By 1865, with all the necessary lines upgraded,

the GWR entered into arrangements with the Sirhowy Railway to obtain running powers over their line from Tredegar Junction Lower to Nine Mile Point and then over the MRCC line to Risca and on to Newport for their traffic to the South Wales Railway, which would have further consequences for the later Hall's Road line.

Hall, by this time Lord Llanover, died in April 1867 and when the Ebbw Vale Co. lease expired in 1873 it was unlikely that the southern section of Hall's Tramroad was carrying a significant amount of traffic at the expense of the line through Penar Junction. Also the Ebbw Vale Co.'s interest in extending the Kendon branch northwards to access Ebbw Vale never went any further.

Following the difficulties incurred by the MRCC, the MRCC shareholders eventually succumbed to the advances of the GWR in 1875, having ignored many demands to take up offers to purchase the Sirhowy Company, who in 1876 sold out to the London & North Western Railway (LNWR) as part of their advance through from Abergavenny to Merthyr. At the time, relations between the GWR and LNWR were not good and the latter withdrew the GW's running powers over their line from Tredegar Junction to Nine Mile Point, forcing the GW to convey their traffic via Pontypool to Newport and causing congestion problems on their Taff Vale Extension line. Accordingly, in October 1877, the GWR agreed a lease for 1,000 years with Lady Llanover to upgrade and use Hall's Tramroad from Penar Junction through to Hall's Road Junction at Crosskeys for the future transport of their Aberdare coal traffic through to their main line at Newport, now taken over from the South Wales Railway in 1863 and changed from broad to standard gauge in 1872.

Even before the negotiations with Lady Llanover were completed, the GWR and LNWR came to an agreement under which the GW regained its running

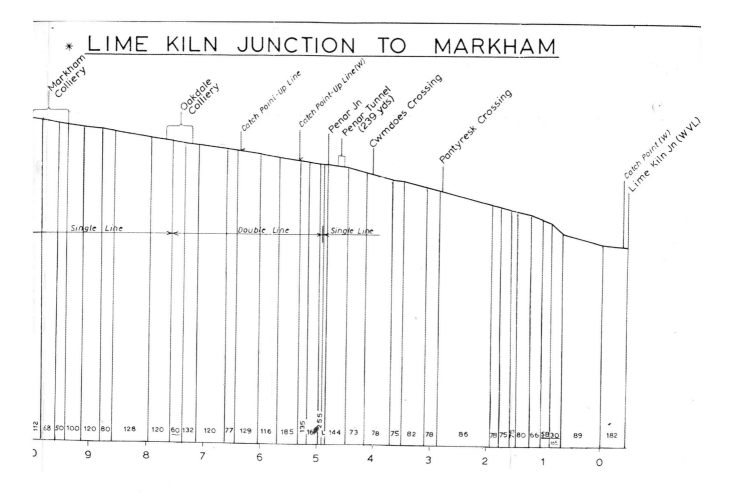

powers along the former Sirhowy line but the only work carried out to upgrade their new line was at Penar Junction, near Pentwynmawr, where first the junction was remade and then four sidings for holding traffic were installed. The upgraded line from the new Penar Junction was opened down to Manmoel Colliery in 1886, with traffic being brought north to pass along the Taff Vale Extension line either towards Pontypool or Aberdare. In 1881, the GWR took powers to upgrade the line south of Manmoel Colliery which included rebuilding Penar Tunnel to take locomotives during which it would be shortened from 407 to 306 yards. It was also intended to do away with Hall's Viaduct at Pontywaun and to make a new junction between Hall's line and the Western Valley line north-west of the viaduct, but these plans were never taken up.

However, in the mid years of the first decade of the new century, plans were announced by the Tredegar Iron Co. (TIC) for the opening of three new collieries to replace the exhausted collieries at the north end of the Sirhowy Valley, these being at Markham, Oakdale (both served off Hall's Road) and at Wyllie on the Sirhowy line. Apparently, at this time the LNWR approached the TIC suggesting that in view of the close proximity of the newly planned Oakdale colliery to the Sirhowy Valley line, they build a connecting line between the two, but this was rejected in view of the existence of the Hall's Road line which was available through to Crosskeys and thence to Newport. In truth, there was a board member of the TIC who was also on the GWR Board and as the TIC were about to sign a contract for the supply of coal to the GWR for its locomotives, they were not going to engage with the LNWR on the matter.

Between 1907-11, the new pits at Oakdale and Markham were sunk, and the railway extended from Manmoel to a point opposite Markham Colliery at 9m.54ch., though it was further extended a train length beyond the new Markham inlet to the branch end at 10m.22ch. in October 1914. The new pits were opened in 1912, by which time the GWR had upgraded the infrastructure, including rebuilding the Penar Tunnel so that a more modern railway existed to serve the collieries remaining open along the line, with the connection into Abercarn Ironworks. From 1909, the original viaduct at Pontywaun over the Western Valley line was rebuilt and realigned in time for the opening of the new Cwmcarn Colliery in 1911 with a nest of three sidings provided at Pontywaun Junction to enable loads to be reduced in serving the new colliery to which there was a steep gradient of 1 in 36, necessitating the splitting of trains. The southern section of the Hall's Road line now carried traffic to and from Cwmcarn traffic on the final mile down to Hall's Road Junction, near Crosskeys on the Western Valley line.

In March 1927, a passenger service was started between Pontypool Road, Penmaen Halt, and Oakdale Halt, just north of Penar Junction, for the conveyance mostly of miners at the local collieries and the section of line between Rhiw-Syr-Dafydd and Colliers Arms was doubled. Oakdale Halt was however closed in September 1932 and the remaining service to Penmaen Halt was also withdrawn. There was also a goods yard with a loading dock at Penmaen, mostly used for loading coal brought in over a tramroad but this seems to have ceased by the end of 1925.

Manmoel, Waterloo, Llanover and other collieries along Hall's Road closed progressively, leaving only the newer collieries at Markham and Oakdale at the northern end of the line. Both became prolific pits, with Markham especially having a glowing reputation for the quality of its locomotive coal supplied to the main GWR and WR depot at Old Oak Common by which the engines working the crack expresses out of Paddington were powered. This traffic however finished in the early 1960s as dieselisation increased and the coal was all treated at the Oakdale Coal Preparation Plant to become prime coking coal for supply to the new Llanwern steelworks, the unwashed coal passing overground over the short distance from Markham to Oakdale where it was washed and blended with the Oakdale produce to make a highly satisfactory blend of prime coking coal which was also later supplied to John Summers at Hawarden Bridge and in later years to Scunthorpe.

In November 1967, under pressure to rationalise routes wherever possible to save on maintenance costs, the Cardiff Division of British Rail saw the opportunity to close the southern section of Hall's Road below Penar Jn. by using the Sirhowy route for the coal from Markham/Oakdale, routing the trains from Penar Jn. to Sirhowy Jn. (and vice versa) over the former Vale of Neath line, but involving reversals at both places. However, what had not been followed through with the NCB was the fact that the two remaining collieries on the Sirhowy route at Nine Mile Point and Wyllie were in the final stages of closure and when these both closed in 1968/9, there was no originating traffic left on the Sirhowy line, other than that from Oakdale, the Aberdare traffic having been diverted via the Abercynon line, Radyr and Cardiff when the Vale of Neath line was closed as a through route in 1964. The southern section of Hall's Road was therefore re-opened in May 1970 (with some re-instatement necessary) so that the Sirhowy route could be closed in its entirety. The Hall's Road route remained open until the closure of Oakdale in 1989. In the meantime Markham coal had been taken by underground link into Oakdale in 1979, as had that from North

Celynen, raising Oakdale to become the largest producing pit in the South Wales coalfield, but like all the others it failed to survive the 1984-5 strike for more than four years, and the last train, an MGR to Llanwern, ran on 26 August 1989. Odd remnants are all that now remain of the line, such as a crossing and bridge north of Crosskeys.

LOCATION ANALYSIS

MARKHAM COLLIERY

Markham Colliery (more fully Markham's Navigation Colliery) was opened between 1910 and 1913 when the first coal was raised, by the Tredegar Iron & Coal Company, and was named after one of the company's directors, Sir Arthur Basil Markham. The colliery had its origins in the fact that the company's pits in the north end of the Sirhowy Valley were

rapidly becoming exhausted at the start of the twentieth century, when they decided to probe the untapped steam coal seams of the Lower and Middle Coal Measures in the central Sirhowy Valley. Leases to the mineral rights in Lord Tredegar's land between Hollybush and Ynysddu were obtained and three new pits sunk at Markham, Oakdale and Wyllie. The Tredegar Company set up a subsidiary company, the Markham's Steam Coal Company, specifically to run this pit, which had a mineral take of 1.8 square miles, limited in the south by Oakdale, in the north-west by Pochin and Elliott and in the east by a geological fault. Sinking of the two shafts began in 1910, the first coal being raised in 1913 from seams up to 60 feet thick.

Two pits were sunk, 40 yards apart and 6 yards in diameter. The No. 1 South Pit was 609 yards deep and No. 2 North Pit 615 yards, accessing the Old Coal (Five-Feet Gellideg) seam, the Brithdir seam, the No. 2 Rhondda, the Four-Feet and Nine-Feet seams at varying depths. Both shafts were used to wind coal, handling either 24 men or 3 tons of coal per wind, using electrically driven

A panoramic view of the Sirhowy Valley, the first showing Markham colliery (centre right) with the Sirhowy line running lower centre with Markham Village Halt visible. At this point the two lines are extremely close, but one is GWR and the other LMS. Opened by the Tredegar Iron & Steel Co., it became a major supplier of locomotive coal to the GWR, and was much prized at Old Oak Common, being used to fuel locos working the GW crack expresses. Courtesy Gerald Davies

MARKHAM COLLIERY, SIRHOWY VALLEY.   W.5538

machinery, one of the first South Wales pits to be so equipped. Much importance was attached to miners' welfare and a model village was laid out in the nearby Sirhowy Valley, equipped with a railway station. The staff level at the opening of the pit in 1913 was 2,591 with an annual production of 300,000 tons. Though generally progress in the first three years was satisfactory, the pit was subject to occasional gas bursts. In 1930, pithead baths were installed at a cost of 6d per man per week, these being renewed in 1940.

By 1935, manpower had dropped to 170 surface and 1,230 underground workers, accessing the Big Vein (Four-Feet), Upper Rhas Las (Upper Nine-Feet) and the Old Coal seams. The principal markets for Markham coal at this time were the Great Western and Italian Railways, the coal being highly rated at the main GWR Old Oak Common depot for use on the crack steam hauled expresses. Manpower held steady for the next 20 years at around 1,300 but was down to 1,000 by 1962 and fell year on year to about 600 by 1985.

Records show 1930 to have been a peak production year at 600,000 tons, but this was halved by Nationalisation and remained at around 300,000 tons until 1961 after which it fell away to around 190,000 until the colliery closure. The fall in production is explained by the fact that the Three-Quarter (Lower Six-Feet) was abandoned in 1959, the Yard (Upper Six-Feet) seam in 1960, and the Big Vein (Four-Feet) seam in 1967. In 1978 the colliery was working the Meadow Vein and Old Coal seams at a depth of up to 713 yards. Various improvements were made to equipment through the 1960s and '70s; the steam winders were converted to electric power during the '60s and in

A closer view of the colliery in its Sirhowy Valley setting with Markham Village, built for the colliery workers on the opposite hillside with the Sirhowy branch running in front.
Courtesy Gerald Davies

Four views of the new colliery in course of construction around 1912, the year of opening. The shafts have been sunk and support buildings completed, but production has not yet started.
Courtesy Gerald Davies

Markham's Collieries, Argoed

1977, part of the coalface became the first in South Wales to be equipped with coalface electric lighting. There were then three coalfaces in operation with 10 miles of underground roadways equipped with 3.25 miles of high speed conveyors. Output per manshift was then 6.2 tons and overall for the colliery 1.8 tons.

In 1979, Markham became part of a £9m development plan for Oakdale Colliery and a new 800 yard underground link roadway was driven between the two pits, enabling Markham coal to be washed, treated and raised at Oakdale. For many years this had been carried out following over-ground transport by rail. A similar linking of North Celynen with Oakdale in 1977 now made Oakdale the largest production unit in the South Wales coalfield. By now, Merry-Go-Round rail operation had been introduced with steelworks markets comprising Llanwern, John Summers (Hawarden Bridge) and

Scunthorpe (after the 1984-5 strike). The colliery produced Type 204 Coking Steam Coal, low volatile, medium to strong caking, suitable for use for steam raising in power stations, though the market for use in ships and locomotives had long since died. The coal was also highly suitable for coking blends in steelworks which was the use now exploited.

In 1981, the pit was working the Meadow Vein and Old Coal seams with a target output per manshift of 10.6tons, equating to 2.7 tons overall. The daily tonnages produced were 720 from the Meadow Vein and 700 from the Old Coal seams. However the production was dirty and only half the yield was saleable after treatment. By now there were only 450 men working underground with about 90 on the surface. By 1983, there was a loss of £3.90 for every ton produced. Following the 1984-5 strike, Markham only reached 76 per cent of its production

The twin shafts stand proud at Markham.
Alastair Warrington Collection.

A view at the bottom of one of the shafts with miners going on duty. Following the cessation of loco coal traffic in 1961/2, all Markham's coal went for washing at nearby Oakdale and was then used to produce prime coking coal for supply to Llanwern. (Courtesy Gerald Davies)

BOND AT MARKHAM'S COLLERIES, Nr TREDEGAR 62.

targets and in June 1985 was losing £30.30 per ton produced, with mounting problems on the coalfaces, so that the colliery was closed in September 1985.

Until 1904, the railway had terminated north of Llanover Colliery (south of Markham) at 9m 12ch (from Hall's Road Jn.), but with the opening of Markham it was extended to 9m 54ch. This however was only half way along the outward sidings and in October 1914, the line was further extended to 10m 22ch, a train length in advance of the north end of the

An interesting wagon label for a 20ton wagon of loco coal bound for Bournemouth shed, dated 9 May 1967, all Southern steam ending on 9 July that year. This would have marked the end of the market in loco coal from Markham, which was a top quality coal much prized at Old Oak Common. Following the end of the market in loco coal, unless there was a market for large coal, all coal from Markham was sent to Oakdale for washing. Previously, wagons of large coal were conveyed front from Markham and taken through to Rogerstone, but as the market in large coal dried up, it would have been crushed and used in the steelworks blend. Alastair Warrington Collection

inwards sidings. These consisted of three long sidings holding 218 wagons which were fed by gravity down through six

DATE OF WEIGHING.............
DATE OF DESPATCH.............
Seller and Place of Weighing:
NATIONAL COAL BOARD   S.W. DIVISION
No. 6 Area   **MARKHAM Colliery**

A/c

To BOURNEMOUTH

MOTIVE POWER DEPOT

4	4	5

Consignee   B. T. C , Western Region

Type of Fuel   LARGE

WAGON NUMBER		SALE WEIGHT OF FUEL
716730	**H**	14 11
TARE 7 3 c		T 11 c

Unfortunately, no trains servicing the colliery ever seem to have been photographed and only views of enthusiast specials have been found. The first is of an SLS Special to the Monmouthshire Valleys on 11 July 1953 with Pontypool Road's 6403 and two auto coaches, and the second eighteen years later is of a three car DMU on a special for the Gloucestershire Railway Society on 19 June 1971. Both trains are standing on the line north of the colliery used for setting back empties into the reception sidings. S.Rickard/J&J Collection & Malcolm James

roads under the loading screens into three outwards sidings beyond, which held 156 wagons.

HAFOD-YR-ISCLAWDD

Hafod-Yr-Isclawdd Colliery, originally owned in 1810 by Sir Thomas Protheroe, may well have been the northern terminus of Hall's Tramroad, though a bitter rivalry existed between the two. Protheroe had applied to the MCC to build a tramroad from this colliery to the canal but the MCC, as always, refused but authorised Protheroe to build his own. In order to do so, it would have run over the same land that Hall was using for his tramroad from Manmoel to the Canal, and after much dissension, Protheroe agreed to use Hall's line and to pay him full charges for so doing. Pre-1835, John Yemm and William Protheroe were joint owners with Sir Thomas Protheroe, but

in that year it was owned by Yemm and William Powell, who became the sole owner in 1839. The mine is shown on the 1843 map and worked the Mynyddislwyn seam, possibly linked with Hafod Trisylod. It was still listed in 1878 but was not in 1888.

MANMOEL COLLIERY

Hall's Tramroad was extended to serve Manmoel (or Manmole) Colliery, owned by Benjamin Hall himself, in 1814. Manmoel Colliery was composed of a series of levels that worked the Mynyddisllwyn seam from early in the nineteenth century. By 1860, ownership had passed to Sir Thomas Phillips and by 1878 to the Manmoel Colliery Co. By 1888, it was owned and managed by Christopher Pond who in 1888 sank the nearby Llanover colliery (see below). In 1896, Manmoel is recorded

Manmoel Colliery was the end of the Hall's Road branch until Markham was developed in 1911, when the branch was lengthened by a mile and a half. Manmoel consisted of a series of levels cut into the hillside from which the coal was worked. Wagons branded C. Pond, the owner being Christopher Pond, can be seen positioned to receive this coal with views looking south and north. Note the precarious angles of the empty wagons on the back sidings. This view looks south, back down the Valley.
Alastair Warrington Collection.

Looking north along the single line branch from Manmoel Colliery.
Alastair Warrington Collection

as employing 17 men underground and 5 on the surface, with 24/6 in 1900, and 40 men in 1903 producing coking, gas house and manufacturing coals. It had declined by 1907 with only eight men employed, but in 1924 was listed as being re-opened and in 1945 was owned by the Manmoel Colliery Company of Argoed, though with only eight men working underground and one on the surface. It was deleted from the Railway Clearing House records in July 1928 and the sidings were removed by July 1930.

Just north of Manmoel Colliery was Pont Abernant y Felin Quarry Siding, beyond which the tramroad/railway ended until 1911. This consisted of a short loop siding on the east side of the running line, the siding shown as in position by 1915, but closed by 1928.

A close-up of the wagons in the sidings at Manmoel Colliery.
(Alastair Warrington Collection)

A new 10 ton wagon for Manmoel Colliery built by Gloucester Carriage & Wagon Works for the owner C. Pond in Nov. 1885, showing the product of Best House, Gas and Smith's Coal. The builders have applied their own version of the correct spelling. (Alastair Warrington Collection)

Llanover Colliery was a deep mine located about half a mile south of Manmoel. It was opened around 1888 by Christopher Pond and closed in 1936, after which it remained to assist with ventilation and pumping at Markham and Oakdale. There were several levels and small mines between Llanover and the next main deep mine at Oakdale. These were Twyn Simon, Courtybella, Gwrhay and Waterloo Levels. Here seen in full production across the Sirhowy Valley where it was located between Markham and Argoed.

LLANOVER COLLIERY

Just south of Manmoel was Llanover Colliery, sunk to a depth of 551 feet to the Brithdir seam by Christopher Pond around 1888. In 1906, it was purchased by the Bargoed Coal Company, and linked to the neighbouring Abernant Colliery. Records show only 57 men employed in 1913, rising to 310 in 1915 and 500 in 1919. In 1923, it employed 472 and with Abernant produced 250,000 tons of coal. Though still employing 500 men in 1927, it was closed as a production unit in 1929 when it was bought by the Markham

Steam Coal Company to serve as a pumping station to protect both Markham and Oakdale collieries. The two pumps available were both original horizontal cylinder types, steam-operated and capable of pumping 60,000 and 120,000 gallons of water per hour respectively. However, they proved incapable of keeping pace with the requirement with many breakdowns, one of which caused

LLANOVER COLLIERY

The layout at Llanover Colliery. (Alastair Warrington Collection)

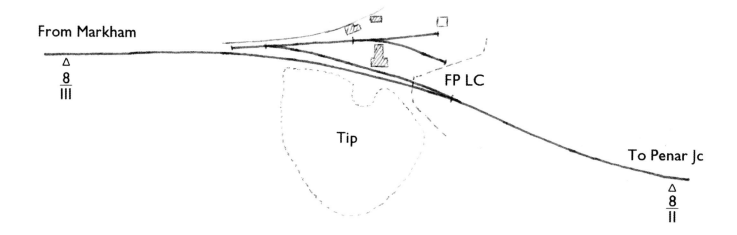

From Markham

$\frac{8}{III}$

FP LC

Tip

To Penar Jc

$\frac{8}{II}$

Llanover Colliery following closure in 1936.
(Alastair Warrington Collection)

80ft of water to rise up one of the Oakdale shafts. As a result, new electric Sulzer pumps were installed at Llanover in 1932, the largest deep well type pumps in the world, each capable of pumping 150,000 gallons per hour.

While the colliery was in production, there were five short inwards sidings at the north end, feeding through the screens to a similar five short outward sidings. Around the east side of the screens was a tramroad bringing in

A VIEW FROM the hillside of Church Crossing, south of Llanover Colliery, at Courtybella (Cwrtybella), Argoed, located on Hall's Road with a siding coming off to the east to serve the Gwrhay Colliery with wagons visible mostly branded W.H. Lever & Co., with one John Edwardson, both companies shown as of Cardiff. (Courtesy Gerald Davies)

CWTYRBELLA CHURCH, NR. OAKDALE.

General View, Argoed

Another view of the same location from nearer ground level showing the Hall's Road line as it curves northwards approaching Church Crossing, for which there is a warning sign on the extreme right, where the siding into Gwrhay Colliery goes off.
(Gerald Davies Colln)

other coal and there was also a long loop siding running alongside the single running line. North of the complex, the connection into the inwards sidings was named Bargoed North GF, though in practice it was known as Llanover North. It was taken out of use in April 1936, when the connection was taken out and the loop converted into a stop-blocked siding. At the south end of the colliery, exit was controlled through Bargoed South GF, known as Llanover South, and as Llanover GF from 1936, when it was retained to serve sidings serving the Pumping Station, the colliery sidings and screens being removed, leaving just three short stop-blocked sidings and a long loop siding.

TWYN SIMON COLLIERY

Immediately south of the outlet from Llanover Colliery was Twyn Simon Colliery, owned by the Bowditch Brothers. Two loop sidings are shown on the east side of the running line which were put into use in July 1922 and ceased operation in August 1931. In production, it had worked the Mynyddislwyn seam for house and manufacturing coals, employing only seven men on closure.

CWRT-Y-BELLA (COURTYBELLA) COLLIERY

At 8m 6ch from Hall's Road Jn. was Church Level Crossing, protected by Courtybella GF, which remained in use until March 1965. South of this was Courtybella Siding, a loop siding on the west side of the single line between 7m.73ch. and 8.3ch., which was probably also removed in 1965 as derelict.

Cwrt-y-Bella Colliery was a level driven into the Mynyddislwyn seam about 1820 by Sir Thomas Protheroe. In 1842 it is on record as employing 130 miners, including ten under the age of thirteen years. Along with the Gwrhay Level, it was owned in 1888 by J. Edmunds and J. Lewis and in 1912 by W. Lewis, who employed a combined 90 miners at both levels in 1913. It remained in existence beyond Nationalisation and was worked as a small level under license from the NCB. In 1842, the Courtybella Colliery School was established by the owner Sir Thomas Phillips, a future Mayor of Newport. He was one of the leading figures in the establishment of schools for colliery children in Wales, and founded the first colliery school in the county.

GWRHAY COLLIERY

As it is clear that Hall extended his tramroad to cater for new mines being brought in to use, it may have been that originally the limit had been the Gwrhay, north of where Oakdale would be developed in 1912. The Gwrhay Colliery is on record as working the Mynyddislwyn seam for house coal in 1809 and was in existence and requiring transport before Manmoel and Hafod-yr-Isclawdd. The earliest record of ownership is 1822 when it was owned by Jeremiah Jones, passing to Moses Moses in 1827 and to Aaron Crossfield in 1841. It was clearly shown on the 1843 map. Between 1858-70 it was owned by Roger Lewis. It was not recorded as operating between 1878-82 when owned by D. Lewis & Co., but was back in business in 1884-93 under Jones, Lewis & Co. In 1900, it was owned by Lewis Lewis and employed ten miners underground with one on the surface. In 1902, ownership passed to the Gwrhay Colliery Co., with 34 men employed, this increasing to 52 in 1905. In 1907, ownership passed to Oakdale Navigation Collieries Ltd. (a subsidiary of the Tredegar Iron & Coal Co.) with 36 men employed. In 1908, it was shown merged with the Waterloo level with 159 men underground and 10 on the surface. Although still shown on a 1921 map, it probably ceased as a production unit when Waterloo Pit came on stream.

WATERLOO LEVEL

The original Waterloo Level, at the Gwrhay, was opened in 1815 to work the Mynyddislwyn seam and was owned in turn by Davies & Morgan, W. Griffiths & Co., Davis Brothers, W.S. Cartwright, and the Waterloo Colliery Co., which became a subsidiary of the TIC. In 1842, when owned by Cartwright, it employed 90 men and the coalface was 1.75miles from the entrance. In 1900, the Old Waterloo (as it had become known to differentiate it from the newer house coal colliery) was owned by the Blackwood Coal Co., employing only thirteen men underground and four on the surface, but by 1907, the figures were 78 and 10. The level closed in 1917, being replaced by the Waterloo pit.

OAKDALE & WATERLOO COLLIERIES

The sinking of the new Oakdale Colliery began in 1907 and the first steam coal from the Black Vein seam was produced in 1911. Waterloo Colliery, Oakdale's house coal partner, was sunk in 1911. The two shafts at Oakdale were 626 and 650 yards deep respectively, some of the deepest in the coalfield, while Waterloo

needed to be sunk to a far shallower level of 282 yards to access the Brithdir seam for best quality house coal. Both collieries were run by Oakdale Navigation Collieries Ltd., a subsidiary of the TIC. Oakdale had cost £300,000 to equip by the TIC who recouped the money from the value of shares in the new Oakdale Company. Oakdale generated its own electricity and later supplied Markham and Wyllie with electric power.

Several geological problems were initially encountered at Oakdale, including coming up against unworkable rider coal (where one seam sits above another) instead of the Rhas Las steam coal seam, though the problem was short-lived; higher levels of water than anticipated; and striking large areas of barren and disturbed grounds. The coalfield was so buoyant in 1914/5 that it was difficult to recruit enough men to work at the coalface, resulting in the colliery management having to pay the highest wages in the coalfield in 1915, Oakdale by now producing some 600,000 tons a year. Because of the large quantities of small coal mined, a washery was built at both Oakdale and Markham in 1918.

Both Oakdale and Markham were provided with garden villages a short distance from the collieries, all houses having bathrooms. Prince Albert visited the area in 1920 and was much impressed with the facilities provided and the quality of the electrical equipment. Welfare arrangements were much improved following representations made by Oakdale at the South Wales Miners' Federation Annual Conference of 1925, which called for underground work to be limited to seven hours per day, improved allowances to be made of free coal to miners' widows, invalid and unemployed miners, and that all injured miners receive full pay. The lock-outs of 1921 and General Strike of 1926 were to cause great hardship to the mining communities across South Wales. The defeats suffered by the miners and the hardening of

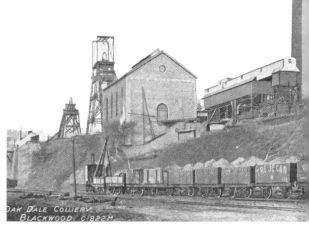

akdale Collieries, Argoed

Oak Dale Colliery, Blackwood. C1822M

Oakdale Colliery, Blackwood, Mon.

Four views of the new Oakdale Colliery taken around 1912, the first showing the creation of the curving embankment into the colliery, the second showing wagons of spoil which will be dumped to help bring ground up to level and the fourth showing the pristine buildings of the new construction. (All Courtesy Gerald Davies)

attitudes among the mine owners caused serious disillusionment with the South Wales Miners' Federation and members began to leave in droves. The lodges in the Tredegar Company pits (under the chairmanship of Aneurin Bevan) decided to hold a 'show card' day in 1929 to quantify membership of the union. When this was carried out at Markham and Oakdale, the management sacked all 47 members of the Federation committee on the grounds that they had interfered with the privacy of the workers. Such was the state of worker/management relations at that time.

After a bumper start to the new decade with production of 900,000 tons in 1930, there was a fall in demand with the Depression so that by 1934/5 it was down by a third to 600,000, and the number employed had fallen from 2,231 in 1930 to 1,843 in 1935. Problems began in 1931 with the colliery only working two or three days a week. There were further problems in 1932 when the colliery was found to be poaching coal belonging to Crumlin Navigation, which resulted in 400 men being laid off and further unrest. Pithead baths costing 6d. per week, and a canteen, were provided from 1936, these being extended in 1941.

In 1939, Oakdale was recorded as working the Meadow Vein (6-7 feet thick), Old Coal, Big Vein (3 feet), Yard and Rhas Las (6-8 feet) seams with a workforce in 1943 of just over 1,500. By comparison, the Brithdir Red Ash seam worked by Waterloo Colliery was only 2ft 10in thick. Problems were being encountered with water from the rocks above the Brithdir seam and four new pumps, each capable of pumping out 80,000 gallons per hour, were installed. More water was met at a depth of 400 yards and more again in the Rhas Las and Old Coal seams, for which further pumps needed to be installed with a 42,000 gallon capacity. There were 24 miles of underground roadways in the mine, some of which were subject to enormous pressure especially in the Rhas Las roadways in an area where the Meadow Vein was being worked 50 yards underneath.

At Nationalisation, Oakdale employed just over 2,000 men, exact figures being 1,772 underground and 320 on the surface, working the Big Vein (machine cut), Meadow Vein (hand and machine

cut), and the Upper Rhas Las. New conveyor systems were installed and the longwall coalface method of coal extraction was introduced into the pit. Production was now down to just under 400,000 tons a year, in comparison with 900,000 in 1930. The period from Nationalisation to the early 1960s was one of relative stability, though it saw the final

Opening of Oakdale Colliery. Special train, composed of four wheeled clerestory coaches, bringing invited guests.

Oakdale Colliery was sunk between 1907-11 when the first coal was raised from the Black Vein seam. It was a major colliery in the Monmouthshire Valleys and remained open until 1989, being the last to close. In 1979 and 1981 respectively, underground connections were made with Markham and Celynen North, making Oakdale the largest production unit in South Wales. (SLS)

Oakdale Colliery, Blackwood

Oakdale Colliery, Near Blackwood

Oakdale colliery just after opening by the Tredegar Iron & Coal Co. with a large supply of its own 10 and 12 ton branded wagons awaiting loading. Very many of these would then be bound for Newport Docks.

system at Oakdale was working on the Meadow Vein seam at a thickness of seven feet on a face length of 465 feet, with a manpower of 60 men along the coalface with a daily advance of 45 inches.

In 1958, the NCB estimated that Oakdale had reserves of 51.5m tons, mostly in the Meadow Vein seam. Water was still a problem and the Old Coal (Five Feet / Gellideg) seam was prone to inrushes of water from underground lakes, one of which overwhelmed the pumps in 1959 and the pit was only saved by diverting the water into old workings. In 1962, the winding engines were converted from steam power to electricity and in 1972 a new central washery was opened. In the mid-1970s there were six coalfaces available to be worked but only four were worked at a time. There were three in the Old Coal seam, one in the Big Vein and two in the Meadow Vein.

The 1970s saw a reduction in the colliery manpower of about 500 miners, with production figures of only 210,000

years of the production of locomotive coal and a change in the early 1960s to the production of prime coking coal for the new Llanwern Steelworks. Staffing levels remained constant at just under 2,000. As an indication of the nature of the coalface operation, a 1956 investigation into power loading at the coalface showed that one

Another view from the same vantage point as the last, but this time from the 1920s showing the single road repair depot which had been constructed on the made-up land alongside the inwards sidings. This depot would be used for housing the colliery shunting loco and internal user wagons as well as other equipment. The picture is dated by the GW 20 ton steel bodied Loco Coal wagons on the inner road, introduced from 1920 under the aegis of Felix Pole when General Manager and used for the conveyance of coal to GWR depots for their steam engines. All other wagons visible are 10 and 12 ton wooden bodied.

With the passage of time and contraction in the number of flows from the colliery, MGR working was introduced, all coal then passing to Llanwern Steelworks. The layout at the colliery was vastly rationalised, a single line sufficing to accommodate the trains involved as can be seen in this 1983 view.

tons in 1974 and 226,000 in 1979/80.

In the late 1970s, the NCB invested an estimated £35m on a modernisation scheme to increase efficiency by reducing non-productive work, eliminating rail charges for over-ground movement of coal to washeries by creating underground links and increasing the amount of men riding underground to raise the time spent at the coalface. Merry-Go-Round working was introduced for the first time, a new rapid loading bunker being installed over the rail track to supply Llanwern, after which all the coal forwarded by rail used this method of transport.

The colliery loading bunker for MGR traffic as seen in the late 1980s. Malcolm James

Colliers Arms Signal Cabin at the north end of the Oakdale complex, which controlled the supply of empty wagons to the Oakdale screens and originally into Waterloo Collieries. Located at 7m.45ch. from Hall's Road Jn., it was opened in 1913 and closed in March 1965. *Gerald Davies*

years without major expansion, the aim being to provide a lifespan of twenty years at a rate of production of 900,000 a year. The plan included driving a new 1,150 yards of roadway to link Oakdale with Markham in 1979 and with Celynen North in 1981. All three pits produced 301A prime coking coals, with a low ash content of 5-9 per cent and a low sulphur content at 0.6-1.5 per cent.

In 1979, it was also agreed to drive 3,179 yards of locomotive roadways and 1,750 yards of conveyor roadways into the former Wyllie Colliery reserves plus a further four roadways from Celynen North. It was estimated that the new complex would have some 24m tons of reserves, half of which would be in the Wyllie area. However, due to adverse geological features, the Wyllie reserves were never reached, a massive setback to the plans for the future of the pit. In 1981, Oakdale was working the Meadow Vein seam, with coalface length varying between 160-241 yards, the Old Coal seam

It was also intended to access 12.3m tons of coal in the former Wyllie Colliery reserves to the south of Oakdale. At that time, Oakdale had a reserve of 12.6m tons which would be exhausted in 10-13

Another view of Colliers Arms from where empty wagons were fed into both Oakdale and Waterloo collieries. This was named after the local public house which can be seen in this photograph. *Garth Tilt*

where the coalface was 221 yards long and the Five Feet seam where the coalface varied between 119-241 yards in length. The saleable yield of coal produced was only 73 per cent and in 1983 the colliery was losing £7.50 on every ton produced. Of a total of 656 men employed at the mine, only 195 were actually working at the coalface, with 192 on development, 268 on other underground activities and 181 on the surface.

The 1984-5 national miners' strike had solid support at Oakdale which made a remarkable recovery when work resumed in March 1985 with 120 per cent of targeted output achieved within a month, output per manshift being just under two tons. Because of problems in the Kent coalfield, Oakdale took on the supply of 5,000 per week to Scunthorpe steelworks, with one MGR train per day. Though in 1985 the colliery made a loss of £7.5m, there was strong hope for the future and new high-tech coalface equipment was installed, with plans to get back to the halcyon days of 900,000 annual production with the level of reserves again quoted as 24m tons, though other collieries in Monmouthshire had closed in the same year. Pit records were being

broken and in one week in November 1986, production reached a record 278,884 tons. Against this positive background, a killer blow was produced when British Coal dismissed the prospect of working the 12.6m tons of Wyllie reserves and abruptly announced the closure of the colliery, stating that if the men failed to accept this, they would lose out on the redundancy to be offered. At the start of the strike in 1984, Oakdale employed 876 men; after the end of the strike and the positive resumption of work this had

A combined train of hoppers (probably for Newport Gwent Coal Concentration Depot) and 21ton Minfits for Llanwern waits to depart as the crew kill time in the days before all traffic was conveyed by MGR. The gates of Rhiw-Syr-Dafydd crossing are closed against the train until departure.

Easing its train under the loading bunker, Type 3 37256 prepares another train of MGR wagons to Llanwern.

risen to 1,400 but the final 1989 figure had again fallen to 873. The closure of Oakdale in August 1989 saw the end of coal mining in Monmouthshire. Demolition of the colliery was completed by the end of March 1990.

Approaching Rhiw-syr-Dafydd with a train of empty MGR wagons is Type 5 diesel 56073. These will be loaded from the bunker and taken to Llanwern Steelworks in this 1980s view. Michael Mensing

The same train, having crossed the level crossing, approaches the loading point at Oakdale.
Michael Mensing

The Oakdale to Scunthorpe MGR service 7E95 which ran in the 1970s and 80s, here loading behind Class 56 56017. Don Gatehouse

History in the making! Five views of the last coal train to leave not only Oakdale, but the Monmouthshire Valleys. This was on 26 August 1989 when my good friend Malcolm James of Rogerstone got up very early to drive to Oakdale and record the historic occasion. The first three views show the last train drawing forward through the loading plant and then the very last wagon to be loaded. The last two views show the train waiting for the crossing gates to be opened at Rhiw-syr-Dafydd and the train passing over the crossing, the 7am service to Llanwern. Malcolm James

Enthusiast specials were sometimes run over colliery lines in South Wales as here with a Class 50 seen at the south end of Oakdale on 12 August 1979. Alastair Warrington Collection

This DMU Special has originated in the London Division and has run through to Colliers Arms, where the track has been recently re-ballasted. Alastair Warrington Collection

There is little colliery activity for the passengers in this weekend special of 5 October 1968 to view with just a few loaded wagons still standing under the screens, before the days of MGR at Oakdale.
Alastair Warrington Collection

A view approaching Colliers Arms.
Alastair Warrington Collection

A section of the overhead loading equipment straddling the double track alongside the colliery.
Alastair Warrington Collection

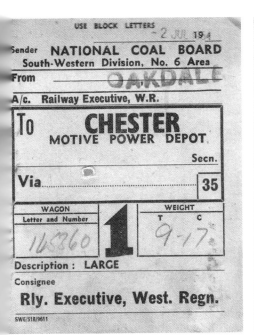

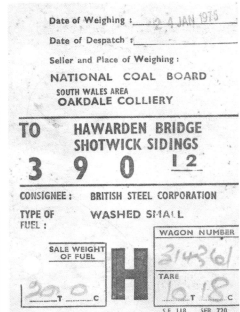

From the days when Western Valley Collieries supplied engine sheds with locomotive coal. Here a wagon label for a 16ton wagon 165360 bound for Chester Shed on 2 July 1954, conveying 9 tons 17cwt of large coal for engine use, when the railway was run by the Railway Executive.

Alastair Warrington Collection

The coal in this wagon of Washed Duff has emanated from Markham Colliery and been washed at Oakdale No. 1 Washery. The date of 3 May 1965 is in the second year of the concentration of Bituminous Coal shipment at Barry Docks, previous to which the coal would probably have been shipped at Newport. The wagon is 75926, a 16 ton unfitted wagon, this basic type being used for all shipment coal as fitted wagons fouled the coal hoists at the docks. Duff was low volatile and would have been bound for a power station, possibly Battersea to where a lot of the coastwise shipment coal was sent from Barry. *Alastair Warrington Collection*

Starting in the early 1970s, Oakdale began supplying coking coal to John Summers of Hawarden Bridge. As a complete trainload ran per day, a special authorisation was made to use 21ton Minfits for the traffic, which were otherwise confined to working in South Wales and Mon. This gave both a trainload of fitted wagons which could run as Class 6, the second highest freight classification at the time (Class 4 being applied to a few flows such as Milford Haven to Provan LPG) , and enabled loads of 20tons per wagon to be achieved as here in wagon no. 314361. The wagons after discharge were also returned empty in trainloads, and later became part of the MGR programme. These wagons were all in a series starting 31XXXX .

Alastair Warrington Collection

PENRHIW COLLIERY

This colliery (full name Penrhiw & Woodfieldside Colliery) was possibly opened as early as 1815 and was located just south of the future Oakdale Colliery, lasting until Oakdale had been in existence for some 14 years. It consisted of a pit and a level into the Mynyddislwyn seam. The earliest record of ownership is in 1893 by W. Baker, who formed the Penrhiw & Woodfieldside Co. to run the mine, which in 1896 employed 79 men underground and 12 on the surface. In 1900, the company was listed with a head office at Bristol. In 1918, it was shown owned by the Penmaen Colliery Co., employing 21 men with an annual production of 12,000 tons in 1923. The colliery seems to have been closed by the company in the following year.

WOODFIELD COLLIERY

South of Penrhiw Colliery and Rhiw Syr Dafydd where a level crossing would

A view of Woodfield Colliery at Blackwood showing the entrance to the mine with drams standing outside and railway wagons in the siding beyond.
(Wayne Hopkins/Alastair Warrington Collection)

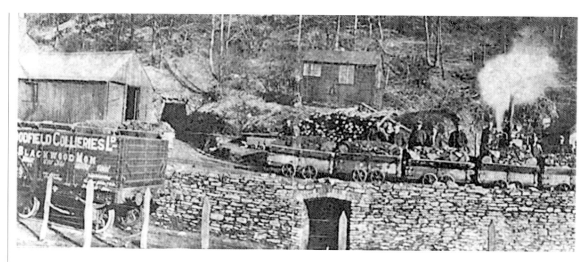

be developed, was Woodfield Colliery, with a location shown as Pontllanffraith. It consisted of two shallow pits into the Mynyddislwyn seam which were 180 and 213 feet deep respectively. It was opened by Powell and Protheroe in 1823 and its traffic passed over Hall's Tramroad to the canal, presumably via Hall's basin. Ownership is shown in 1842 by Sir Thomas Protheroe only with 64 men employed but in 1851 by Thomas Powell only, though it may well be that joint ownership continued throughout. Records for 1860 and 1865 show it owned by J. Powell, in 1890/3 by Thomas Jones of Pontlottyn, in 1895 by W. Baker, in 1905 by B.P. Harris and in 1913 by Woodfield Collieries Co.

Ltd. of Blackwood. It appears to have amalgamated with the Penrhiw Colliery in that year as a joint staffing figure of 57 men with a production of house coal is shown. By 1917, it was in the hands of the Penmaen Colliery Co. which was outside the Monmouthshire & South Wales Coal Owners Association. A figure of 100 men employed is available for 1919, presumably again for the two collieries. Woodfield closed in 1924 and was abandoned in 1928, filled in 1946 and capped in 1976.

The railway layout at Woodfield consisted of a long loop siding with another shorter one on the east side. In April 1915, the running line between Penar Jn. and Oakdale was doubled. Oakdale SB was opened in March 1927 to control the inwards and outwards siding at Woodfield Colliery, between which a new Oakdale Halt was opened also in March 1927 at 6m 67ch, together with a LC at the north end of the single platform, access to which was provided by single crossovers between the running lines. Oakdale Halt was closed in September 1932 when the passenger service to/from Pontypool was withdrawn. The connections into and out of the closed Woodfield Colliery and the crossovers between the running lines were all taken out of use in September 1946 and removed the same day. In June 1980, the line was singled south of 6m 60ch, the previous

A Woodfield Collieries wagon No. 276, advertising the Best House, Gas and Smiths Coal, the usual description displayed on wagons. The wagon was built by Ince Waggon & Ironworks Co. Ltd. (Alastair Warrington Collection)

location of Oakdale SB and the exit from Woodfield Colliery.

PENMAEN HALT

Almost a mile south of Oakdale Halt was Penmaen Halt at 5m 75ch which was open between 1927-32 for the passenger service with Pontypool. A plan of the layout for 1875 shows a single running line with a level crossing near the 6mp, and Penmaen Siding with a loading dock controlled by a ground frame at 5m 73ch. The line curved sharply south-east between the 6 and 5¾mp and at the north end of the curve was the entrance to Tir Philkins Colliery (see below).

PENMAEN COLLIERY

The exact location of this colliery is not clearly defined but may have been in the same area as the Tir Philkins Colliery. The mine consisted of two main pits 17 yards deep with two air shafts of 8 yards depth. It was bounded by Rock Colliery to the north, Lys Pentwyn Level to the east, Woodfield Level to the south and Buttry Hatch Level to the west and like all house coal pits in that area worked the Mynyddislwyn seam. It was operating as early as 1812, when it was owned by John Gibson and Thomas Ellwood. In 1841, the owners were Ellwood and Thomas Powell and by 1843 there was reference to an Old and New mine, jointly owned by Thomas Powell and Thomas Protheroe. The Old Penmaen was closed before 1878 and the New was abandoned in December 1896 when owned by the New Penmaen Colliery Co. of Pontypool.

TIR PHILKINS COLLIERY

This pit was opened by Thomas Powell between 1857-61 on the closure of his nearby Llyspentwyn mine (1827-54). It was sunk 109 yards to the Mynyddislwyn house coal seam and worked both this and the rider seam. Thomas Powell died in 1863 and ownership passed to a new company, Messrs. H.& W. Powell, but

Shortly after leaving Oakdale, Hall's Road passes through part of Blackwood where the former Penmaen Halt was located. Type 3 diesel 37895 heads the 13.40 Oakdale to Llanwern MGR service on 19 September 1988, with the remains of the platform visible. Michael Mensing

Penmaen Halt can be seen beyond the bridge, from where the previous two pictures were taken, in this 14 July 1986 shot, the train service from Pontypool to Oakdale, calling at Penmaen and Oakdale, having been withdrawn in 1932. Alastair Warrington Collection

by January 1873, the owner was George Powell, all forerunners of the Powell Duffryn company. Reports for that year indicate that there were Old and New Tir Philkins pits and that they were working more regularly than other pits in the area, the New pit accessed off the Vale of Neath line near Penar Jn. Records from the Abercarn canal weighing machine for May 1863 show 4,160 tons of large, 538 of branch and 29 of small carried from Tir Philkins over the canal, which would have arrived in the 5 ton trams then operating on Hall's Tramway. A newspaper report of April 1880 states that almost all the house coal pits in the Blackwood area had been worked out, and that the chief colliery in the area – the New Tirphilkins Pit at Pontllanffraith – would be closed very shortly due to exhaustion, the men currently working their one month's notice. In 1888, the Powells sold the mine to E. Beddoe, who abandoned the Mynyddislwyn seam in June 1880 and created a drift mine. In 1893, it was owned by J. Tedstone of Hollybush and was working the Mynyddislwyn Rider seam. In 1896, it is shown owned by Wm. Hopkins & Co. of Penmaen Farm, still working the same seam, with only one man working

underground and one on the surface. In 1900, the owner was E.T. Phillips of Cardiff with three men underground and one on the surface, but the mine was not listed as in existence in 1902.

Further records for the ownership of the private siding show that in November 1918 it passed to Messrs. Stephens & Cousins, in June 1919 to the Kincoed Colliery Co. Ltd., in February 1921 to Bush Collieries Ltd., and in October 1924 to the Llwyn Glo Colliery Co. Ltd., before termination in November 1925 when the private siding was purchased by the GWR. All traffic from the complex was brought to the outward siding by tramroad.

PENAR JUNCTION

Penar Junction, the junction between Hall's Tramroad and the new Taff Vale Extension line, was created in 1857 as a flat junction with the single line tramway crossing the double track Pontypool to Quakers Yard line, with no other lines or sidings involved, but the Penar Tunnel a

A view looking across the junction from the end of the northern section of Hall's Road towards Penar Tunnel and the start of the southern section.
Michael Hale/GW Trust

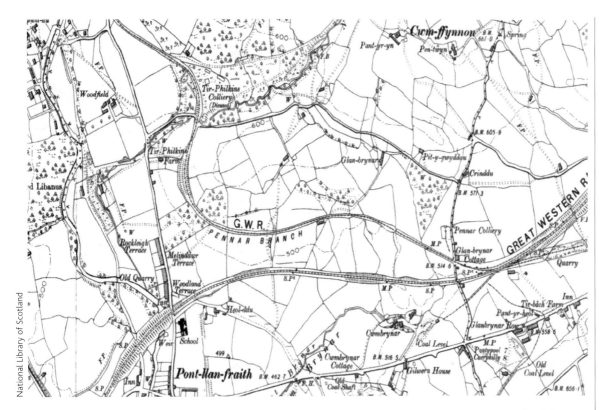

National Library of Scotland

short distance south on Hall's Road.

A plan of the junction for 1882 shows that the flat junction had been removed and the through route of Hall's Road across the TVE taken out. The tramroad between Oakdale and Penar Jn. had been doubled but at the junction, trains could now only run into a siding alongside the westbound TVE line or continue along that line itself, with connections to run

As seen on 4 June 1963, the Vale of Neath lines approach Penar Junction with the southern section of Hall's Road feeding in on the extreme left and crossing the Vale of Neath lines in front of the SB to form the northern portion to the right. Four holding sidings (all empty) are on the right of the Vale of Neath lines. Garth Tilt

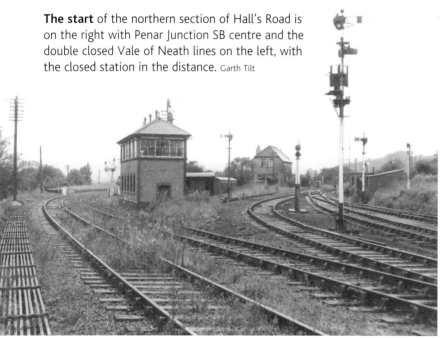

The start of the northern section of Hall's Road is on the right with Penar Junction SB centre and the double closed Vale of Neath lines on the left, with the closed station in the distance. Garth Tilt

Four views of the junction as seen on 24 July 1966, when the Vale of Neath was closed as a through route but Hall's Road was still operative. The first shows the end of the southern section of Hall's Road (left) which then crosses the Vale of Neath line in front of Penar Junction SB to form the northern section. The Vale of Neath line runs behind the box. Garth Tilt

back through onto the eastbound line to Pontypool.

In 1900, the GWR brought a new layout into being with a double junction through from Hall's Road north to south and a nest of four sidings alongside the westbound TVE line. This layout remained in existence until the closure of the Vale of Neath as a through route in 1964, the TVE having by now ceased to be referred to as such.

From 20 November 1967 under route rationalisation plans, trains from Oakdale reversed at Penar Junction where a loop was created using the previous Vale of Neath running lines and ran back to Sirhowy Junction and south to Tredegar Junction Lower to proceed on the Sirhowy Valley line to Risca and Newport. However, with the closure of the remaining collieries in the Sirhowy Valley, the Cardiff Division realised the error of their ways and trains reverted to their original routing between Penar Junction and Hall's Road Junction. The Vale of Neath line was again closed as was the whole of the Sirhowy Valley line, achieving far greater savings.

The northern section with a water column where engines could take water while waiting to cross to the southern section. Garth Tilt

Another view of the end of the northern section looking south towards the signal box and the former Vale of Neath line.
Garth Tilt

The Control Office at Penar Junction.
Garth Tilt

The south portal of Penar Tunnel. After the tunnel, the track curves to the right. The tunnel was only commissioned in September 1912, previous to which traffic passed via Penar Junction and the Taff Vale Extension. Garth Tilt

Penar Tunnel was just south of Penar Junction. Originally built to allow the passage of horses and trams, the tunnel was partly opened out, shortened, widened and rebuilt to be 239 yards in length by the GWR when they converted the line into a standard gauge railway. This was the north portal quite close to Penar Junction, the tunnel straight throughout with the south end easily visible. Garth Tilt

Type 3 diesel 37894 emerges from the north end of Penar Tunnel with a train of empty MGR hoppers for Oakdale in the early 1980s. The mouth of the tunnel is obscured by the oblique angle of the sun. Michael Mensing

PENAR TUNNEL

The original Penar Tunnel was built by Benjamin Hall for the passage of horses and trams from the several local collieries to the Crumlin Canal. When the GWR took over the line in 1877, the tunnel was found to be too low and narrow for the passage of steam engines and so would require rebuilding. When this was finally undertaken at the start of the new century in preparation for the movement of coal from the new Markham and Oakdale pits, it was found that the tunnel could be shortened by about half to 239 yards in length but required a complete rebuild to accommodate steam engines. This was not fully completed until September 1912, before which the line south from Penar Junction to Hall's Road was unusable. During the period from the opening of Markham and Oakdale, traffic to and from those collieries, and also others open north of Penar Junction (for instance, Llanover), passed via the Taff Vale Extension Line from Penar Junction, but after September 1912 was able to run south from Penar Junction to Hall's Road Junction where it joined the Western Valley line on to Rogerstone Yard and Newport.

When Standard Class 9 2-10-0s worked services to Markham and Oakdale in the early 1960s, their clearance through Penar Tunnel was extremely restricted with only about 1½in between the engine chimney/cab and the tunnel roof, so that the driver and fireman had to lie face down on the cab floor for ventilation through the tunnel in the up direction when running engine leading. It was more normal when working back down the Valley tender-first.

At a later time of day the tunnel mouth is in full light as Class 56 diesel No. 56067 emerges from Penar Tunnel with a train of MGR wagons for Oakdale in 1989, the last year of operation.
Michael Mensing

CWMDOWS COLLIERY

Having turned south-east and passed through Penar Tunnel which was opened out and shortened by the GWR, having been built to accommodate a horse and trams, Hall's Road turned north-east to serve Cwmdows Colliery, also known as Twyngwyn No. 2 Colliery, before arriving at Hall's basin alongside the canal.

Cwmdows Colliery was a level working the Mynyddislwyn top seam at a thickness of 42ins. It was in operation as early as 1811 and was one of the first collieries to be served by Hall's Tramroad, when owned by Braithwaite & Head. In 1820, Head sold the colliery to Sir Thomas Protheroe who in 1829 sold it on to Mrs. Monkhouse. In 1841, the owner is recorded as Morrison & Co. The mine came under strong criticism for employing miners as young as six, some completely uneducated. At that time, the colliery consisted of two mines, one a level, the other a shaft 113 yards deep. Together they employed 87 men and were owned by Morrison and Powell, and in 1865 by Martin and Morrison.

Between 1917-25, the colliery was owned by the Twyn Gwyn Colliery Co. and in 1918 employed 74 men underground and 15 on the surface, with a total of 89 in 1923, 123 in 1927, but only 92 in 1928. It was not listed among mines operative in 1935 but continued as a licensed mine after Nationalisation being owned from 1949-57 by W.A. and E.V. Lucas and in 1960 by S.W. Evans and L.J. Lewis.

Cwmdows was located on a branch off Hall's Road leading north to Kendon Pit at Newbridge. The branch came off Hall's Road at 3m 30ch due to the contours of the land and ran north parallel with it for a mile before swinging north and splitting, a short branch running to Cwmdows and a much longer branch to Kendon Pit.

PANTYRESK CROSSING

Pantyresk Crossing at Abercarn lay on a tight curve on the single line and was protected by traffic lights. Other views can be seen in the Last Train section.

Pantyresk Automatic Crossing near Abercarn.
Malcolm James

TWYN GWYN COLLIERY

Twyn Gwyn Colliery was on the west side of Hall's Road where a loop had been added by 1880 between Cwmdows South SB at 4m 16ch and Cwmdows North SB at 4m 39ch. Two sidings passed under the screens and there was a separate tramroad which passed over a bridge at the north end to a loading dock on the other side of the line. Like most other collieries in the area, it worked the Mynyddislwyn house coal seam from 1842. In 1878, it was owned by T. Stroud and in 1893-6 by the Twyn Gwyn Coal Co. of Newbridge, employing eleven men underground and one on the surface. The Twyn Gwyn Co. were shown as of Pontypool in 1900 by when the employment had expanded to 33 men underground and 8 on the surface.

Twyn Gwyn No. 1 closed in 1916 when it employed 27, with the No. 2 Pit employing a further 36 men, and 70 in 1919. No. 2 Pit closed in May 1929 when it was reported that 120 men had lost their jobs with the closure of one of the oldest house coal levels in the district. It had worked the Mynyddislwyn Top seam at a depth of 42ins for house and gas coal.

The original access to Twyn Gwyn Colliery was via a connection at 4m 20ch, but this was taken out in October 1931. A new loop had been installed between Cwmdows South at 4m 16ch and Cwmdows North at 4.39ch in February 1927, access into the colliery now being via a backshunt at the North end. Signal boxes were provided at both North and South but these were also closed in October 1931 until further notice and again in May 1935. The loop between the North and South SBs was left in position but was taken out of use in October 1940 and removed in December 1944.

KENDON COLLIERY

Though not actually on the main trunk of Hall's Road, being on the branch that came off at 3m 30ch, Kendon and Cwmdows feature significantly in Hall's management of his tramroad in the early days of his basin alongside the canal. Kendon colliery was located further north at Crumlin and consisted of a series of levels that worked the Upper and Lower Mynyddislwyn seams and date back to the early days of the tramroad in 1810. Records show that the Old Mine at Kendon closed in 1839 during the Chartist uprising. In 1842, Kendon was owned by Martin Morrison but by 1848, when owned by John Bees, was only producing 56 tons of coal per month. Morrison sold the levels to William Davis who sold on to Charles John in 1850 and in 1860 it was owned by Edmund Jones. The first of the 'modern' levels was opened around 1878 by C. Morgan and was operated through to 1941; a second level opened in 1932 and closed in 1944.

The New Kendon Level opened in the 1890s and closed in the 1920s, with other owners including H.C. Davies, the Waterloo Colliery Co., Davies Bros. and the Kendon Colliery Co. It was always a small concern and in 1896, when owned by Davies Bros., it employed only six men underground, with ten in 1900, fifteen in 1907 and eleven in 1908/9. In 1918, when owned by Henry Davies, manpower was down to six. The level was still in operation in 1938 under the ownership of A.J. Biss, when four men were employed underground and one on the surface.

KENDON BRANCH JUNCTION to PONTYWAUN JUNCTION

South of the junction with the Kendon Branch, there was nothing on Hall's Road until Pont Hall Siding approaching the viaduct crossing the Western Valley line and accessing the junction and sidings serving Cwmcarn Colliery. It might be wondered why the GWR in facing the costs of upgrading the Hall's Road line south of Kendon Branch Jn. did not opt to link the line into their Western Valley line. I can only presume that in the early years of the twentieth century, traffic

On 7 May 1960, the RCTS ran a tour of the Monmouthshire Valleys with a 64XX and three auto coaches. The train is here seen descending Hall's Road between Abercarn and Pontywaun Jn.

On a murky Valleys day, 22 March 1962, the one photograph that has emerged of a steam working on Hall's Road north of Pontywaun Viaduct, showing a 42XX climbing above the Western Valley line with a train of empties. The train is partly composed of wagons of pitprops in Opens with some in 16ton Minerals and will be bound for either Markham or Oakdale colliery, or both. The Western Valley line can be seen in the centre, showing how high Hall's Road has climbed above it since deviating south of Crosskeys. (C.H.A. Townley/Industrial Railway Society)

levels on their Western Valley line, which was only double track carrying both freight and passenger, was so heavy that they needed a relief line, which could now be provided by the upgraded Hall's Road. South of the point at which Hall's Road joined the Western Valley line just south of Crosskeys, there were three and four track sections reflecting the heavy traffic levels and this was matched above Crosskeys by having both the Western Valley and Hall's Road lines.

An 1876 plan of the Hall's Road south of Kendon Branch Junction shows a short siding on the west side of the line and a loop before reaching Pantyresk Crossing, Abercarn, neither being shown on a plan for 1905. Further south there appears to have been a link from the tramroad into the Abercarn Tinplate and Chemical Works though most of their traffic would have been to/from the MRCC and GWR line.

Approaching the Viaduct carrying Hall's Road over the Western Valley line between the 8 and 7¾ mp on the Western Valley line, was Pont Hall Quarry Siding running from a quarry to the west of the tramroad to a loading dock alongside it. This was opened in 1909 with a private siding agreement by E. Marsh dated December 1909 and terminated in December 1935. The siding and South GF controlling access were taken out of use in June 1936 and removed the same month.

The original tramroad viaduct crossing the Western Valley line and the River Ebbw was a few chains south of the new viaduct built by the GWR. The new viaduct was 173 yards long and stretched much further on both ends than did the original tramroad viaduct, the east end of which was just clear of the river bank.

Having crossed the new viaduct as a single line, the new GWR line opened out to become a double track junction with the new line to Cwmcarn Colliery which opened in 1911 at Pontywaun Junction.

The original Hall's Road Viaduct at Pontywaun which was demolished by the GWR about 1912 when the new section south of Penar Junction was brought into use. The Western Valley line is in the foreground.
Author's Collection

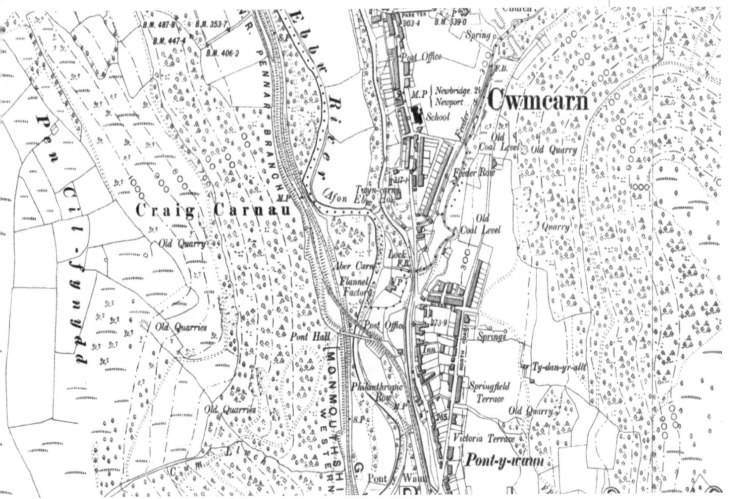

National Library of Scotland

The old and new viaducts in 1912 with the old in process of demolition. Author's Collection

A view of the viaduct, showing it is now really a bridge on six supports, with the now singled Western Valley line running beneath, as seen on 14 March 1990. Michael Mensing

A view north-west along the viaduct, shortly after closure. Note the apparent re-ballasting that has taken place which may have been necessary when the line was brought back into use following the closure of the section from Penar Junction to Hall's Road Jn. from November 1967 to May 1970, even though the photograph was twenty years later.
Michael Mensing

PONTYWAUN JUNCTION TO CWMCARN COLLIERY

(Pontywaun was previously spelt Pontywain which may well have been an English version. However, as it is now spelt as Pontywaun, this has been used throughout.)

The Western Valley line crossed the River Ebbw north of Crosskeys station and immediately north of the river bridge an 1880 drawing shows Cox's Quarry Siding on the up side between the 7¼ and 7½ mp. Just beyond the 7¾ mp, the Hall's Tramroad crossed the river and the Western Valley line on a 173 yard viaduct to now run on the south side of the main line. A crossing loop was provided on the original tramroad at this juncture.

A 1909 drawing for the Cwmcarn area shows no changes on the Western Valley line, other than a realignment of the track under the Hall's Road viaduct, but several changes on the Hall's Road branch which ran on the north side of the River Ebbw with the Western Valley line on the south side with the 173 yards long viaduct across the river. A new branch off the Hall's Road line was created in 1911 to serve Cwmcarn Colliery (opened in 1865), a SB being located at Pontywaun Jn., opened in that year and closed in 1934. Double track was provided between Hall's Road Jn. and Pontywaun Jn. from May 1915 and three loop sidings provided for handling the traffic to and from Cwmcarn Colliery.

A siding on the Hall's Road branch south of the WV line, gave access to a loading dock for stone traffic from a tramroad-worked Pont Hall Quarry Siding which was open from 1909 to 1936.

Crosskeys North SB was moved from its previous location to the other side of the river bridge to control the northern access to Cox's Quarry Siding at 7m 34ch by 1934. A new layout was implemented from October that year to the sidings on the Hall's Road branch with the junction between the Cwmcarn and Oakdale lines now placed south of the Pontywaun Sidings, now reduced to two between the two running lines, Pontywaun SB being reduced to a GF. Cwmcarn Colliery is now shown as owned by the Ebbw Vale Steel, Iron & Coal Co. from 1913, and they also had a siding, called North Siding, south of the colliery, between 1914 and 1938.

From Pontywaun Junction, the line proceeded as a single track in a north-east direction to a new Cwmcarn Colliery, opened by the Ebbw Vale Iron, Steel & Coal Co. in 1911. At Pontywaun North, a GF gave access to a siding installed in April 1914 for the Ebbw Vale Co.'s use called North Siding, which closed in 1938 when the GF was removed.

The first pit at Cwmcarn was sunk in 1836 by the Monmouthshire Iron & Coal Co. as one of their Abercarn pits. There was also a tramroad to convey the coal mined to the Monmouthshire Canal near Pontywaun Bridge. The company intended to sink six pits but with the trade slump of 1839 it went under and the two pits already sunk remained closed until the Abercarn pit reopened in 1845. The new owners concentrated on the Abercarn pit, though a Cwmcarn pit is listed in 1865 owned by the Cwm Carn Company, being also known as the Beesom Makers Pit. It was situated a mile further down the valley than the future Cwmcarn pit, opened in 1876 with which it was not connected and had been closed by 1880. It worked the No. 1 Rhondda Rider seam (also known as the No. 1 Rock Vein) at a depth of 132 feet. The seam was only 18ins thick at the south end but widened to 36 inches further north.

One of the two shafts of the newer colliery existed from 1876 when at a cost of £60,000 it was sunk as a downcast ventilation pit for Abercarn Colliery. It was sunk to the Five-Feet/Gellideg seam, also known as the Old Coal seam which was reached at a depth of 815ft with the Black Vein seam found at a depth of 740ft. A second shaft was sunk by the Ebbw Vale Steel, Iron & Coal Co. in 1909 to

The daily Rogerstone to Cwmcarn Colliery train ran in the early afternoon with Ebbw Jn.'s 4265 in charge and is seen here reducing its load by splitting the train at Pontywaun Sidings, alongside the Monmouthshire Canal, on a very dull 22 March 1962.
C.H.A. Townley/Industrial Railway Society

Pontywaun Sidings – originally three, then two but now reduced to one – used by trains serving Cwmcarn Colliery to reduce their load. The train above has left these empty wagons in the siding and has proceeded to the colliery. The track to Cwmcarn Colliery is in the foreground, that to Oakdale runs behind the cabin on the right and these are now signalled as separate single line routes from Hall's Road. The Crumlin Canal can be seen in the centre. C.H.A. Townley/Industrial Railway Society

The engine working at Cwmcarn Colliery where the empty mineral wagons have been placed at the north end and the loaded which have been gravitated down will be formed up into the return train to Rogerstone Yard.
C.H.A. Townley/Industrial Railway Society

the Black Vein seam from which the first coal was raised in June 1912, from when Cwmcarn worked as a separate unit to Abercarn.

The railway line linking the colliery with Hall's Road at Pontywaun ran along the south side of the Nantcarn Valley. The wagons would be taken past the colliery by the GWR engine and then gravity fed through the screens for loading and removal. The coal produced was classed as 301B prime coking coal, with early markets for locomotives and steamships and later for steelworks and power stations.

In 1913, Cwmcarn Colliery employed 292 men out of a total of 5,397 employed by the Ebbw Vale Company at their eight pits. By 1918, this had risen to 590 men underground and 125 on the surface, showing the increased production at the colliery in those five years. By 1935, the totals had risen to 800 men underground with 100 on the surface, but by 1943-5 this had reduced to 532 underground

and 90 surface working on the Black Vein, Five-Feet, Meadow Vein and Big Vein seams. The Big Vein (or Four-Feet) seam was worked between 1923-29 and again in the 1950s and '60s, the average thickness being 36ins. The Upper-Three-Quarter seam was extensively worked in the 1920s and during the 1940s and 1960s. It was located just over 15 feet below the Big Vein and also averaged about 36ins in thickness. The Lower-Six-Feet seam was some 13 feet below the Upper-Six-Feet with a thickness of 28ins. Attempts to work the Meadow Vein and Old Coal seams during the 1940s met with poor success due to geological difficulties. The Meadow Vein had a thickness of 36ins. and the Old Coal seam a top thickness of 21ins, then 8ins of dirt and a bottom thickness of a further 25ins.

At Nationalisation, Cwmcarn employed 526 men underground and 79 on the surface, working the Nine-Feet, Five-Feet, Yard/Seven-Feet, Four-Feet and Two-Feet-Nine seams. Colliery production fell

The daily service from Rogerstone Yard to Cwmcarn Colliery with Ebbw Jn.'s 5209 in charge has reduced its load of empties at Pontywaun Siding and is now on the final climb to the colliery.
Gerald T. Robinson

A view looking down on the colliery from the hillside with No. 5209 marshalling its train of loaded wagons for conveyance to Rogerstone Yard.
Gerald T. Robinson

during the mid-1950s and out of total employment of 561, only 253 of them worked at the coalface, and by 1961 only 190 worked at the coalface out of a total of 453, one service per day from Rogerstone sufficing to provide all the empty wagons necessary and clear the output which in 1961 was 772,000 tons. At this time, there were major problems with water breaking into the Big Vein seam on occasions and washing everything away, so that all working on that seam had to be abandoned. It was also feared that large amounts of water had gathered in the abandoned Cwmbran Colliery workings and could bear into the nearby Cwmcarn workings, to prevent which a borehole was driven through into the old workings and the water safely drained off, though it was still coming through 16 years later when the Cwmcarn Colliery was closed in 1968. Two pumps were used to raise this water up the shafts, both pumping 250 gallons per minute for ten hours each day, giving an idea of the volume of water concerned.

Cwmcarn Colliery was closed on 30 November 1968 as uneconomic. The shafts were filled with washery waste (known as 'tailings') from Hafodyrynys, Bedwas, Nantgarw and Celynen South washeries. The area was later grassed over to become part of the Cwmcarn Scenic Forest Drive. At closure, 100 of those employed there moved to nearby Celynen South, with others joining Oakdale and Bedwas. The branch line from Pontywaun Jn. to Cwmcarn Colliery became redundant, though the line to Oakdale remained in use. Cwmcarn station on the Western Valley line closed in April 1962 following which that line was subsequently singled.

An interesting account is available from Ray Lawrence of the method of working at Cwmcarn Colliery where the coal was hand filled onto conveyors at the coalface on the dayshift only. On the other shifts, the coal would be undercut up to four feet deep by a coal cutter and allowed to fall loose. The colliers on the dayshift would then load the coal onto the conveyor at the coalface. They would also hack down the coal that had not fallen with a mandrill and erect supports in the form of wooden props to protect themselves. The area (or stent) that they would work depended on the thickness of the coal but was normally between seven and nine yards long. The coalface conveyor would then take the coal to other conveyors and eventually to a 'dump end' where it would be loaded into trams. When 28 trams were ready, they were attached by a rope to a haulage engine to take them to pit bottom where they were wound up the pit.

The next shift going onto the coalface would then partly dismantle the conveyor and push it forward ready for the next cycle of operations, and they were called the turnover gang. The roof supports were taken down and moved forward with the advancing coalface, and the roof behind was allowed to fall, except for the two roadways either side of the coalface which were used for ventilation and to bring men and materials in and coal out. They were normally called the 'dump road' (where the conveyor was) and the 'tail road' (where the supplies such as timber came in).Towards the end of the life of the colliery, another method called 'narrow work' was used, when headings or roadways were driven into the coal; boreholes were then driven into the coal and explosives used to loosen it. The coal was then loaded into Samson loaders which consisted of two rotating steel 'gathering arms' that scooped the coal back onto a metal conveyor that was part of the machine, the coal then being dumped onto a belt conveyor and out to the 'dump end'. This method was used near to the outcrop of the coal and could encounter areas of coal 30ft thick. The coal could also rise in parts almost vertically making it very dangerous to work at the risk of it falling on top of you. As you neared the outcrop of the seam, the coal would go from rising at 2½:1 to 1½:1. These details would have

Pontywaun Sidings with the running lines leading from Hall's Road Jn. to Cwmcarn Colliery (right) and the Penar Branch (left), with overgrown sidings between, as seen on 24 July 1966. Garth Tilt

been provided by Ray Lawrence's father who worked at Cwmcarn Colliery, and to whom I am very grateful for this insight into the detail of colliery operations.

Trains proceeding to Cwmcarn Colliery needed to reduce their load due to the incline of 1 in 36 beyond Pontywaun Junction. In the 1909 layout for this location, three loop sidings are shown where trains would reduce loads of empties and also make up fuller loads of outwards loaded traffic. These sidings lay on the up side of the double line with Pontywaun Junction SB at the north end, opened in 1911 and closed in October 1934. The track down to Hall's Road Junction, south of Crosskeys, was doubled in May 1915. Also in October 1934, separate reversible single running lines were brought into use from Hall's Road Junction, one line to/from Cwmcarn Colliery, the other to/from Hall's Road, thus enabling Pontywaun Jn. SB to be closed. To achieve this, the most westerly of the three sidings at Pontywaun was upgraded to be used as the Hall's Road running line, this reducing the yard to two sidings, and enabling the junction at Pontywaun to be completely removed.

HALL'S ROAD JUNCTION

Between Pontywaun and Hall's Road Junction, just below Crosskeys, a plan

Approaching the end of Hall's Road as seen on 24 July 1966 where the two bi-directional running lines are flanked by two sidings, the connections into which can be seen centre. From 1934 the single line on the left ran to the Penar Branch while that on the right served Cwmcarn. Garth Tilt

for 1875, two years before the line was taken over by the GWR, shows the former tramroad (now upgraded to a standard gauge railway) to have been a single track. Following taking over by the GWR in 1877, there was a siding on the west side about mid-way owned by the

Abercarn Coal Company, the agreement dated June 1890. This passed to the United National Colliery Co. in May 1893 and was probably removed by 1904. Near the junction with the Western Valley line there were two substantial loop sidings on the east side of the line, where traffic to

The end of the Penar Branch at Hall's Road Junction with the Western Valley line on the right. The wagons in the siding are probably cripples awaiting movement to Newport Dock Street Wagon Shops, as on 24 July 1966. Garth Tilt

go forward on the GWR line would have been held. In previous years there was also a point at which the contents of trams coming down Hall's Road (which was on a higher level) would have been tipped into larger trams standing below on the Western Valley line, but the exact location of this is not known. At the junction, which was only between the Hall's Road line and the down main line, there was also a level crossing with a SB on the east side of the line. How empty wagons got back onto Hall's Road is not shown on the plan.

A plan for 1886 shows a much more practical layout at the junction which had by then been installed by the GWR with a full junction between the Western Valley line and Hall's Road and a loop created on the latter to hold a train waiting passage onto the main line; the two other sidings had been retained but shortened. In December 1912, a connection off the Hall's Road down line (north of the junction) was made into the Down Loop installed in 1886 between Hall's Road and Lime Kilns providing much needed relief accommodation to down loaded trains.

In 1915, the loop on Hall's Road approaching the junction became a second running line as the track was doubled back to Pontywaun Junction and in 1934 crossovers were installed between the running lines on the branch. This layout lasted until December 1967 when the line between Hall's Road and Pantywaun was singled with a loop alongside approaching the junction, the previous two additional sidings being removed.

In November 1967, the Hall's Road line between Penar Junction and Cwmcarn Branch Junction (the previous Pantywaun Jn.) was closed and trains for Oakdale were diverted via the Sirhowy Valley, using the link line between Gelligroes Jn. (Tredegar Jn. Lower) to Sirhowy Jn. where trains reversed and then ran over the previous Vale of Neath line to Penar Jn. where they again reversed onto Hall's Road for Oakdale. This enabled Hall's Road Jn. SB at Crosskeys to be closed. A

year later in November 1968, Cwmcarn Colliery closed and the line between there and Hall's Road Jn. and on over the Down Loop to Lime Kiln was closed. The closure by the NCB of Wyllie and Nine Mile Point in 1968/9 meant that the only traffic now using the Sirhowy Valley were the trains to Oakdale (Aberdare traffic having been diverted via the Cardiff Valleys when the Vale of Neath was closed as a through route in 1964). As greater savings were possible by now closing the Sirhowy Valley line below Tredegar Jn. Lower, the Hall's Road line between Penar Junction, Hall's Road Jn. and on over the Down Loop to Lime Kiln was reopened in 1970, and Oakdale trains reverted to this route and the Vale of Neath section between Penar Jn. and Sirhowy Jn. finally closed. In 1981, the Western Valley line was singled north of Gaer Jn. as far as Lime Kiln where the Down Loop from the previous Hall's Road box remained in use as an up and down running line for Oakdale trains until that colliery closed in August 1989.

With the re-introduction of the passenger service in 2008, a section of double line was re-instated between north of Crosskeys and north of Rogerstone and this has now been extended through to Aberbeeg to allow a half hourly interval service to be introduced.

Hall's Road dropped down to the level of the Western Valley line south of Crosskeys station and joined up at Hall's Road Junction, until December 1967 when the junction was made at Lime Kiln and Hall's Road Jn. box was closed.
(Michael Mensing)

LAST TRAIN ON THE PENAR BRANCH– MONMOUTHSHIRE RAILWAY SOCIETY SPECIAL

Following the running of the last coal train over the Penar Branch from Oakdale Colliery to Llanwern on 25 August 1989, the branch stood derelict until the Monmouthshire Railway Society agreed with the railway authorities to run a final special five-car DMU service – the 'Caerwent Cannonball' – over the line on 12 May 1990. Malcolm James of Rogerstone recorded the train at some interesting locations on the day.

Approaching Pantyresk Crossing, Abercarn, on the journey up to Oakdale Colliery. The crossing had to be carefully negotiated due to doubts about the functioning of the automatic equipment, and was flag controlled on the day.

The train en route to Oakdale Colliery is seen leaving Penar Tunnel.

The returning train passing Penmaen Halt south of Oakdale where passenger services from Pontypool Road operated between 1927-32.

The returning train south of Pantyresk Crossing with a view of part of Abercarn.

The returning train has just come off the extended Hall's Road branch, the connection to/from which was moved south from Hall's Road to Limekiln in December 1967.